CHEWY GOOEY

CRISPY CRUNCHY

MELT-IN-YOUR-MOUTH

COOKIES BY

ALICE MEDRICH

CHEWY GOOEY

CRISPY CRUNCHY

MELT-IN-YOUR-MOUTH

COOKIES BY

ALICE MEDRICH

PHOTOGRAPHS BY

DEBORAH JONES

ARTISAN

Published by Artisan
A Division of Workman Publishing Company, Inc.
225 Varick Street
New York, NY 10014-4381
www.artisanbooks.com

Library of Congress Cataloging-in-Publication Data
Medrich, Alice.
Chewy gooey crispy crunchy melt-in-your-mouth cookies /
by Alice Medrich.
p. cm.
ISBN 978-1-57965-397-2
1. Cookies. I. Title.
TX772.M432 2010
641.8'654—dc22
2010019491

DESIGN BY MORLA DESIGN
ART DIRECTION AND PHOTOGRAPHIC STYLING BY SARA SLAVIN

Printed in China
First printing, October 2010

PRECEDING SPREAD: Robert's Brownies Transposed (page 226)
PAGE 8: New Classic Coconut Macaroons 2.0 (page 166)

10 9 8 7 6 5 4 3 2 1

CONTENTS

INTRODUCTION

Cookies are easy, enticing, and fun. They invite creativity and reward experimentation—no rocket science required. Yet, even in this era of culinary obsession, chefs ignore cookies, and home cooks cling to the recipe on the bag of chocolate chips. So I asked myself: What if cookies reflected our modern culinary sensibility—our spirit of adventure and passion for flavors and even our dietary concerns—without losing their universal friendly appeal? What if cookies were hip (but not too hip)? And why not celebrate the physical and sensual appeal of cookies by grouping them by texture? *Chewy Gooey Crispy Crunchy . . .* is my response to these, life's larger cookie questions.

I began by revisiting my own repertoire, always asking, "Do I still like these? Do they appeal to modern tastes?" I changed leavenings, baking temperatures, and pan liners to improve textures. I sometimes cut sugar or butter (for more flavor!), or added more spice, or new spices. I tried olive oil, herbs, and pepper. I adjusted salt to offset sweetness and heighten flavors. I tuned up cookie classics like snicker doodles, sugar cookies, coconut macaroons, even brownies, with a shower of grated cinnamon stick or nutmeg, or with fragrant sugars spiked with cardamom, garam masala, chili powder, or star anise. How many times

did I say, "These are good, but let's do it again with a little more of this, or add some pepper, or what about whole wheat or oat flour"? Indeed, "What about this? What about that?" was my constant mantra.

Even plain flour gave me pause. I've always insisted that bleached flour makes more tender cookies. But now, after a career-long, oft-stated commitment to simple ingredients and pure flavors, I confronted my bleached-flour habit. Tinkering and tasting, I found that I *could* get tender, even melt-in-your-mouth cookies with unbleached flour, and that the plainest cookies not only *tasted* but also *smelled* better when I used it! I revised my recipes (as necessary) for unbleached flour.

What else is new? Classic crispy wafers called tuiles come in flavors from vanilla bean to saffron, lavender, tarragon, and thyme. Nutty Cocoa Cookie Bark flaunts Parmesan and pine nuts. Or forget the cheese and make it kitschy and kid-friendly for the holidays with crushed peppermint sticks and drizzled white chocolate!

My collection of bittersweet brownies remains priceless, including Less-Is-More Overnight Brownies. Look for Buckwheat Linzer Cookies with cacao nibs as well as Spicy Linzer Bars. You'll also find an inspired handful of gooey caramel-filled Latin American cookies called Alfajores.

My classic chocolate chip cookies with melted butter are here, but so are shatteringly crisp, ultrathin chocolate chip cookies that redefine the genre. Look for cookies with whole grains such as Great Grahams (addictive!) and Whole Wheat Chocolate Chip Cookies—right next to superb Wheat-Free Chocolate Chip and Wheat-Free Double-Oatmeal Cookies—and more. Indeed, I adored the creative challenge of making delicious cookies without wheat and I used a variety of strategies to that end. Sometimes I used a single non-wheat flour; other times I blended flours and starches. Rather than seek or rely on a one-size-fits-all blend of flours, I wanted the best taste and texture for the particular cookie at hand.

Meanwhile, if you think you know meringues, try Banana Pecan Meringues, Peanut Butter Clouds, or meringues loaded with salted nuts and milk chocolate chunks, then think again. You'll also find ethereal French Macarons—and everything you need to know to make them successfully.

My recipes are organized by texture. If you love crispy cookies, go directly to the "Crispy" chapter, then check out "Crunchy," just in case. Browse the "Chunky" chapter for cookies or bars chock-full of nuggets and bumps. If what you are looking for has nothing to do with texture, go to "Smart Search" (pages 365–67) to find quick-and-easy cookies, wheat-free cookies, cookies with whole grains, or cookies for Weight Watchers, for example.

I aimed for the highest standard: if a cookie that was lower in fat, wheat-free, or whole grain was just "pretty good," then it wasn't good enough! Thus cookies that meet these criteria are not segregated, and omnivorous cookie lovers should not ignore them.

Most of my recipes are short and simple, but each includes the essential details to ensure great cookies. Throughout the book you will find loads of information and help if you need to brush up on beating or folding egg whites, piping meringue, handling phyllo dough, and other common cookie tasks.

A personal collection such as this is not meant to be encyclopedic. I hope you find this one whimsical yet practical, quirky but comforting, eccentric but engaging. I hope that *Chewy Gooey Crispy Crunchy* will pull new bakers into the kitchen for the first time and inspire seasoned hands to ever greater heights of cookie creativity.

USER'S GUIDE

No matter what kind of cookie you choose, you will get the most from this book if you read the information in this chapter before you start with any of the recipes. If you simply can't wait that long, read "Quick Start" while you are preheating the oven.

Cookie recipes are the simplest in the baker's repertoire: ingredient lists are brief and familiar, and instructions are few and uncomplicated. But simplicity does not mean a recipe can be executed casually, that the details are whimsical, or that the measurements are flexible. In reality, cookies are tiny pastries. As such, they are subject to all the rules of baking: mundane acts of measuring and mixing, cookie sheet preparation, oven temperature, and timing make the difference between tough and tender cookies and between ordinary and extraordinary cookies. If you've ever eaten ten chocolate chip cookies made by ten different bakers all using the same recipe, you know what I mean.

Experienced cooks have their own measuring, mixing, and baking habits. Cooks (even those of us who are professional bakers or cookbook authors) do not measure and mix the same way. And each of us has our special tricks. The information that follows will get you into my kitchen and my head by explaining why I do what I do and why some of my methods may be different from what you are accustomed to or what you find in other books.

DECODING RECIPE LANGUAGE

A good recipe uses specific descriptive language to tell you what to do, when and for how long to do it, and with what utensil. It includes visual cues to look for so you know you are on the right track. All of this is designed to help you achieve results that resemble those that we got in my kitchen. If you change the details, you will change the results—for better or for worse!

The order of the recipe is designed so that the most important steps of the recipe can proceed without interruption. This explains why the flour and dry ingredients are often blended first, even if they are used later. Blending them first means that you can keep the flow of a recipe moving (and you don't end up with a dough or batter that has pockets of unmixed salt or baking powder).

Phrases like *just until* are important. When the recipe asks you to mix just until the dry ingredients are blended, or warm the chocolate just until it is melted, or bake just until the edges are brown, you know that more mixing, warming, or baking is not better and your cookies could suffer.

The texture of your cookie is also affected by how you mix: terms like *stir, fold, beat,* and *whip* are used to guide you. When a recipe calls for mixing, stirring, or folding, you are meant to act gently (but decisively) to incorporate ingredients without destroying or changing the texture of the batter. For beaten egg whites or any type of meringue, the goal is to preserve as much of the air in the batter as possible—excessive or vigorous mixing or the wrong stroke will deflate these batters. For denser, richer batters (like those for chocolate chip cookies or butter cookies), excess or vigorous mixing may add too much air or activate too much gluten.

When a recipe calls for beating, whipping, or mixing vigorously, you are meant to aerate the mixture and/ or make sure that the ingredients are emulsified. This is done with an electric mixer or by hand, depending on the recipe. Egg whites are whipped at medium to high speed with an electric mixer with the whisk attachment. Heavier, richer batters and doughs are mixed with the flat beater or paddle attachment, or by hand with a spatula at a brisk pace. Aeration and emulsification caused by mixing briskly with a paddle or spatula are less obvious than the effect of whipping egg whites, but they do occur.

When a recipe calls for "1 cup nuts, chopped," measure the whole nuts and then chop them. If the recipe calls for "1 cup chopped nuts," it is the chopped nuts that should be measured. The difference between the weight of 1 cup of whole almonds and that of 1 cup of chopped almonds is not a make-it-or-break-it detail for most cookies, but doing what the recipe is actually asking you to do can make the process easier for you—it is more efficient, for example, to measure and then chop!

Finally, note that all measures given in ounces always refer to weights rather than volume (see page 15 for a fuller explanation).

Certain recipes in each chapter are accompanied by additional information that pertains to all of the similar recipes in the chapter. "Stick Chat" (page 33) gives techniques and tips that apply to all of the "stick cookies" in the "Crispy" chapter, for example. Similarly, tuiles are featured, with lots of extra information about tuiles and similar wafers.

QUICK START

Here are the five most important things to know about making the cookies in this book successfully. More details about methods and techniques can be found in "FAQs" (opposite).

1 | Too much flour is the biggest problem in homemade cookies. Use an electronic scale or measure with measuring cups as follows: Spoon the flour lightly into the cup until it is heaped above the rim. Sweep the flour level with a finger or spatula without tapping or shaking the cup. Dipping the measuring cup directly into the flour container will give you too much flour, resulting in heavy, doughy cookies.

2 | Use a national brand of unbleached all-purpose flour, unless another type of flour is called for.

3 | Check your oven temperature with a thermometer and correct for discrepancies when you preheat the oven (or have your oven recalibrated).

4 | Always preheat the oven before putting cookies in.

5 | Use medium to heavy baking sheets that don't warp. Avoid those with dark surfaces, including those that are nonstick.

FAQs

Successful baking is all in the details. The simplest things can make the difference between a perfectly tender cookie and a doughy paperweight, between a soggy cookie and one that is sublimely crisp. Each recipe spells out the important details for that cookie, but here is the background.

What makes cookies tough?

Tough cookies often result from badly measured flour, the wrong kind of flour (bread flour or whole-grain flours rather than all-purpose flour), too much mixing after the flour has been added to the moist ingredients in the batter, or too much flour used to keep the dough from sticking to the rolling pin or the countertop. Other culprits include too much kneading and rerolling of scraps and baking at too high or too low a temperature or for too long.

The fix? Use the flour called for in the recipe, measure it accurately, mix it just enough (as called for in the recipe), avoid excessive rerolling, roll out between sheets of wax paper or plastic wrap, and check your oven and timer. You may also increase tenderness with a finer granulation of sugar, either by using superfine sugar or grinding regular sugar to a finer consistency in a food processor.

MEASURING INGREDIENTS

What does *mise en place* mean, and what can it do for me?

Mise en place means "to put into place." You've seen TV chefs whipping through their recipes in front of an audience with all of their ingredients measured out and ready to use. That's *mise en place*. The TV chef's helper probably did the *mise,* but doing your own assures that you have everything you need so you don't have to run to the store or ransack the pantry while your butter melts or melted chocolate congeals. *Mise en place* promotes calm and focus in the kitchen. Who doesn't need that?

How important is careful measuring?

A creative approach to measuring does not always spoil cookies. You may use a liberal hand with raisins, nuts, chocolate chips, coconut, or even vanilla. Feel free to substitute dried fruits and nuts one for another and to experiment with extracts and flavors.

But for cookies with great textures, and to avoid dry, tough, and leaden cookies, you must carefully measure the baking soda, baking powder, salt, and, most of all, flour. I cannot emphasize enough how many cookie problems can be prevented by knowing how to measure flour correctly.

Is it better to measure with a scale?

A cup of flour can weigh anywhere from 4 ounces to well over 6 ounces, depending on a number of factors, including whether the flour was compacted, loosened, or sifted; whether the measuring cup was dipped into the flour or the flour was lightly spooned into the cup; and, finally, whether the measure was leveled by tapping or shaking the cup or simply by sweeping a knife across the rim. Given so many variables, your results will be more consistent from batch to batch and closer to the results that I got in my kitchen if you weigh most ingredients— not just flour—instead of using measuring cups. Weighing is also faster and produces fewer dirty dishes than measuring with cups.

What kind of scale is best?

Electronic scales that register in decimals or fractions are inexpensive and easy to use. Weights in my recipes are given in decimals. If your scale registers fractions, see the chart on page 384 to convert decimals to fractions. In most cases, for convenience, I have rounded weights to increments of 0.125, or ⅛ ounce.

If I don't have a scale, how should I measure flour with cups?

For 1 cup of flour, measure the flour (without sifting* it) using a 1-cup dry measure as follows: Gently loosen the flour in the sack or canister with a spoon, but avoid excessive stirring or whisking or your cup of flour will be too light. Spoon the flour lightly into the measure, without packing it, until it is heaped above the rim. Don't shake or tap the cup. Sweep a straight-edged knife or spatula or your finger across the rim of the cup to level the measure. Your level cup should weigh about 4½ ounces.

What are dry and liquid measures, and how are they used?

Dry measures refer to measuring cups designed to measure dry ingredients; these are meant to be filled to the rim and leveled as described above. When using dry measures, use a 1-cup measure to measure 1 cup, a ½-cup measure to measure ½ cup, and so forth.

Liquid measures are designed to measure liquid ingredients. These are clear plastic or glass pitchers marked with measurements on the sides. To measure, set the measure on the counter—no one can hold a cup level in the air. Pour liquid up to the appropriate mark with your head lowered to read the measurement at eye level.

---

*Ignore the "pre-sifted" label on flour sacks. Pre-sifting eliminates stones and foreign matter, but it cannot prevent the flour from compacting again en route to your grocer's shelf.

Can I use the ounces printed on my liquid measuring cup instead of a scale?

Alas, no. The ounces printed on the sides of glass measures are fluid ounces for measuring volume, not weight. One cup of anything is always 8 fluid ounces, but 8 fluid ounces of raisins does not weigh the same as 8 fluid ounces of honey or 8 fluid ounces of cornflakes. There are only a few exceptions where fluid ounces and weight ounces are the same: 1 cup of butter or water (and some but not all other thin liquids) equals 8 fluid ounces and also weighs 8 ounces on the scale. In my recipes ounces refer to weight unless otherwise noted.

CHOOSING/PREPARING INGREDIENTS

How soft is softened butter?

If the recipe calls for softened butter and you are mixing with an electric mixer, allow the butter to soften at room temperature (or in the microwave at 30 percent power for a few seconds at a time) until it is pliable but not completely squishy, 65° to 70°F. If you are mixing with a large spoon or rubber spatula, it is easier if the butter is softened to the consistency of mayonnaise but not melted, 75° to 80°F.

What's the best way to melt chocolate?

Unsweetened, bittersweet, or semisweet chocolate should be coarsely chopped before melting. White and milk chocolate should be finely chopped.

If you are melting chocolate by itself, with nothing else added to it, the goal is to heat the chocolate gently until it is warm (not hot) and perfectly fluid. To this end, the cutting board, bowl, and all utensils should be dry, as small amounts of moisture or liquid may cause the chocolate to thicken or seize instead of melting smoothly. (Note: If you are melting chocolate with butter or cream or other ingredients for a specific recipe, dry utensils are not critical and the individual recipe will tell you how warm or hot the mixture should be.)

While most cookbooks advise using a double boiler or a microwave for melting chocolate, I find it both safe and flexible to use an open water bath—a wide skillet of hot (see note below for white or milk chocolate), not even simmering water with a heatproof (preferably stainless steel) bowl of chocolate set directly into it. It is easy to keep an eye on the water and turn it down or off if it begins to boil, easy to watch and stir the chocolate as it melts, and easy to use a bowl that is the right size for the quantity of chocolate or the recipe. Should you prefer to use the classic double boiler instead, it is perfectly OK if the upper container touches the water below. The key to *not* burning chocolate has more to do with paying attention to the temperature of the chocolate and the water than whether or not the bowl touches the water! With either method, stir the chocolate frequently, dip a finger in now and then

to gauge temperature, and remove the bowl when the chocolate is melted, or almost melted. Easy!

Note: To melt white or milk chocolate (both of which are more heat sensitive than dark chocolate), bring the skillet of water to a simmer, then remove it from the burner and wait 60 seconds before setting the bowl of chocolate into it and stir frequently; the hot water will do the job safely without live heat under the pan.

How do I toast coconut?

Have a medium bowl ready near the stove. Spread the coconut in a wide heavy skillet over medium heat. Stir constantly until the coconut begins to color slightly. Turn the heat down (once hot, coconut burns quickly) and continue to stir until the coconut bits are mostly light golden brown flecked with some white. I often take the pan off the heat early and continue to stir, letting the residual heat of the pan finish toasting the coconut slowly and evenly. The whole process takes less than 5 minutes. Immediately scrape the coconut into the bowl.

How do I toast sesame seeds?

Spread the seeds in a dry wide skillet and stir constantly over medium heat until they just begin to color. Turn the heat down (seeds burn quickly once they get hot) and continue to stir until the seeds are fragrant and medium golden brown, with a nice toasted flavor. I usually take the pan off the heat early and continue to stir—the hot pan finishes the toasting gently and evenly. The whole process takes less than 5 minutes. Immediately scrape the seeds onto a plate to cool completely before using.

How do I toast nuts?

To toast nuts, spread them in a single layer on an ungreased cookie sheet. Bake in a preheated oven (350°F for almonds and hazelnuts; 325°F for pecans and walnuts) for 10 to 20 minutes, depending on the type of nut and whether they are whole, sliced, or slivered. Check the color and flavor of the nuts frequently and stir to redistribute them on the pan. When chopped toasted nuts are called for, toast them whole or in large pieces, then chop them. Almonds and hazelnuts are done when they are golden brown when you bite or cut them in half. To rub the skins from toasted hazelnuts, cool them thoroughly, then rub them together in your hands or in a tea towel or place them in a large coarse-mesh strainer and rub them against the mesh until most of the skins flake off. Pecans and walnuts are done when fragrant and lightly colored.

How do I grind nuts?

To pulverize or grind nuts in a food processor without making paste or nut butter, start with a perfectly dry processor bowl and blade at room temperature (not hot from the dishwasher) and nuts at room temperature.

(Frozen or cold nuts will produce moisture that turns the nuts to paste, as will nuts still hot from the oven.) Use short pulses, stopping from time to time to scrape the sides of the processor bowl with a skewer or chopstick. If you observe these rules, there is no particular need to add flour or sugar from the recipe to the nuts to keep them dry, although that is a good precaution.

Why do some recipes that call for bittersweet or semisweet chocolate also specify the cacao percentage?

Modern bittersweet and semisweet chocolates include such a wide range of cacao percentages that it has become necessary for recipes to be more specific about the chocolate called for. Whenever chocolate is melted and blended into dough or batter, the cacao percentage of the chocolate affects not only the flavor intensity and sweetness of the finished product, but also its texture and moistness. Using chocolate with 70% cacao in a recipe that was created for a chocolate with only 60% cacao can result in dry, bitter cookies. You will have greater success with your cookies if you use chocolate within the range of cacao content called for.

Does cacao content matter when chocolate is used as chips or chunks?

Cacao percentage affects the texture and moistness of cookies only if it is melted and blended into the dough. If you are mixing unmelted chocolate chips or chunks into cookie dough, you can choose chocolate with any cacao percentage that you like or think will taste good in your cookies, keeping in mind that the higher the cacao percentage, the stronger and more bittersweet the flavor of the chocolate.

When a recipe calls for chocolate chips or chunks, can I hand-chop a bar of chocolate instead of using premade chocolate chips or chunks?
Commercial chocolate chips (and some but not all commercial chocolate chunks) hold their shape after melting because they are made with less cocoa butter than a good bar of chocolate. Because of this, cookies may themselves hold a better shape. However, if you don't care whether the chocolate chips or chunks hold their shape when they melt or your cookies are a bit flatter, you may certainly chop your own chocolate. Many chefs (including me) do just that so they can use any kind of chocolate they like as chunks. See page 351 for more information about chocolate chips and chunks.

MIXING

How important is mixing technique?
Cookie flavor and texture are a function of the type and amount of ingredients in the recipe. But mixing time and technique have a surprisingly significant effect as well.

There are two critical stages of mixing. Most recipes begin with mixing the butter with sugar. The consistency of the butter and how long and vigorously it is beaten with the sugar affect the texture and the intensity of the flavor in subtle yet wonderful ways. I find that shortbread, chocolate chip, and oatmeal cookies are best when the butter is melted completely and simply stirred with the sugar. Butter cookies have a superior flavor and texture when the butter is just softened and beaten, by hand or with an electric mixer, but only until smooth and creamy. Sugar cookies are at their best when pliable butter is beaten with sugar with an electric mixer until light and fluffy.

Flour is normally added at the end of the recipe. This is the second critical mixing phase for most cookie recipes. How long and vigorously the flour is mixed into the dough has an important—and not at all subtle—effect on cookies! Once flour is added to the moist ingredients, excess mixing makes tough cookies. This happens because gluten (certain proteins in wheat) begins to develop and makes the dough stronger and more elastic. Strong dough is great for breads but terrible for cookies. The goal then is to blend the flour thoroughly into the dough or batter with as little mixing as possible. The trick is to be sure that the flour is first mixed thoroughly with other dry ingredients (especially leavening and sometimes spices and salt) and that it is aerated and fluffed up rather than compacted and clumped, so that it will blend easily into the dough. Toward this end, I mix dry ingredients together with a wire whisk, which aerates at the same time as it mixes.

To add the flour without excessive mixing, I like to turn the mixer off (if I am using one) and add all the flour mixture at one time and then commence mixing at low speed. This works if your bowl is relatively tall—at least as tall as it is wide—to prevent the flour from flying out of the bowl when the mixer is turned on. Otherwise, add the dry ingredients gradually enough to avoid flying flour, but without taking any more time than necessary. Or mix in the flour with a spoon or your hands. In any case, mix only long enough to blend in the flour.

If the dough is relatively stiff, as with butter or sugar cookies, scrape the dough into a mass and knead it with your hands a few times just until smooth and with any traces of dry flour incorporated.

CHILLING AND RESTING THE DOUGH

Why chill and rest cookie dough?

Cookies are so simple to make that it seems a shame to deny the convenience, and the instant gratification, of mixing and baking on the spur of the moment whenever possible.

In the case of slice-and-bake or roll-and-cut cookies, chilling makes the slicing, rolling, and cutting possible. But even cookies spooned and dropped right onto the pan may be improved with chilling/resting. Gluten developed in mixing or rolling out dough is relaxed while the dough rests, so cookies become more tender. Moisture in the dough is absorbed by the dry ingredients and dissolves some of the sugar. This causes extra caramelization (browning), which improves flavor. Flavors become more developed and better integrated when dough has rested, and some cookies end up both more tender and crisper. Although wheat-free or gluten-free cookies that are made with non-wheat flours don't have the same gluten or toughness problem, resting benefits these doughs as well. I've found that letting dough with non-wheat flours and starches rest and absorb moisture causes the starches to gelatinize and cook more thoroughly, and this eliminates the unpleasant raw starch flavor that plagues many gluten-free treats. For me this was a trial-and-error discovery that made my experiments turn out much better.

The appearance of cookies may be enhanced by chilling as well: cookies spread less on the pan and some develop an appetizing sheen on the surface. Nuts, chocolate chips, and other additions often poke through the dough and show themselves off more after chilling.

If chilled cookie dough is too stiff to scoop, let it soften at room temperature. A chilled log of dough may need to soften briefly at room temperature as well.

Can I cheat on the chilling time?

When the recipe says, "If possible, chill the dough . . . ," then cheat if you must. Your cookies will still be tasty and delicious. But compare cookies mixed and baked immediately with cookies baked after an overnight chill and you may change your cookie-making habits forever. If you are always in a hurry and still want the best cookies, keep portioned scoops of cookie dough on hand in the freezer or fridge to satisfy spur-of-the-moment desires or choose recipes that do not recommend a chilling period.

Can cookie dough be frozen?

Consult the list on page 366 for cookie doughs that can be frozen. As a rule most stiff doughs (as opposed to wetter batters and meringues, etc.) can be frozen—and for at least 3 months, before they deteriorate in quality. The quality of the cookies baked from frozen dough depends on how well you wrap the dough and whether your freezer actually keeps things frozen.

For slice-and-bake cookies, freeze cookie dough after shaping it into logs rolled up in parchment or wax paper. Wrap the logs again in heavy-duty foil. Then put them into an airtight freezer bag or sealed freezer container.

For rolled-and-cut cookies, form patties as directed in the recipe and wrap them in plastic wrap. Wrap again in foil and then put them into a freezer bag or sealed freezer container.

For drop cookies (oatmeal, chocolate chip, gingersnaps), freeze the whole mass in a freezer bag and then put that into another freezer bag or sealed container; or you can shape the dough into cookie-size portions by freezing them on a cookie sheet, then double-bagging them in freezer bags.

For convenience, tuck a note in the container to remind you of baking time and temperature. Thaw frozen dough in the refrigerator several hours or overnight.

ROLLING, CUTTING, SHAPING, SCOOPING

What is the best way to roll and cut cookies?

Traditionally, cookie dough is rolled out on a well-floured board with a floured rolling pin and lots of flour sprinkled everywhere to prevent it from sticking. All that excess flour tends to toughen the cookies, and the procedure is tricky for inexperienced bakers anyway.

A better, easier, and less messy technique is to roll the dough between sheets of wax paper, plastic wrap, or a cut-apart heavy resealable plastic bag.

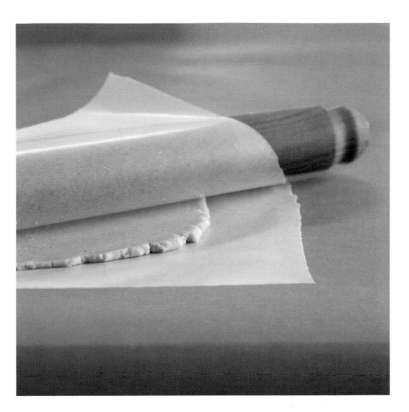

Cookie dough softens quickly once it comes out of the refrigerator. If you have more than one patty of dough to roll out, remove them one at a time, a few minutes apart, so they won't be too soft to work with when you get to them.

Let the dough sit at room temperature until supple enough to roll but still quite firm. It will continue to soften as you work. Roll the dough to the required thickness between the sheets of plastic wrap or wax paper or the cut-apart plastic bag. Roll from the center up to, but never over, the edge of the dough, rotating the dough as you work. Turn over the dough and attached sheets now and then to check for deep wrinkles. If necessary, peel off and smooth a wrinkled sheet over the dough before continuing to roll it. When the dough is thin enough, slide the whole assembly onto a tray and refrigerate it while you roll out the remaining pieces of dough.

To cut out cookies, remove the first piece of dough from the fridge, peel off the top sheet, and place it on the counter in front of you. Flip the dough, still attached to the other sheet, over onto the loose sheet and peel off the attached sheet. Cut shapes close together to minimize scraps, dipping the edges of your cookie cutters in flour as necessary to prevent sticking. Use the point of a paring knife to remove scraps between cookies.

If the dough gets too soft at any time—while rolling, removing paper or plastic, cutting, removing scraps

between cookies, or transferring cookies—slide a cookie sheet underneath the bottom sheet of paper or plastic and refrigerate the dough for a few minutes, until firm. Repeat with the remaining pieces of dough. Gently press all of the accumulated dough scraps together (don't overwork them with too much kneading) and reroll.

Is there a shortcut for rolling soft dough?
When you want to get most of the work done now, and then cut and bake at the last minute, an alternative to chilling dough and then rolling it out is to roll it out and then chill it! As soon as the dough is mixed, roll it very gently between sheets of parchment or heavy plastic from a large resealable plastic freezer bag that has been cut apart. The dough will be so soft that you barely need any

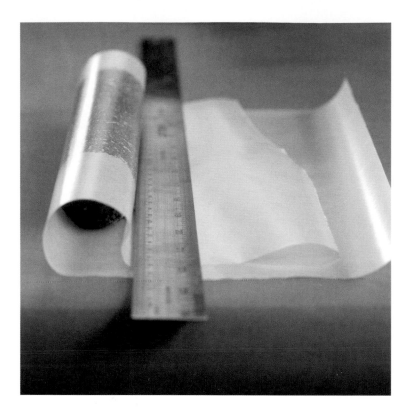

pressure on the pin. Be extra-careful not to let the edges of the dough become thinner than the center: thus the pin should never be rolled over the edge of the dough. Once the dough is rolled out, you can smooth it by rubbing the surface with the rolling pin. Slide the dough, still between the sheets, onto a cookie sheet and refrigerate it until it is cold and firm enough to cut, or for as long as you like. Stack more rolled-out sheets on top if necessary. Remove the cold sheets one at a time.

How should dough scraps be handled?

Squishing and rerolling dough scraps over and over again toughens the final cookie. To minimize this effect, first cut cookie shapes as close together as possible (for the smallest amount of scrap). Second, set aside all scraps from cutting out cookies from each piece of rolled-out dough. Then gather all of the accumulated scraps and press them together (with as little kneading or working as possible). Roll them out, chill the sheet, and cut shapes as close together as possible. Repeat once or twice . . . but no more.

What's the best way to shape a log of cookie dough for slice-and-bake cookies?

Place an 18-inch length of wax paper horizontally on the counter in front of you. Form a rough log lengthwise in the center of the paper, 2 or 3 inches shorter than the recipe calls for. If the dough is soft or gooey, just scrape it into a vaguely long uneven shape. Pull the top edge of the paper over the log (toward you) to cover it. Hold the edge of a ruler (or straightedge) along the length of the log, on top of both layers of paper, pressing against the counter. With your other hand, grip the bottom layer of the paper while pushing the ruler away from you, to squeeze and lengthen the log. When the log is the desired length, roll it up in the paper and twist the ends. Refrigerate until needed. For round cookies, slice logs in the obvious way. For oval cookies (see photo, page 317), make dough logs thinner than the recipe might call for and slice on the diagonal.

What are the best ways to portion cookies?

Cookies bake more evenly if they are all the same size. Here are three ways to get there:

> A cookie scoop (there are several sizes) with a squeeze-release handle is a good tool for forming equal-size lumps of cookie dough quickly and easily. See page 360 for more information.

> A scale is also a great way to produce equal-size lumps of dough: divide the weight of the entire batch of dough by the number of cookies desired in order to find the weight for each portion. Or pinch off a piece of dough the size you want and weigh it. Then duplicate that weight for the rest of the cookies.

> A grid is a great low-tech method for portioning cookies: pat the dough into a neat square patty, evenly thick (say, about ¾ inch thick), and chill it. Cut the patty into equal squares: for 36 cookies, cut a 6-by-6 grid, for example. Shape each piece into a ball, a crescent, or what you will.

PAN PREPARATION

What is the best way to prepare cookie sheets?

My recipes offer options for pan preparation in order of preference, weighing quality of outcome with convenience for the baker.

Pan liners are convenient because they rarely need greasing, they can be preloaded while cookie sheets are still in the oven, and you can slide them off of the pan and onto racks for cooling (or even set the lined pan itself on racks to cool), rather than removing hot cookies one by one from hot pans.

Parchment paper is probably the best all-purpose pan liner. Cookies don't stick to it and its slight insulating effect promotes even baking, prevents chocolaty batters and meringues from scorching, and generally mitigates the effects of poor quality baking sheets, which might be too dark or too thin. Precut sheets of parchment (see Resources, page 362) are vastly easier to use (and reuse) than the rolls that come in a box because these sheets lie flat on the pan, instead of curling up.

That being said, parchment is not always the first choice. Assuming good quality cookie sheets (see page 360), a few cookies (for example, certain chocolate chip cookies and oatmeal cookies) are noticeably more crusty and caramelized around the edges—in contrast to their chewy centers—if baked directly on the pan. One caveat: if your cookie sheets are so thin or dark that your cookies tend to burn on the bottoms before the tops are baked, you are better off using parchment paper liners.

To get the advantages (browning, caramelized flavor, and contrast of texture) of baking directly on the pan *as well as* the convenience of a liner, you can use foil. Placed dull side up, foil conducts heat and produces results similar to an unlined pan. Use regular weight foil unless heavy-duty foil is called for. Recipes call for the dull side up only when it makes a significant difference in results.

Silicone liners or mats (such as Silpat) are especially convenient for very thin fragile wafers and lace cookies, but they provide too much insulation to be good all-purpose liners. I avoid black or other dark-colored reusable pan liners because they produce cookies with a boringly uniform soft texture.

When it is necessary to grease pans or liners, use a brush or wad of paper towel to coat them lightly, but thoroughly, with flavorless vegetable oil or melted butter.

What is the best way to line baking pans?
Why line baking pans? It is easier to line pans than to grease them, and lined pans make the removal of bars or brownies easier too.

You can simply line the pan across the bottom and all the way up two opposite sides with foil or parchment.

But a second method (which I prefer) is to line the bottom and all four sides of the pan. Use a sheet of foil or parchment 4 inches wider and longer than the bottom of the pan. Turn the pan upside down and center the liner on it with 2 inches extending on all sides. Fold the excess over the sides of the pan. Fold and crease the corners over as though wrapping a present. Slip the liner off the pan. Turn the pan right side up and insert the liner. To remove brownies or bars from the pan, simply lift the edges of the foil or parchment.

BAKING

What kind of oven was used to develop these recipes?

My recipes were developed and tested in a conventional (nonconvection) gas oven. To bake in a convection oven, check your oven's operating manual for instructions. It may tell you to bake at a temperature 25 degrees lower than the recipe calls for and check doneness a little bit early.

Do I have to preheat the oven?

Oven temperature affects the texture and flavor of cookies as well as the baking time. Cookie dough put into an oven that is not hot enough may spread too much, dry out, or toughen. As well, different kinds of dough do better at different temperatures. All things considered, you will get better results if cookies go into an oven that is already heated to the optimal temperature. It takes most ovens about 15 minutes to reach a set temperature.

If your cookies are baking faster or slower than the recipe suggests, your oven may not be accurate. Test the oven with an oven thermometer and compensate accordingly or have a professional calibrate and reset the dial. All of your baking will turn out better.

Where should the racks be placed in the oven?

My recipes suggest that you bake in the center of the oven if you are baking one sheet of cookies at a time, or in the lower third for one pan of brownies or bars. When baking two sheets at a time, position the racks in the upper and lower thirds of the oven, reversing the cookie sheets from upper to lower and from front to back about halfway through the baking period so that the cookies bake evenly.

In a convection oven, you will be able to bake more than two trays at a time and may not have to rotate them if the oven bakes evenly.

Why rotate the pans while baking?

Even if you are baking one sheet of cookies at a time in the center of the oven, chances are your oven is hotter in the back than the front (if not also different from one side to the other!). Turning the pan around halfway through the baking time produces cookies that are baked about the same regardless of where they were in the oven. If you are baking two sheets at once, rotating from top to bottom (as well as back to front) will prevent your top sheet from overbaking before your bottom sheet is done. Seems fussy, I know.

Do I need to cool the cookie sheets between batches?
A common rule in cookie baking says that you must always cool cookie sheets before putting a new batch of raw cookies on the sheet. Warm sheets start the dough melting slowly before it goes into the oven, which can cause deformed cookie shapes, too much spreading, or altered baking times.

There is, however, a little-known exception to the rule: if raw cookies are already formed and laid out on a parchment or foil pan liner, you may slide the liner onto a hot or warm cookie sheet so long as you put the sheet into the oven *immediately*. Cookies may get done a few seconds earlier . . .

Take advantage of this exception to the rule to produce scads of cookies with only one oven and two cookie sheets. While cookies are baking, keep forming cookies and laying them out on parchment or foil liners spread out on the counter. When hot cookies come from the oven, slide the hot liners onto cooling racks and slide the new liners, laden with unbaked dough, onto the hot sheets and into the hot oven immediately. Baking times may be a bit shorter, but the cookies will not suffer. Repeat the performance until you drop or all the dough is used up—whichever comes first.

Can I bake small cookies and large cookies at the same time?
If you are baking a variety of different-size cookies from one type of dough, group cookies of similar size on each sheet so that all the cookies on the sheet will be done at the same time. The smaller cookies will be done earlier.

Can I make cookies larger or smaller than the recipe directs?
If your cookies are larger or smaller than the recipe calls for, the baking time and yield will necessarily be different. If you make extra-large cookies, leave more space between them for spreading.

What is the best way to cool cookies?
If you bake on parchment- or foil-lined pans, slide the liner from the hot cookie sheet onto a cooling rack, leaving the cookies attached. Or, if you have enough pans and racks, do what the professionals do: set the hot cookie sheet itself on the rack and allow the cookies to cool on the lined pan. However, if your cookies seem slightly overbaked or verging on overbaked (no one is perfect), slide the liners off immediately rather than letting the cookies cool on the pan. Every second counts.

If baking directly on the pan, use a thin, flexible metal pancake turner to transfer each cookie from the pan to cooling racks. Some cookies can be transferred from the pan immediately; others require 1 to 2 minutes of cooling before they are firm or sturdy enough to move without breaking. If the first cookie you transfer breaks or bends, wait a minute or so and try again.

What if cookies stick to the parchment or foil liner?
A few cookies tend to stick to parchment paper or foil. Allowing the cookies to cool completely before removing them usually solves this problem. And if the cookies are fragile (like lace cookies and certain delicate macarons), they should be removed by turning an edge of the parchment or foil over and peeling it carefully from each cookie, rather than trying to lift the cookies from the liner. If cookies still stick or leave a bit of their bottoms on the liners when removed, they are probably underbaked. Bake them a bit longer next time.

STORING

How should cookies be stored and for how long?
Cool cookies thoroughly before stacking or storing in a closed container. Othewise, they will become soggy (even moldy!) or misshapen from trapped steam.

Most cookies should be stored in airtight containers: tins, jars, resealable plastic bags, or cookie jars with tight-fitting lids. Certain cookies (such as those that are crunchy on the outside and moist within) should be stored in loosely covered containers that allow some air to get in. Different kinds and flavors of cookies should be stored separately or they will all taste pretty much the same and have the same texture after a day or two. Fragile cookies should be stored in wide containers where they can lie flat with parchment or wax paper between layers. If you have iced or decorated your cookies, make sure the decoration is completely dry before layering the cookies between sheets of wax paper.

Some cookies keep for a remarkably long time—how long depends on how often the container is opened and whether the cookies have inclusions or whole grains that can turn rancid. Certain butter cookies, shortbreads, meringues, and biscotti may keep for 3 months or more in an airtight tin. Unless indicated otherwise, the cookies and bars in this book may be frozen for at least 2 or 3 months.

Depending on the filling, thumbprint cookies and other filled cookies may soften in storage. Fill on the day of serving if possible. Lightly sieved powdered sugar may seep into the cookie; sieve shortly before serving. Cookies rolled in powdered sugar may need to be redusted before serving.

CRISPY

Thin is the hallmark of "crispy" that sets snappy tuiles, wafers, and my favorite cookie sticks apart from thicker, sandier, or crunchier butter cookies or biscotti. Thin appears to describe mere physicality or shape, but it profoundly defines the entire experience of enjoying a crispy cookie: the dainty first impression, the sharp audible crack with each bite, and (with luck) the frisson of pleasure and surprise that such a fragile-looking cookie could be so very flavorful. Thinness affects behavior too: a long thin cookie forces you to take many small bites rather than one large one; your pleasure is prolonged and you focus on flavor. Fragile tuiles and shards of cocoa cookie bark—as crisp as potato chips—are more likely to be picked up one by one with two fingers than taken up in handfuls. (Did someone lift a pinky?) Canny bakers take note. Crispy wonderfulness is easily lost if thicker cookies are shaped from the same mixture, or if cookies are underbaked.

SESAME STICKS

Irresistible to sesame lovers, these thin, addictively crunchy yet delicate cookies pack a wallop of flavor.
(Photograph on page 28)

Makes thirty-six to forty-six 4- or 5-inch sticks

INGREDIENTS

1¼ cups (5.625 ounces) unbleached all-purpose flour

⅔ cup (4.625 ounces) sugar

⅓ cup (1.625 ounces) lightly toasted sesame seeds (see page 16)

⅓ cup (1.125 ounces) ground blanched almonds

Scant ¾ teaspoon salt

6 tablespoons cold unsalted butter

1 teaspoon pure vanilla extract

2 tablespoons cold water

EQUIPMENT

A 5-by-9-inch loaf pan (optional), lined on the bottom and sides with foil (see page 24)

Cookie sheets, lined with parchment paper or greased

By Hand Put the flour, sugar, sesame seeds, almonds, and salt in a large mixing bowl and whisk to blend. Cut the butter into the flour mixture with a pastry blender or two knives until the butter is reduced to small pieces. With the fingertips of both hands, lightly toss and rub the mixture together until the mixture resembles coarse meal. Combine the vanilla and water in a small pitcher or cup. Stir the flour and butter mixture with a fork while drizzling the water and vanilla into the bowl. Continue to toss and stir lightly with the fork or your fingers until all of the dry ingredients are slightly damp. The dough should remain crumbly and stick together only when pinched (see Tips for Sticks, page 33).

In a Food Processor Combine the flour, sugar, sesame seeds, almonds, and salt in the food processor and pulse until thoroughly mixed. Cut the butter into ½-inch cubes and add to the processor. Pulse until the mixture looks like coarse crumbs. Combine the vanilla and water and drizzle them into the processor bowl. Pulse just until the mixture resembles damp crumbs—they should stick together only when pressed (see Tips for Sticks, page 33).

If using a loaf pan, dump the mixture into the lined pan and spread it evenly. Press it very firmly, making a thin layer. Or dump the mixture onto a sheet of foil on a baking sheet and distribute it evenly over an area about 4 by 9 or 10 inches. Press it firmly, squaring up the edges, to make an even compact layer about ½ inch thick. Fold the foil over the dough and wrap it tightly. Refrigerate for 2 hours or overnight.

Preheat the oven to 350°F. Position racks in the upper and lower thirds of the oven.

Unwrap the dough and transfer it to a cutting board. Use a long sharp knife to cut the dough crosswise into ¼-inch (or thinner if possible) slices. Use the knife to transfer each slice to the lined or greased cookie sheets, placing the slices 1 inch apart. The slices will be fragile and require the support of the knife in transit; the results will be worth your careful effort.

Bake for 12 to 18 minutes, until the cookies are golden with golden brown edges. Rotate the pans from top to bottom and from front to back halfway through the baking time to ensure even baking.

For lined pans, set the pans or just the liners on racks to cool; for unlined pans, use a metal spatula to transfer the cookies to racks. Cool the cookies completely before stacking or storing. May be kept in an airtight container for several days.

UPGRADES

Coconut Sticks Crispy crunchy. Sweet with loads of coconut flavor. Pair with tropical fruit sorbets, citrus sherbets, raspberries and cream . . . a cup of espresso. | Substitute 1 cup (3 ounces) unsweetened dried shredded coconut (see page 352) for the sesame seeds and the almonds. Decrease the salt to a rounded ¼ teaspoon.

STICK CHAT

The Coconut Sticks upgrade and the several other "stick" cookies in these pages are stars in this collection. The recipe and the method came about as I was trying to make an extra-flavorful crunchy coconut butter cookie. To get more coconut flavor and crunch, I reduced the amount of butter. Then, to produce a tender cookie with less butter, I changed the mixing method and made the cookies extra-thin. The long thin shape made the cookies dainty and elegant, wonderfully crispy, and (happy surprise) produced more intense and complex flavors in the bargain.

It makes sense. Thin cookies have loads of surface area. They brown easily, so the flavors of caramelized sugar, browned butter, toasted flour, nuts, and seeds permeate the entire cookie. Ingredients such as coconut (or hazelnuts in Hazelnut Sticks, page 34) that often require pretoasting to bring out their flavor actually toast while the cookies are baking, so it is not necessary to toast them separately. Sesame seeds proved an exception (see Sesame Sticks, page 30): lightly toasting them beforehand improves the cookie enough to make it worth the quick extra step.

Mixing the dough by hand—which I prefer—is like making pie dough by hand, but much more forgiving. And "by hand" is less work here rather than more. Meanwhile, the process is tactile, quiet, fast, and easy to control. It produces the best cookies, and you don't have to get out (or wash) the food processor.

Tips for Sticks It is essential that you *not* make a smooth cohesive dough here. All you want is a damp crumbly mass that sticks together only when you press it together. (If it doesn't, sprinkle and toss with only a tiny bit more liquid—not too much—just wetting your fingers and retossing the dough might be enough.)

HAZELNUT STICKS

I love the flavor of toasted hazelnuts, but I don't love toasting and skinning them. Here the hazelnuts go into the dough raw and emerge toasted along with the cookies.

Makes thirty-six to forty-six 4- or 5-inch sticks

INGREDIENTS

⅔ cup (3.33 ounces) raw hazelnuts
1¼ cups (5.625 ounces) unbleached all-purpose flour
½ cup plus 1½ tablespoons (4 ounces) sugar
Slightly rounded ¼ teaspoon salt
6 tablespoons cold unsalted butter
1 teaspoon pure vanilla extract
2 tablespoons cold water

EQUIPMENT

A 5-by-9-inch loaf pan (optional), lined on the bottom and sides with foil (see page 24)
Cookie sheets, lined with parchment paper or greased

By Hand Finely chop the hazelnuts and transfer them to a large mixing bowl. Whisk in the flour, sugar, and salt. Cut the butter into the flour mixture with a pastry blender or two knives until the butter is reduced to small pieces. With the fingertips of both hands, lightly toss and rub the mixture together until it resembles coarse meal. Combine the vanilla and water in a small pitcher or cup. Stir the flour and butter mixture with a fork while drizzling the water and vanilla into the bowl. Continue to toss and stir lightly with the fork or your fingers until all of the dry ingredients are slightly damp. The dough should remain crumbly and stick together only when pinched (see Tips for Sticks, page 33).

In a Food Processor   Combine the hazelnuts, flour, sugar, and salt in the food processor and pulse until the hazelnuts are finely chopped. Cut the butter into ½-inch cubes and add to the processor. Pulse until the mixture looks like coarse crumbs. Combine the vanilla and water and drizzle them into the processor bowl. Pulse just until the mixture resembles damp crumbs—it should not be a smooth mass, but it should stick together when pressed (see Tips for Sticks, page 33).

If using a loaf pan, dump the mixture into the lined pan and spread it evenly. Press it very firmly, making a thin layer. Or dump the mixture onto a sheet of foil on a baking sheet and distribute it evenly over an area about 4 by 9 or 10 inches. Press it firmly, squaring up the edges, to make an even compact layer about ½ inch thick. Fold the foil over the dough and wrap it tightly. Refrigerate for 2 hours or overnight.

Preheat the oven to 350°F. Position racks in the upper and lower thirds of the oven.

Unwrap the dough and transfer it to a cutting board. Use a long sharp knife to cut the dough crosswise into ¼-inch (or thinner if possible) slices. Use the knife to transfer each slice to the lined or greased cookie sheets, placing the slices 1 inch apart. The slices will be fragile and require the support of the knife in transit; the results will be worth your careful effort.

Bake for 12 to 18 minutes, until the cookies are golden with golden brown edges. Rotate the sheets from top to bottom and from front to back halfway through the baking time to ensure even baking.

For lined pans, set the pans or just the liners on racks to cool; for unlined pans, use a metal spatula to transfer the cookies to racks. Cool the cookies completely before stacking or storing. May be kept in an airtight container for several days.

CAFÉ DE OLLA STICKS

Inspiration for these crispy cookie sticks came from the memory of a spicy anise-scented cup of coffee (*café de olla*) that I tasted more than thirty years ago at the San Angel Inn outside of Mexico City. Food memories are powerful. The cookies are good too.

Makes thirty-six to forty-six 4- or 5-inch sticks

INGREDIENTS

1¼ cups (5.625 ounces) unbleached all-purpose flour

½ cup plus 1½ tablespoons (4 ounces) sugar

⅔ cup (2.67 ounces) ground blanched almonds

Scant ¾ teaspoon whole aniseed, crushed in a mortar

¾ teaspoon ground cinnamon

1¾ teaspoons freshly and finely ground coffee beans

Slightly rounded ⅛ teaspoon freshly ground black pepper

Slightly rounded ¼ teaspoon salt

6 tablespoons cold unsalted butter

2 tablespoons cold brewed espresso or very strong coffee

1 teaspoon pure vanilla extract

EQUIPMENT

A 5-by-9-inch loaf pan (optional), lined on the bottom and sides with foil (see page 24)

Cookie sheets, lined with parchment paper or greased

By Hand Put the flour, sugar, almonds, aniseed, cinnamon, ground coffee, pepper, and salt in a large mixing bowl and whisk thoroughly to blend. Cut the butter into the flour mixture with a pastry blender or two knives until the butter is reduced to small pieces. With the fingertips of both hands, lightly toss and rub the mixture together until it resembles coarse meal. Combine the brewed coffee and vanilla in a small pitcher or cup. Stir the flour and butter mixture with a fork while drizzling the coffee mixture into the bowl. Continue to toss and stir lightly with the fork or your fingers until all of the dry ingredients are slightly damp. The dough should remain crumbly and stick together only when pinched (see Tips for Sticks, page 33).

In a Food Processor Combine the flour, sugar, almonds, aniseed, cinnamon, ground coffee, pepper, and salt in the food processor and pulse until thoroughly mixed. Cut the butter into ½-inch cubes and add to the processor. Pulse until the mixture looks like coarse crumbs. Combine the brewed coffee and vanilla and drizzle into the processor bowl. Pulse just until the mixture resembles damp crumbs—it should not be a smooth mass, but it should stick together when pressed (see Tips for Sticks, page 33).

If using a loaf pan, dump the mixture into the lined pan and spread it evenly. Press it very firmly, making a thin layer. Or dump the mixture onto a sheet of foil on a baking sheet and distribute it evenly over an area about 4 by 9 or 10 inches. Press it firmly, squaring up the edges, to make an even compact layer about ½ inch thick. Fold the foil over the dough and wrap it tightly. Refrigerate for 2 hours or overnight.

Preheat the oven to 350°F. Position racks in the upper and lower thirds of the oven.

Unwrap the dough and transfer it to a cutting board. Use a long sharp knife to cut the dough crosswise into ¼-inch (or thinner if possible) slices. Use the knife to transfer each slice to the lined or greased cookie sheets, placing the slices 1 inch apart. The slices will be fragile and require the support of the knife in transit; the results will be worth your careful effort.

Bake for 12 to 18 minutes, until the cookies are a darker brown at the edges. Rotate the sheets from top to bottom and from front to back halfway through the baking time to ensure even baking.

For lined pans, set the pans or just the liners on racks to cool; for unlined pans, use a metal spatula to transfer the cookies to racks. Cool the cookies completely before stacking or storing. May be kept in an airtight container for several days.

VANILLA SUGAR COOKIES

Golden edges. Sweet snap. Crisp, crunchy perfection. Rolling the dough between sheets of paper or plastic avoids the addition of extra flour and thus ensures crisp but tender cookies. Perfectly crisp sugar cookies are an invitation to cut out hearts, diamonds, daisies, or dragons and decorate! When my daughter was tiny, we decorated vanilla sugar hearts for her preschool classmates each year on her birthday. Later I regularly cut out 8-inch fashion doll cookies for a kitchen full of little girls (and their moms) to dress in ball gowns and bikinis, with colored sugars, miniature M&M's, and swanky silver shot, with mink stoles made of chocolate jimmies . . .

Makes about ninety 2½-inch cookies or fifty-five 3½-inch cookies

INGREDIENTS

4 cups (18 ounces) unbleached all-purpose flour

1 teaspoon baking powder

½ teaspoon salt

½ pound (2 sticks) unsalted butter, slightly softened

2 cups (14 ounces) sugar

2 large eggs

1 tablespoon pure vanilla extract or prepared vanilla bean paste or (better still) ¾ teaspoon ground whole vanilla beans (see page 359)

Sugar or Vanilla Sugar (page 336) for sprinkling

EQUIPMENT

Cookie sheets, lined with parchment paper or greased

Cookie cutters

Combine the flour, baking powder, and salt in a bowl and mix together thoroughly with a whisk or a fork.

Beat the butter and sugar in a large bowl with an electric mixer until light and fluffy, 3 to 4 minutes. Beat in the eggs and vanilla. On low speed, beat in the flour just until incorporated. Scrape the dough into a mass and knead it with your hands a few times until smooth. Divide the dough into 4 pieces and form each into a flat patty. Wrap and refrigerate the patties until firm enough to roll, preferably several hours or overnight.

Preheat the oven to 350°F. Position racks in the upper and lower thirds of the oven.

To Roll and Cut Cookies Remove 1 patty from the refrigerator and let it sit at room temperature until supple enough to roll but still quite firm. It will continue to soften as you work. Roll the dough between two sheets of wax paper or plastic sheets from a cut-apart resealable plastic bag to a thickness of ⅛ inch. Turn the dough over once or twice while you are rolling it out to check for deep wrinkles; if necessary, peel off and smooth the paper over the dough before continuing to roll it.

When the dough is thin enough, slide it (still between the sheets) onto a cookie sheet and refrigerate. Repeat with the remaining patties, sliding each rolled-out piece on top of the others in the fridge. Remove the bottom (coldest) sheet of dough from the refrigerator. Peel off the top sheet of paper and set it on the counter. Invert the dough onto it and peel off the second sheet.

Cut cookie shapes as close together as possible to minimize scraps, dipping the edges of the cookie cutters in flour as necessary to prevent sticking. Use the point of a paring knife to lift and remove scraps as you transfer cookies to cookie sheets. Place the cookies at least 1½ inches apart on the lined or greased cookie sheets. If the dough gets too soft at any time—while rolling, cutting, removing scraps between cookies, or transferring cookies—slide a cookie sheet underneath the paper or plastic and refrigerate the dough for a few minutes, until firm. Repeat with the remaining pieces of dough. Gently press all of the dough scraps together (don't overwork them with too much kneading) and reroll. Sprinkle cookies with sugar or Vanilla Sugar.

Bake for 8 to 10 minutes, or until pale golden at the edges, rotating the pans from top to bottom and from front to back halfway through the baking time to ensure even baking. Repeat until all the cookies are baked.

For lined pans, set the pans or just the parchment liners on racks to cool; for unlined pans, use a metal spatula to transfer the cookies to the racks, waiting 1 or 2 minutes if necessary to let the cookies firm up before moving them. Cool the cookies completely before stacking, decorating, or storing. May be kept in an airtight container for at least 1 month.

UPGRADES

Cardamom Sugar Stars These are fragrant in any shape. Be sure to allow the edges to turn lightly golden in the oven for extra flavor and snap. | Make Vanilla Sugar Cookie dough, adding 1 teaspoon of ground cardamom with the sugar. Cut with star or snowflake cookie cutters. Sprinkle cookies with Cardamom Sugar (page 336) instead of plain sugar or Vanilla Sugar before baking.

Sugar and Spice Cookies Substitute any of the spiced sugars (page 336) for the sprinkled sugar or Vanilla Sugar.

COOKIE TREATMENTS

IMPRINTING

The dough for Basic Butter Cookies (page 310), Mexican Wedding Cakes (page 306), and Peanut Butter Cookies (page 324) can be imprinted, scored, or marked before baking with cookie stamps or ordinary household or kitchen objects such as meat-tenderizing mallets, forks, graters, kids' toys, and other found objects. For deep impressions, form the dough into a ball, then press with the chosen imprinter until the cookie is as thin as desired. Test the imprinter to see if it sticks to the cookie dough; grease and/or dust it with flour if necessary. For the best impressions, refrigerate imprinted cookies for at least 30 minutes before baking.

PIPING AND DRIZZLING

Cookie icing is always an option, but for piped and drizzled cookie decorations that dry hard and taste good too, nothing beats pure melted chocolate (see page 15). It's simple to use (although it must be kept warm) and requires no tempering. (Melted untempered chocolate rarely blooms or discolors if drizzled or piped [but not spread or dipped] on the surface of cookies. The explanation is part science—having to do with the fats migrating from the cookie to the chocolate drizzle—and part magic as far as I am concerned.) Use white chocolate, milk chocolate, or dark chocolate bars (or professional pieces of chocolate called *pistoles, callets,* or *fèves*) rather than ordinary chocolate chips, which do not melt well.

You can even tint melted white chocolate with oil-based or powdered food colorings (see Resources) designed especially for the purpose. Ordinary food coloring, which is water based, is incompatible with chocolate. Pipe or drizzle on the cookies after they have baked and cooled.

DIPPING

From butter cookies to biscotti, alfajores to amaretti, cookies dipped in chocolate always raise the bar. For the best results, dip cookies in Easy Chocolate Cookie Dip (page 344) or Tempered Chocolate Cookie Dip (page 345).

DECORATING WITH COLORED SUGARS AND CANDIES

For fancy party favors, Christmas decorations, or any other show-off cookies, where each cookie is a unique work of art.

Gather an assortment of colored sprinkles, sugars, miniature M&M's, jelly beans, and silver shot. Melt chocolate (see page 15) or prepare cookie icing (see page 342) and scrape it into the corner of a resealable plastic bag. Snip the tip of the bag with scissors. Pipe chocolate on a cookie wherever you want to affix a particular type of sprinkle, then press the cookie gently, piping side down, into a saucer of the sprinkles. Set the cookie aside to dry. To add a second type of decoration, pipe on the same cookie and press into another saucer, and so forth. Embed larger decorations in chocolate or icing by hand, one by one. Let the decorations dry completely before storing the cookies between layers of wax paper or sliding each into a cellophane bag.

MAKING SANDWICHES

In addition to the Alfajores (page 192), French Macarons (page 276), Linzer Cookies (page 194), and other sandwich cookies in this book, you can fill almost any cookie you like with the fillings or frostings on pages 338–44, or with Nutella, jams or preserves from your pantry, or even pure melted chocolate. For dainty sandwiches, make cookies a little thinner than usual.

Rich fillings like pure chocolate ganache or Nutella have little or no moisture, so they don't cause cookies to soften. By contrast, the moisture in jams and preserves, Lemon Curd, and Dulce de Leche softens cookies in a short time; put sandwiches together with these fillings shortly before serving (except for French Macarons, which are meant to meld with their filling).

Basic Butter Cookies (page 310), Almond Sablés (page 318) and any variations with nuts or whole wheat are excellent with jam. Pair blackberry preserves with walnut or hazelnut cookies, raspberry or apricot with almond cookies, strawberry with peanut cookies, pineapple with macadamia cookies, and so forth. Use 1 teaspoon of jam for each sandwich; 1 cup fills about forty-eight 2½- to 3-inch sandwich cookies.

Try Vanilla Sugar Cookies (page 38) and Basic Butter Cookies (or nut variations) sandwiched with 1 to 1½ teaspoons melted bittersweet or semisweet chocolate; Brown Sugar Butter Cookies and Bourbon Pecan Butter Cookies (both on page 312) with white chocolate; and Chocolate Espresso Cookies (page 204) filled with milk chocolate. No tempering is necessary because the chocolate will not actually be seen. Let cookies sit at room temperature or refrigerate briefly to harden the chocolate. Six ounces of chocolate fills about twenty-four sandwich cookies.

Vanilla ice cream is a sublime filling for all kinds of cookies—use your imagination. Soften the ice cream in the refrigerator just until it is soft enough to scoop and press between cookies without breaking them. Refreeze until serving. If the sandwiches are rock hard, let them soften briefly before serving. Count on about 3 tablespoons of ice cream for a 3-inch cookie. One pint fills about 10 sandwiches.

WHEAT-FREE BUTTER COOKIES

Finally, after *so* much testing . . . here are wheat-free cookies with a clean lovely flavor and tender buttery crunch. You can produce heaps of different cookies with this simple dough. Feel free to add chopped nuts of any kind (raw or roasted), citrus zest, spices, bits of dried fruit, raisins or currants, or cacao nibs. In short, flavors or inclusions that are delicious in wheat-based butter cookies or sugar cookies will be successful in these. You can use this dough to make crusts for wheat-free toffee bars. You can even make cutout cookies (page 46) for decorating with kids. Wheat-free magic.

Makes about thirty-six 2½-inch cookies

INGREDIENTS

⅓ cup plus 1 tablespoon (2 ounces) white rice flour, preferably superfine (see Note)

1¼ cups plus 2 tablespoons (5 ounces) oat flour (see Note)

¼ teaspoon salt

⅛ teaspoon baking soda

⅔ cup (4.625 ounces) sugar

2 ounces cream cheese, cut in chunks

12 tablespoons (1½ sticks) unsalted butter, softened, cut into chunks

1 teaspoon pure vanilla extract

EQUIPMENT

Cookie sheets, lined with parchment paper or greased

In a medium bowl, combine the flours, salt, and baking powder, and mix thoroughly with a whisk or fork. In a large bowl, using the back of a large spoon or an electric mixer, mix the sugar with the cream cheese, butter, and vanilla just until smooth and creamy. Add the flour mixture and mix just until it is incorporated. (Don't overmix; while there is no risk of gluten developing, excess mixing reduces the binding power of the cream cheese and produces a finished cookie with a less perfect texture.)

Divide the dough between two sheets of wax paper and form two 8-inch logs about 1½ inches in diameter. Wrap them tightly in the wax paper and refrigerate for at least 2 hours, preferably longer or overnight.

Preheat the oven to 325°F. Position racks in the upper and lower thirds of the oven.

Use a sharp knife to cut the cold dough log into ¼-inch-thick slices. Place the cookies at least 1½ inches apart on the lined or greased baking sheets. Bake for 12 to 15 minutes, until the cookies are golden brown at the edges and well browned on the bottom. The tops will remain fairly pale. Rotate the pans from top to bottom and from front to back halfway through the baking time to ensure even baking.

For lined pans, set the pans or just the liners on racks to cool; for unlined pans, use a metal spatula to transfer the cookies to racks. Cool completely before stacking or storing. May be kept in an airtight container for at least 2 weeks.

NOTE

The weight of a cup of non-wheat flour or starch can vary wildly—even more than wheat flour—depending on your measuring style. And wild variation can make an otherwise excellent cookie quite dreadful. Weighing is the surest way to get consistently good results. But if you must measure with cups, do it like this: Set the measuring cup on a sheet of wax paper. Spoon the flour or starch lightly into the cup until it is heaping. Sweep a knife across the rim of the cup to level it without tapping or packing. (Pick up the wax paper and fold it in half to pour excess flour back into the bag.)

WHEAT-FREE CUTOUT COOKIES

This is the only recipe you need when cutout shapes are wanted for kids, decorating (see page 41), special events, or holidays. You won't need to make an additional batch of wheat cookies to please the others, because these will please everyone. Since the dough spreads slightly in baking, choose cookie cutters with simple rather than highly intricate or detailed shapes.

Makes about thirty-six 2½-inch cookies

INGREDIENTS

1 recipe Wheat-Free Butter Cookie dough (page 44)

EQUIPMENT

Cookie sheets, lined with parchment paper or greased
Cookie cutters

Form the dough into 2 flat patties. Wrap and refrigerate the dough for at least 2 hours, and preferably overnight. The dough may be frozen for up to 3 months.

Preheat the oven to 325°F. Position racks in the upper and lower thirds of the oven.

Remove 1 patty from the refrigerator and let it sit at room temperature briefly, until supple enough to roll but still quite firm. It will continue to soften as you work. Roll the dough between 2 pieces of wax paper, or between heavy plastic sheets from a plastic bag, to a thickness of ⅛ inch. Turn the dough over once or twice while you are rolling it out to check for deep wrinkles; if necessary, peel off and smooth the paper or plastic over the dough before continuing to roll it. When the dough is thin enough, peel off the top sheet of paper or plastic and keep it in front of you. (If the dough is sticky, dust it with a little oat flour.) Invert the dough onto the sheet in front of you and peel off the second sheet. Cut cookie shapes as close together as possible to minimize scraps, dipping the edges of cookie cutters in oat flour as necessary to prevent sticking. Use the point of a paring knife to lift and remove scraps as you transfer cookies to cookie sheets. Place cookies 1½ inches apart on cookie sheets. If the dough gets too soft at any time— while rolling, cutting, removing scraps between cookies, or transferring cookies—slide a cookie sheet underneath the paper or plastic and refrigerate the dough for a few minutes until firm. Repeat with the second piece of dough.

Press all of the dough scraps together gently and reroll them as necessary. (There is no need to worry that rerolling scraps will produce tough cookies.)

Bake for 8 to 12 minutes, until golden brown at the edges but deep brown on the bottom, rotating the cookie sheets from top to bottom and from front to back halfway through the baking time to ensure even baking. Repeat until all the cookies are baked.

For lined pans, set the pans or just the liners on racks to cool; for unlined pans, use a metal spatula to transfer the cookies to racks. Cool completely before stacking or storing. May be kept in an airtight container for at least 2 weeks.

GOLDIES

This recipe originally produced a very sweet bar called a Scandinavian Blondie. Repurposed, it now makes gorgeous brown-edged golden cookies shaped like sand dollars. Enjoy them plain or sandwich them with a little rich milk chocolate or not-too-bitter semisweet chocolate . . . or a slather of Vanilla Dulce de Leche (page 337).

Makes seventy-two 2-inch cookies

INGREDIENTS

1½ cups (6.75 ounces) unbleached all-purpose flour

4½ tablespoons (1.35 ounces) cornstarch

3 large eggs

¾ cup plus 2 tablespoons (6.125 ounces) sugar

¾ teaspoon salt

1 tablespoon pure vanilla extract

12 tablespoons (1½ sticks) unsalted butter, melted and still warm

EQUIPMENT

Cookie sheets, lined with parchment paper or greased

Preheat the oven to 325°F. Position racks in the upper and lower thirds of the oven.

Combine the flour and cornstarch in a medium bowl and whisk together thoroughly with a wire whisk.

In a large mixing bowl, combine the eggs, sugar, salt, and vanilla. Beat with an electric mixer on high speed until the mixture is thick and pale, 2 to 3 minutes. Beat in the melted butter. Fold in half of the flour mixture. Fold in the remaining flour mixture.

Drop rounded teaspoons of batter 2 inches apart on the lined or greased cookie sheets. Bake until the cookies are deep golden brown around the edges, 16 to 20 minutes, rotating the pans from top to bottom and from front to back halfway through the baking time to ensure even baking. For lined pans, set the pans or just the liners on racks to cool; for unlined pans, use a metal spatula to transfer the cookies to racks. Repeat until all of the cookies are baked. Cool the cookies completely before stacking or storing. May be kept in an airtight container for at least 2 weeks.

UPGRADES

Lemon Goldies Quietly lemony and just right with a cup of tea. Finely grate the zest of 2 medium lemons into the melted butter before adding it.

ULTRATHIN CHOCOLATE CHUNK COOKIES

A theatrical departure from mainstream chocolate chip cookies, these are large and decidedly flat. They shatter dramatically when you bite them, releasing loads of caramel brown sugar flavor and bursts of bittersweet chocolate. I created this recipe for the original Scharffen Berger Chocolate Factory Store in Berkeley. These cookies will not spread as they should in a convection oven, so make them only if you have a conventional oven.

Makes fifteen 5-inch cookies

INGREDIENTS

1⅓ cups (6 ounces) unbleached all-purpose flour

½ teaspoon baking soda

10 tablespoons (1¼ sticks) unsalted butter, melted

½ cup (1.5 ounces) quick rolled oats

½ cup (3.5 ounces) granulated sugar

¼ cup (1.75 ounces) packed dark brown sugar

2 tablespoons plus 1 teaspoon (2 ounces) light corn syrup

2 tablespoons whole milk

½ teaspoon salt

7 ounces bittersweet or semisweet chocolate, chopped into chunks, or
   1 generous cup chocolate chips or chunks

EQUIPMENT

Cookie sheets, lined with foil, dull side up

Preheat the oven to 325°F. Position racks in the upper and lower thirds of the oven.

Combine the flour and baking soda in a small bowl and mix together thoroughly with a whisk or fork.

In a large bowl, whisk together the melted butter, oats, sugars, corn syrup, milk, and salt. Mix in the flour mixture. If the batter is warm from the butter, let it cool before adding the chocolate. Stir in the chocolate chunks. If possible, let the dough rest for at least several hours at room temperature or (better still) overnight in the fridge. The rest makes for an especially crisp and extra-flavorful cookie!

Divide the dough into 15 equal pieces (each a scant ¼ cup or about 1.75 ounces). Lay out 3 sheets of aluminum foil, cut to fit your cookie sheets, on the counter. Arrange 5 pieces of dough (4 in a square and 1 in the center) well apart on each sheet of foil, remembering that the cookies will spread to 5 inches. Flatten each piece of dough until it is about 3½ inches in diameter. Slide two of the sheets onto baking sheets.

Bake for 20 to 25 minutes, until the cookies are thin and very brown. If they are too pale, they will not be crisp. Rotate the pans from top to bottom and front to back halfway through the baking time to ensure even baking. Slide the foil with cookies onto racks to cool completely before removing the cookies from the foil. Repeat with the third batch—you can even slide the next foil and cookie dough onto a hot baking sheet as long as you put the pan in the oven immediately. Cool the cookies completely before stacking or storing. May be kept in an airtight container for at least 3 days.

VANILLA BEAN TUILES

Out of the oven, the deep fragrance of ground vanilla beans will stir memories from childhood: sweet cream-filled vanilla wafers, giant scoops of vanilla ice cream, vanilla-custard-filled éclairs . . .

Makes about forty 2½-inch tuiles

INGREDIENTS

3 tablespoons unsalted butter, melted and still warm, plus extra for greasing the pan liners

⅔ cup (4.625 ounces) sugar

3 large egg whites

¼ cup plus 3 tablespoons (2 ounces) unbleached all-purpose flour

¾ teaspoon ground vanilla beans (see page 359)

⅛ teaspoon salt

EQUIPMENT

Cookie sheets, lined with silicone baking mats or heavy-duty foil, dull side up

Offset spatula (optional)

Stencil (see page 60) with a 2½-inch-diameter circle (or other shape) cut from it (optional)

Small cups or a rolling pin for shaping the cookies (optional)

Preheat the oven to 300°F. Place racks in the upper and lower thirds of the oven. If using foil, smooth it to remove any wrinkles, which would distort the cookies. Grease the silicone mats or the foil lightly but thoroughly with melted butter.

In a small bowl, whisk together all of the ingredients until blended. Let the batter rest for at least 10 minutes or cover and refrigerate for up to 3 days.

Drop level teaspoons of the batter 2 inches apart onto the cookie sheets. Using a small offset spatula (and a template, if using) or the back of a spoon and a circular motion, spread the batter evenly in 2½-inch rounds (or ovals or other shapes) about ⅟₁₆ inch thick.

Bake, watching carefully, for 10 to 15 minutes, until the tuiles are golden brown half to three-quarters of the way to the center but still pale in the center. Rotate the pans from top to bottom and from front to back halfway through the baking time to ensure even baking. If the cookies are not baked long enough, they will not be completely crisp when cool.

If Using Silicone Mats As soon as you can coax a thin metal spatula under a cookie without destroying it, transfer it to a rack to cool flat. Or shape it by draping it over a rolling pin, nestling it into a little cup, or twisting it with your fingers. Working fast, remove the remaining tuiles; reheat if necessary.

If Using Foil Slide the foil sheet of cookies onto a rack to cool flat. Or, for curved tuiles, grasp the edges of the foil when the sheet comes from the oven (without touching the hot pan or the cookies) and roll it into a fat cylinder, gently curving the attached cookies like potato chips. Crimp or secure the foil with a paper clip. When cool, unroll the foil carefully and remove the tuiles. Alternatively, remove individual tuiles from the foil while they are hot (as soon as you can coax a thin metal spatula under a cookie without destroying it) and shape them as described above. Flat or curved, tuiles are easiest to remove from the foil when they are either very hot or completely cool.

Repeat until all of the tuiles are baked. To retain crispness, put the cookies in an airtight container as soon as they are cool. May be stored airtight for at least 1 month.

UPGRADES

Cinnamon Stick Tuiles You may be astonished at the flavor and aroma to be had from simply grating a stick of cinnamon with a Microplane grater—and at how easy it is. | Substitute 1½ teaspoons freshly grated stick cinnamon (or a slightly rounded ½ teaspoon ground cinnamon) for the ground vanilla beans.

Citrus Tuiles If you can find them, Meyer lemons will produce an exceptional floral fragrance and flavor. Or use mandarin orange, tangerine, blood orange, or regular orange zest. | Substitute 1 tablespoon finely grated lemon zest (I use a Microplane zester), preferably from an organic or unsprayed fruit, for the vanilla beans.

Fresh Thyme or Tarragon Tuiles Back porch gardeners will love this excuse to use more herbs in more interesting ways. The flavors of thyme or tarragon are clean and bright and lively in these sweet crisp wafers, and the aroma of butter, herbs, and sugar is divine coming out of the oven. | Stir ¾ teaspoon fresh thyme, lemon thyme, or small tarragon leaves (or pieces of larger tarragon leaves) into the very warm butter. Cover and allow to infuse for 5 minutes. Proceed as directed, using the butter and herbs instead of plain melted butter.

Saffron Tuiles These are exotic and impressively aromatic. Serve them with a creamy dessert such as panna cotta or a bowl of fresh sweet strawberries. | Stir a scant ⅜ teaspoon crushed saffron threads into the very warm butter. Cover and allow to infuse for 5 minutes. Proceed as directed, using the saffron butter instead of plain melted butter.

OPPOSITE: Fresh Thyme Tuile (above)

LAVENDER, JASMINE, OR ROSE TUILES

Pretty scented cookies to savor with tea. Serve Lavender or Rose Tuiles with fresh berries. The floral sultry flavor of jasmine makes a compelling partner for oranges and tangerines, or for honey ice cream.

Find dried lavender in the spice section of a good supermarket or gourmet shop or by mail order (see Resources, page 362). If you grow your own, make sure it is culinary lavender—the variety *Lavandula x intermedia,* also called *Provence lavender*—as other varieties can be unpleasantly pungent and resinous. Use lavender with a light hand to avoid a soapy or medicinal flavor.

Makes about forty 2½-inch tuiles

INGREDIENTS

3 tablespoons unsalted butter, melted and still very warm, plus extra for greasing the pan liners

⅜ teaspoon crushed dried culinary lavender, jasmine tea, or rose tea

⅔ cup (4.625 ounces) sugar

3 large egg whites

¼ cup plus 3 tablespoons (2 ounces) unbleached all-purpose flour

⅛ teaspoon salt

EQUIPMENT

Cookie sheets, lined with silicone baking mats or heavy-duty foil, dull side up

Offset spatula (optional)

Stencil (see page 60) with a 2½-inch-diameter circle (or other shape) cut from it (optional)

Small cups or a rolling pin for shaping the cookies (optional)

Preheat the oven to 300°F. Position racks in the upper and lower thirds of the oven. If using foil, smooth it to remove wrinkles. Grease the silicone mats or the foil lightly but thoroughly with melted butter.

Stir the lavender or tea into the very warm melted butter, cover, and allow to infuse for 5 minutes.

In a small bowl, whisk the infused butter mixture together with the sugar, egg whites, flour, and salt.

Drop level teaspoons of the batter 2 inches apart onto the cookie sheets. Using a small offset spatula (and a template, if using) or the back of a spoon and a circular motion, spread the batter evenly into 2½-inch rounds (or ovals or other shapes) about 1/16 inch thick.

Bake, watching carefully, for 10 to 15 minutes, until the tuiles are golden brown half to three-quarters of the way to the center but still pale in the center. Rotate the pans from top to bottom and from front to back halfway through the baking time to ensure even baking. If the cookies are not baked long enough they will not be completely crisp when cool.

If Using Silicone Mats As soon as you can coax a thin metal spatula under a cookie without destroying it, transfer it to a rack to cool flat. Or shape it by draping it over a rolling pin, nestling it into a little cup, or twisting it with your fingers. Working fast, remove the remaining tuiles; reheat if necessary.

If Using Foil Slide the foil sheet of cookies onto a rack to cool flat. Or, for curved tuiles, grasp the edges of the foil when the sheet comes from the oven (without touching the hot pan or the cookies) and roll it into a fat cylinder, gently curving the attached cookies like potato chips. Crimp or secure the foil with a paper clip. When cool, unroll the foil carefully and remove the tuiles. Alternatively, remove individual tuiles from the foil while they are hot (as soon as you can coax a thin metal spatula under a cookie without destroying it) and shape them as described above. Flat or curved, tuiles are easiest to remove from the foil when they are either very hot or completely cool.

Repeat until all of the wafers are baked. To retain crispness, put the cookies in an airtight container as soon as they are cool. May be stored airtight for at least 1 month.

TUILES

Tuiles (or "toolies," as young culinary students have been heard to say) are properly pronounced "tweel." The *s* is silent. If you don't speak French, you just can't win sometimes. But if you actually make these cookies, you win big! They are a quintessential cookie experience: ultrathin, elegant, addictive, very flavorful, and infinitely flexible (literally and figuratively) once you get the hang of them. They appear to be a project at first, and then you'll find that you want to make them again and again. This explains why there are so many tuiles in this book. I couldn't stop. You'll want to try them curved, rolled into little cigarettes, or shaped as tiny ice cream cones for a fancy party. You will invent your own flavors.

What's important to know about making tuiles? Timing is important: The cookies are very thin, so if you've never baked such thin cookies before, you might start by baking one sheet at a time on one rack in the center of the oven. Then you can graduate to handling two pans, remembering that you must rotate the pans, front to back and top to bottom, when you do. Measure flour scrupulously (see page 14 or use an electronic scale). Too much flour in such delicate cookies will toughen them.

Pastry chefs use a small offset spatula to spread tuile batter into thin rounds with or without a template. Absent a template (which requires that you use a little offset spatula), home bakers may find it easier to smear the tuile batter out to the desired diameter with the back of a small spoon using a circular motion.

HOW TO MAKE AND USE A STENCIL FOR TUILES

Cut stencils for tuiles out of any thin piece of plastic—such as a cottage cheese container lid or a flexible plastic place mat or cutting mat, or one normally used as a cutting board. Rounds, ovals, long cat's tongues, or any shape without intricate or fine detail will work perfectly: I've seen starfish, cacti, zigzags, spirals, and bunny rabbits. To use a stencil, hold it flat against the pan liner. Smear a little batter across the opening with a small offset spatula. Lift the stencil and repeat.

MORE EFFICIENT TUILE BAKING

While cookies are baking, you can continue to spread batter on extra pan liners set on the counter (or on extra pans if you have them). Slide the batter-laden liners onto cookie sheets and into the oven as soon as the oven is empty. You do not have to wait for the pans to cool between rounds so long as the liners are already filled with batter when you slide them onto the pans and the pans go into the oven immediately.

TO MAKE DAINTY ICE CREAM CONES FROM ANY TUILE BATTER

Position a rack in the center of the oven. Make the batter and preheat the oven as described. Line pans with greased silicone baking mats. Have ready a wooden cone or a plastic cone made by rolling and taping a piece of flexible plastic cutting mat.

Drop batter 3 inches apart onto the lined pans and spread each to a diameter of 4 inches. Bake (in this case, just one pan at a time, in the center of the oven) until the tuiles are mostly golden brown with pale splotches, 10 to 14 minutes, watching carefully. Rotate the tray from front to back halfway through the baking time.

Have a triple layer of paper towels or a folded dishtowel next to you. After a few seconds, or as soon as the tuile is cool enough for you to slide a metal spatula under without deforming it, flip it upside down on the hot silicone liner and roll it quickly around the cone form without burning your fingers. Press the edges in place for a couple of seconds. Transfer the cone to the paper towels. Repeat with the remaining tuiles, working as quickly as you can. If the cookies get too stiff to roll, reheat them in the oven until pliable again. While the second sheet is baking, transfer the cones to a rack to finish cooling. Reuse the cookie sheets and liners, making sure the liners are cool between batches, until all of the batter is used. Cool the cones completely before storing them. May be kept in an airtight container at least 1 week.

COCOA TUILES

Addictive as potato chips, these thin, crispy, elegant cookies have terrific chocolate flavor. They are wonderful plain, but you can embellish them endlessly (see Nutty Cocoa Cookie Bark with Parmesan and Sea Salt, page 63, or Holiday Cookie Bark, page 64).

Makes twenty-four to thirty 2½-inch tuiles

INGREDIENTS

4 tablespoons butter, melted and still very warm, plus extra for greasing the pan liners

½ cup (3.5 ounces) sugar

¼ cup (0.8 ounce) natural (nonalkalized) cocoa powder, sieved after measuring

⅛ teaspoon salt

2 large egg whites

1 tablespoon plus 1 teaspoon unbleached all-purpose flour

EQUIPMENT

Cookie sheets, lined with silicone baking mats or heavy-duty foil, dull side up

Offset spatula (optional)

Stencil (see page 60) with a 3-inch-diameter circle (or other shape) cut from it (optional)

Small cups or a rolling pin for shaping the cookies (optional)

Preheat the oven to 350°F. Position racks in the upper and lower thirds of the oven. If using foil, smooth it to remove any wrinkles. Grease the silicone mats or the foil lightly but thoroughly with melted butter.

In a small bowl, whisk together the melted butter, sugar, cocoa, and salt. Whisk in the egg whites. Add the flour and whisk only until combined. Let rest for at least 10 minutes or cover and refrigerate for up to 3 days.

Drop level teaspoons of the batter about 3 inches apart onto the cookie sheets. Using a small offset spatula (and a template, if using) or the back of a spoon and a circular motion, spread the batter evenly into 3-inch rounds (or ovals or other shapes) about 1/16 inch thick. Bake, watching carefully, for 10 to 12 minutes, until the edges are ever so slightly darker (look closely to see this color change) than the rest of the cookie. Rotate the pans from top to bottom and from back to front halfway through the baking time to ensure even baking. If the cookies are not baked enough, they will not be completely crisp when cool.

If Using Silicone Mats As soon as you can coax a thin metal spatula under a cookie without destroying it, transfer it to a rack to cool flat. Or shape it by draping it over a rolling pin, nestling it into a little cup, or twisting it with your fingers. Working fast, remove the remaining tuiles; reheat if necessary.

If Using Foil Slide the foil sheet of cookies onto a rack to cool flat. Or, for curved tuiles, grasp the edges of the foil when the sheet comes from the oven (without touching the hot pan or the cookies) and roll it into a fat cylinder, gently curving the attached cookies like potato chips. Crimp or secure the foil with a paper clip. When cool, unroll the foil carefully and remove the tuiles. Alternatively, remove individual tuiles from the foil while they are hot (as soon as you can coax a thin metal spatula under a cookie without destroying it) and shape them as described above. Flat or curved, tuiles are easiest to remove from the foil when they are either very hot or completely cool.

Repeat until all of the wafers are baked. To retain crispness, put the cookies in an airtight container as soon as they are cool. May be stored airtight for at least 1 month.

UPGRADES

Nutty Cocoa Cookie Bark with Parmesan and Sea Salt Addictive shards of nut-topped cocoa tuile have a rustic appearance, a dainty texture, and loads of chocolate flavor. A hint of Parmigiano-Reggiano adds complexity—umami—but not enough to give itself away. You can omit the Parmesan and/or salt if you must; the cookies will still be very good. Or, instead of the Parmesan, you can sprinkle each sheet with 1/2 teaspoon of crushed dried rosemary (leaves, not ground) or 1/2 teaspoon crushed aniseed. Vin Santo, a rare cream sherry, or a ten-year-old Malmsey Madeira makes a divine partner for these. (Photograph on page 65)

Position a single rack in the center of the oven. Set aside ¼ cup (1 ounce) each slivered raw almonds, raw pine nuts, raw hazelnuts (medium finely chopped), raw pistachios (medium finely chopped), 2 to 3 teaspoons finely grated Parmesan cheese or (even better) a small chunk of Parmesan, and a little flaky sea salt such as Maldon or fleur de sel.

Make the batter as directed. Pour half of the batter onto each of two cookie sheets. Use an offset spatula to spread an even rectangle of batter about 9 by 13 inches and less than ⅛ inch thick. For even baking, be sure the batter in the center is no thicker than the edges. Sprinkle each sheet evenly with half (2 tablespoons) of each nut and half of the Parmesan. (I prefer to grate a chunk of Parmesan directly over each sheet by eye—very, very lightly—with a Microplane zester.) Crushing larger flakes of salt between your fingers, sprinkle 2 tiny pinches over each sheet.

Bake one sheet, watching closely, for 11 to 13 minutes, until the batter turns a faintly darker shade of brown and the Parmesan turns golden brown. Rotate the pan from back to front halfway through the baking time to ensure even baking. Set the baking sheet on a rack to cool completely. Repeat with the second sheet. When cool, slide a thin spatula between the sheet and the liner. The cookie should be completely crisp—not at all flexible (when completely cool). Break the cookie into random shards. If any pieces are not completely crisp, return those pieces to a 350°F oven for 4 to 6 minutes. To retain crispness, put the bark in an airtight container as soon as it is cool. May be kept airtight for at least 2 weeks.

Holiday Cookie Bark Bake and cool Nutty Cocoa Cookie Bark, without nuts, Parmesan, or salt. Coarsely crush enough peppermint or cinnamon hard candies or candy canes to measure ⅓ cup. Set aside. Following instructions on page 15, melt 2 ounces finely chopped white chocolate (not chocolate chips). Drizzle and drip half of the chocolate generously over each sheet of bark. Sprinkle candy generously over the drizzles. Refrigerate sheets for 10 minutes to set the chocolate. Break as directed and shake off any excess candy.

OPPOSITE: Nutty Cocoa Cookie Bark with Parmesan and Sea Salt (page 63)

COCONUT WAFERS

If you love all things coconut, these flavorful wafers (also known as *tuiles*) are for you. Make them flat, curved, or rolled into dainty ice cream cones (see page 61). Make sure to bake them fully so they will be crisp.

Makes about forty 3-inch tuiles

INGREDIENTS

3 tablespoons unsalted butter, melted and still very warm, plus extra for greasing the pan liners

Scant 1 cup (3 ounces) unsweetened dried shredded coconut (see page 352)

⅔ cup (4.625 ounces) sugar

3 large egg whites

¼ cup plus 1 tablespoon (1.5 ounces) unbleached all-purpose flour

⅛ teaspoon salt

1 tablespoon rum

EQUIPMENT

Cookie sheets, lined with silicone baking mats or heavy-duty foil, dull side up

Offset spatula (optional)

Stencil (see page 60) with a 3-inch-diameter circle (or other shape) cut from it (optional)

Small cups or a rolling pin for shaping the cookies (optional)

Preheat the oven to 300°F. Place racks in the upper and lower thirds of the oven. If using foil, smooth it to remove any wrinkles, which would distort the cookies. Grease the silicone mats or the foil lightly but thoroughly with melted butter.

In a small bowl, whisk together all of the ingredients until blended. Let rest for at least 10 minutes or cover and refrigerate the batter for up to 3 days.

Drop rounded teaspoons of the batter 2 inches apart onto the cookie sheets. Using a small offset spatula (and a template, if using) or the back of a spoon and a circular motion, spread the batter evenly into 3-inch rounds (or ovals or other shapes) about 1/16 inch thick. Bake, watching carefully, for 12 to 15 minutes, until the tuiles are mostly golden brown with pale splotches. Rotate the pans from top to bottom and from back to front halfway through the baking time to ensure even baking.

If Using Silicone Mats As soon as you can coax a thin metal spatula under a cookie without destroying it, transfer it to a rack to cool flat. Or shape it by draping it over a rolling pin, nestling it into a little cup, or twisting it with your fingers. Working fast, remove the remaining tuiles; reheat if necessary.

If Using Foil Slide the foil sheet of cookies onto a rack to cool flat. Or, for curved tuiles, grasp the edges of the foil when the sheet comes from the oven (without touching the hot pan or the cookies) and roll it into a fat cylinder, gently curving the attached cookies like potato chips. Crimp or secure the foil with a paper clip. When cool, unroll the foil carefully and remove the tuiles. Alternatively, remove individual tuiles from the foil while they are hot and shape them as described above. Flat or curved, the tuiles are easiest to remove from the foil when they are either very hot or completely cool. Repeat until all of the wafers are baked.

To retain crispness, put the cookies into an airtight container as soon as they are completely cool. May be stored airtight for at least 1 month.

UPGRADES

Coconut Banana or Coconut Pineapple Wafers Crush enough unsweetened freeze-dried banana or pineapple pieces to make 1½ tablespoons of powder. Add the powder to the batter with the other ingredients.

CHOCOLATE WAFERS 3.0

Ages ago I developed a simple crisp "plain" chocolate wafer made with cocoa, perfect with a dish of ice cream or a cup of coffee. I've packed them into lunch boxes, made icebox cakes with them, and smashed them up for cheesecake crusts. But new ideas and changes in the quality of ingredients periodically send me back to the drawing board to reinvent even my favorite recipes. The cookies are now better than ever: superbly crisp yet tender, with exceptional cocoa flavor. They are not too sweet and not too rich. Clarity of flavor came with editing out the eggs in the original and extra-tender crispness came with the inclusion of a little milk. I prefer to use natural (nonalkalized) cocoa rather than Dutch process for this recipe.

Makes fifty to sixty 1¾-inch wafers

INGREDIENTS

1½ cups (6.75 ounces) unbleached all-purpose flour

¾ cup (2.4 ounces) unsweetened cocoa powder

1 cup plus 2 tablespoons (7.875 ounces) sugar

¼ teaspoon salt

¼ teaspoon baking soda

14 tablespoons (1¾ sticks) unsalted butter, slightly softened

3 tablespoons whole milk

1 teaspoon pure vanilla extract

EQUIPMENT

Cookie sheets, lined with parchment paper or greased

Food processor

Combine the flour, cocoa, sugar, salt, and baking soda in a food processor and pulse several times to mix thoroughly. Cut the butter into about 12 chunks and add them to the bowl. Pulse several times. Combine the milk and vanilla in a small cup. With the processor running, add the milk mixture through the feed tube and continue to process until the mixture clumps around the blade or the sides of the bowl. Transfer the dough to a large bowl or a cutting board and knead a few times to make sure it is blended evenly.

Form the dough into a log about 14 inches long and 1¾ inches in diameter. Wrap the log in wax paper or foil and refrigerate until firm, at least 1 hour, and up to 3 days.

Preheat the oven to 350°F. Position racks in the upper and lower thirds of the oven. Cut the log of dough into slices a scant ¼ inch thick and place them 1 inch apart on the lined or greased sheets.

Bake for 12 to 15 minutes, rotating the pans from top to bottom and back to front halfway through the baking time to ensure even baking. The cookies will puff up and deflate; they are done about 1½ minutes after they deflate. For lined pans, set the pans or just the liners on racks to cool; for unlined pans, use a metal spatula to transfer the cookies to racks.

If the cookies are not baked long enough, they will not be completely crisp when cool. In that case, return them to the oven to bake a little longer and then cool again. May be stored airtight for up to 2 weeks or frozen for up to 2 months.

UPGRADES

Spicy Chocolate Wafers Along with the sugar, add ¾ teaspoon ground cinnamon, ⅛ teaspoon cayenne, and ⅛ teaspoon freshly ground black pepper.

Extra-Bittersweet Chocolate Wafers Finely ground unsweetened chocolate makes extra-flavorful wafers. I like them completely crisp, which takes a little more time after cooling, because the bits of ground chocolate have to harden again. Otherwise the cookies are a little chewy—and also delicious. | In a food processor, combine 1½ ounces good-quality unsweetened chocolate with half of the sugar. Pulse until the chocolate bits are the size of sesame seeds. Add the remaining sugar, the flour, cocoa, salt, and baking soda and pulse to mix. Proceed as directed.

Chocolate Mint Sandwiches For mint and chocolate lovers: dainty sandwich cookies, made with extra-thin Chocolate Wafers. Cutout tops (made *after* the cookies are baked) reveal the cool and creamy mint-laced white chocolate filling within. (Photograph on back cover) | Form the dough into a log about 16 inches long and 1½ inches in diameter. Wrap and refrigerate until firm, then use a thin sharp knife to score the log at 1-inch intervals. Cut 6 very thin slices per inch, placing them 1 inch apart on the lined or greased cookie sheets. Bake as directed. As soon as the cookies come from the oven, press a ⅞-inch cookie cutter (or improvise with a bottle cap) into the centers of half of them. Remove cutouts when the cookies are cool. Cool completely before filling.

To make the filling, place 6 ounces white chocolate, finely chopped, in a microwave-safe bowl and microwave on medium power for 3 minutes. Use a rubber spatula to stir the chocolate and then microwave it at 5- to 10-second intervals, stirring after each one, until most of the chocolate is melted. Stir until completely melted. Mix in 3 drops mint oil. Taste and add more drops, one at a time, until it tastes the way you want it. Spread ½ teaspoon of the filling almost to the edges of a cookie without a hole and set a cookie with a hole on top. Repeat until all of the cookies are filled.

When the filling is set, the cookies may be stored airtight for up to 2 weeks or frozen for up to 2 months. Makes about forty-eight 2-inch sandwich cookies.

MAYA'S LEMON THINS

My friend Maya Klein (Portland culinary consultant, superb cook, and occasional partner in crime) invented these tender, crisp, and very lemony cookies for my first cookie book some years ago. They remain perfect cookies to serve with tea. For best results, make them thin thin thin!

Makes sixty-four 2½-inch cookies

INGREDIENTS

¼ cup fresh lemon juice

12 tablespoons (1½ sticks) unsalted butter, cut into several pieces

2½ cups (11.25 ounces) unbleached all-purpose flour

¼ teaspoon baking soda

1 large egg

1 large egg yolk

1 cup (7 ounces) sugar

1 tablespoon plus 1 teaspoon finely grated lemon zest

¼ teaspoon salt

EQUIPMENT

Cookie sheets, lined with parchment paper or greased

A 2½-inch cookie cutter, round or other shape

Heat the lemon juice in a small nonreactive saucepan over high heat. Boil for about 5 minutes, or until thick and syrupy and reduced to about 1 tablespoon. Add the butter and stir until melted. Set aside.

Combine the flour and baking soda in a medium bowl and mix together thoroughly with a whisk or a fork.

Using a spoon or a rubber spatula, mix the egg, egg yolk, and sugar in a large bowl until homogenous. Mix in the butter mixture, lemon zest, and salt. Add the flour mixture and stir just until incorporated. Cover and chill for at least 20 minutes.

Divide the dough into 4 pieces. Roll each piece $\frac{1}{16}$ inch thick between 2 sheets of plastic from a cut-apart resealable plastic bag or wax paper. Slide a cookie sheet under the plastic sheets and dough. Refrigerate until firm, at least 15 minutes and up to 2 days.

Preheat the oven to 400°F. Position racks in the upper and lower thirds of the oven.

Remove 1 piece of dough from the refrigerator. Peel off the top sheet of plastic or paper and set it in front of you. Invert the dough onto it and peel off the second sheet. Use a cookie cutter to cut out 2½-inch cookies or any desired size or shape. Place cookies 1 inch apart on the lined or greased cookie sheets. Repeat with the remaining dough. Scraps may be pressed together and rerolled.

Bake for 6 to 7 minutes, or until lightly browned at the edges. Rotate the pans from top to bottom and from front to back halfway through the baking time to ensure even baking. For lined pans, set the pans or just the liners on racks to cool; for unlined pans, use a metal spatula to transfer the cookies to racks. Cool the cookies completely before stacking or storing. To retain crispness, put the cookies in an airtight container as soon as they are cool. May be stored airtight for at least 1 week.

UPGRADES

Lemon Poppy Seed Thins   Add ¼ cup poppy seeds with the flour mixture.

Lemon Ginger Thins   Omit the lemon juice and the boiling step. Melt the butter and add 2 tablespoons finely grated fresh ginger. Set aside until needed. Mix 1 teaspoon of ground ginger with the flour and baking soda. Proceed as directed.

HAZELNUT MOLASSES COOKIES

Thin, crispy, and elegant, with flavors that are lovely, subtle, and balanced.

Makes one hundred 2½-inch cookies

INGREDIENTS

1⅔ cups (7.5 ounces) unbleached all-purpose flour

½ cup (2.5 ounces) raw hazelnuts, skin left on

1 teaspoon baking soda

½ pound (2 sticks) unsalted butter, slightly softened

¾ cup (5.25 ounces) sugar

¼ teaspoon salt

½ teaspoon pure vanilla extract

½ teaspoon grated orange zest (optional)

¼ cup light unsulfured molasses

EQUIPMENT

Cookie sheets, lined with parchment paper or greased

Food processor

Put the flour, hazelnuts, and baking soda into a food processor and process until the nuts are finely ground. Set aside.

In a mixer bowl, combine the butter, sugar, salt, vanilla, and zest, if using. Beat until fluffy.

On low speed, beat in half of the flour mixture followed by all of the molasses. Add the remaining flour and beat just until blended.

Shape the dough into a cylinder about 14 inches long and 1¾ inches in diameter lengthwise on an 18-inch-long sheet of wax paper. Wrap tightly. Refrigerate until firm enough to slice, 2 to 3 hours or overnight.

Preheat the oven to 350°F. Position racks in the upper and lower thirds of the oven. Cut slices ⅛ inch thick from the cylinder. Place the slices about 1½ inches apart on the lined or greased cookie sheets. Bake for 10 to 12 minutes, until golden brown with darker edges, rotating the pans from top to bottom and from front to back halfway through the baking time. The cookies will puff up and then settle down before they are done. For lined pans, set the pans or just the liners on racks to cool; for unlined pans, use a metal spatula to transfer the cookies to racks. Cool the cookies completely before filling, stacking, or storing. May be kept in an airtight container for up to 1 week.

UPGRADES

Hazelnut Molasses Sandwich Cookies Melt 8 ounces bittersweet chocolate. Sandwich two cookies back to back with about ½ teaspoon melted chocolate. Let the chocolate set and harden. Store in an airtight container. Makes about 50 sandwich cookies about 2½ inches in diameter.

Spicy Hazelnut Thins Omit the orange zest and add 1 teaspoon ground cinnamon, 2 teaspoons ground ginger, and ½ teaspoon ground cloves to the butter and sugar.

HONEY SNAPS

Crispy, crunchy honey cookies that don't turn limp, chewy, or sticky (honey tends to do all this to cookies) are hard to find. To make these, I adapted a recipe for brandy snaps given to me by the late Berkeley cooking teacher Elizabeth Thomas. If you don't want to curl them into cylinders, just skip that step and call 'em lace cookies. Served plain, they are delicious with tea. Or fill them with lightly sweetened vanilla whipped cream as for Elizabeth's Brandy Snaps (page 77) and serve them immediately.

Makes thirty-six 4-inch cylinders or wafers

INGREDIENTS

4 tablespoons unsalted butter, plus extra for greasing the pans

3 tablespoons honey

¼ cup (1.75 ounces) sugar

¼ teaspoon ground ginger

¼ cup plus 3 tablespoons (2 ounces) unbleached all-purpose flour

2 pinches of salt

EQUIPMENT

Cookie sheets

Preheat the oven to 400°F. Position a rack in the center of the oven. Butter the cookie sheets.

In a small saucepan, heat the butter, honey, sugar, and ginger over low heat until the butter is melted. Remove the pan from the heat and stir in the flour and salt. Mix well.

Drop 6 level teaspoons of the batter onto each of the baking sheets, allowing plenty of room for spreading. Place one sheet at a time in the oven and bake for 3 to 5 minutes, until the cookies are golden. While they are baking, butter the handle of a wooden spoon.

Exchange the sheet of unbaked cookies for the sheet of baked ones. Allow the cookies to cool for a few seconds, then lift one with a metal spatula onto the wooden spoon handle (or a cooling rack if you don't want to curl them). Curl the hot cookie into a cylinder around the handle with your fingers and slide it to the end of the spoon. Form the second cookie near the bowl of the spoon and transfer the first one to a cooling rack. Repeat, forming and removing cookies as fast as you can. If they harden before you can roll them, return the cookie sheet to the oven for a few seconds to soften and then roll them. If the first set of cookies does not spread or curl properly, add a tiny bit of extra butter and/or honey to the batter before continuing. Do not bake more than 6 cookies at a time, or you will not be able to keep up! Cool the cookies completely before storing. To retain crispness, put the cookies in an airtight container as soon as they are cool. May be stored airtight for several days.

UPGRADES

Cinnamon Snaps The cinnamon flavor starts subtly before it really kicks in and begins to warm the palate. Finally, the buttery, spicy sweetness is reminiscent of the taste of cinnamon toast. | Substitute golden syrup for the honey. Add 1 rounded teaspoon freshly grated stick cinnamon (if possible) or ½ teaspoon regular ground cinnamon to the melted butter mixture.

Elizabeth's Brandy Snaps Substitute 3 tablespoons of golden syrup for the honey, if desired. Add 2 teaspoons of brandy to the batter before the flour mixture. After baking, shape the hot cookies into cylinders as described. Whip 1 cup of whipping or heavy cream with 1½ to 2 tablespoons sugar and ¼ teaspoon pure vanilla extract until stiff. Refrigerate if not using immediately. Just before serving, fit a pastry bag with a medium star tip and fill with the cream. Pipe the cream into the snaps and serve immediately to prevent them from softening.

TROPICAL LACE COOKIES

These cookies are pretty and delicious with creamy desserts, including ice creams, sorbets, panna cotta, even just a bowl of ricotta cheese. Or top with cream, sour cream, or crème fraîche. Freshly grated nutmeg or cinnamon adds a top note of spice; always good.

Makes sixteen to twenty 4-inch cookies

INGREDIENTS

3 tablespoons unsalted butter, plus additional melted butter for greasing foil-lined pans

¾ cup (5.25 ounces) packed grated piloncillo, palm sugar, light muscovado sugar, or regular brown sugar

1 tablespoon dark rum

1 large egg

⅛ teaspoon salt

2 tablespoons unbleached all-purpose flour

½ cup (2 ounces) finely chopped pecans, walnuts, or almonds, sliced almonds, or unsweetened dried shredded coconut

A nutmeg or cinnamon stick for seasoning (optional)

EQUIPMENT

Cookie sheets, lined with parchment paper, silicone baking mats, or heavy-duty foil

Small cups or a rolling pin for shaping the cookies (optional)

Preheat the oven to 350°F. Position a rack in the center of the oven. Plan to bake only one sheet at a time. If you are lining your cookie sheets with foil, grease the foil lightly but thoroughly with melted butter.

In a medium saucepan, melt the butter. Stir in the sugar and remove from the heat. Add the rum, egg, and salt and beat until smooth. Stir in the flour and nuts. Let the batter rest for 5 minutes. Drop tablespoons of batter about 3 inches apart on one of the lined pans.

If Using Silicone Mats Spread the batter very thin (about $\frac{1}{16}$ inch) into rounds, ovals, or long tongue shapes.

If Using Foil or Parchment Paper The batter should spread by itself when in the oven. But if the cookies on your first tray do not spread as much as you'd like, spread the batter on subsequent sheets as described above.

Bake until the cookies are browned all over, 8 to 10 minutes, rotating the cookie sheet from front to back halfway through the baking time. Remove the pan from the oven. If desired, grate nutmeg or cinnamon over the tops of the hot cookies. For flat cookies, slide the foil or parchment off the pan onto a rack to cool; let cookies baked on silicone cool for 30 seconds before transferring them to a rack to cool. If the cookies are to be shaped, let rest for 30 seconds, then slide an offset spatula under each and shape as desired by draping the cookies over a rolling pin, nestling them into a cup, rolling them into cornets, or pinching or twisting them into any desired shape before they cool. Cool completely before storing. May be kept in an airtight container for at least 1 week.

GINGER FLORENTINES

Dressy caramel-almond cookies studded with crystallized ginger and drizzled with chocolate are an exotic alternative to the traditional orange and almond florentine combination.

Makes about sixty 3-inch cookies or 30 sandwich cookies

INGREDIENTS

½ cup (3.5 ounces) sugar

¼ cup heavy cream

1 tablespoon honey

5 tablespoons unsalted butter, cut into pieces

Pinch of salt

1 tablespoon plus 1 teaspoon unbleached all-purpose flour

1 cup (3.5 ounces) sliced almonds

½ cup (2.5 ounces) minced crystallized ginger

3 ounces semisweet or bittersweet chocolate, finely chopped

EQUIPMENT

Cookie sheets, lined with heavy-duty foil, dull side up

Candy thermometer

Preheat the oven to 350°F. Position a rack in the center of the oven. Smooth any wrinkles from the foil, which would distort the cookies. Plan to bake one sheet at a time.

In a small saucepan, combine the sugar, cream, honey, butter, and salt. Stir over low heat until the butter is melted and the mixture comes to a simmer. Brush the sides of the pan with a wet pastry brush or wet wad of paper towel to remove any sugar crystals and to prevent the sugar from crystallizing. Attach the candy thermometer to the pan and cook, without stirring, until the mixture reaches 238°F. Remove the pan from the heat and stir in the flour, almonds, and ginger.

Drop level teaspoons (no more) of the batter about 3 inches apart onto one of the foil-lined baking sheets. With the back of a moistened spoon, flatten the cookies to a diameter of about 1½ inches. Bake for 6 to 8 minutes, until the cookies are a deep mahogany brown all over (if the cookies are not baked until deeply brown, they will be soft and sticky between your teeth rather than crisp and tender and they will stick to the foil), rotating the pan from front to back halfway through the baking time to ensure even baking. While the first batch bakes, you can continue to drop and flatten the batter on sheets of foil. Slide the foil onto a cookie sheet each time before baking. When each batch is done, slide the foil sheet of cookies onto a rack to cool completely—a key to success with these very delicate cookies—before removing the cookies.

To remove the cookies without breakage, slide a thin metal spatula completely under each cookie or gently peel the foil from under the cookie. (If you try to lift the edge of a cookie to detach it from the foil, it is likely to break.) The cookies are very fragile at first, less so several hours later. If you are not planning to drizzle them with chocolate immediately, store the cookies in an airtight container as soon as they are cool.

Place the chocolate in a heatproof bowl (preferably stainless steel) set directly in a wide skillet of barely simmering water. Stir constantly until two-thirds of the chocolate is melted. Remove the bowl from the water and stir patiently until the remaining chocolate melts.

Drizzle the tops of the cookies with the chocolate or spread the backs of the cookies with chocolate and then sandwich them together. Let the chocolate set, then store the cookies in an airtight container for up to several days.

CRUNCHY

Crunchy is the brash loud cousin of crispy. Instead of the high-pitched shattering sound of crispy, crunch is all in the bass notes. It's often a thicker cookie with a harder bite and a bigger mouthful. Not so dainty. I'm crazy for crunch. Biscotti come to mind, from the hard, dry-as-bones Italian style to gentler incarnations including the myriad American-influenced biscotti that seem more like slices of well-toasted cake. But crunchy is also a terrific graham cracker, an addictive seed cookie, or a perfect snicker doodle. Some crunchy cookies are pleasingly coarse and crumbly. Some feature loads of nuts. Some teeter on the brink of sablés . . . Loving the crunch, you may not be inclined to dunk, but biscotti and their ilk invite a splash in coffee, milk, or sweet wines. Crunchy cookie batters are dropped from a spoon, pressed from a pastry bag, sliced from a log, rolled out thin, or sliced from thick loaves and double baked.

CORNMEAL AND OLIVE OIL BISCOTTI WITH WALNUTS AND PEARS

Extra-good when made with stone-ground cornmeal, these biscotti have a delicate crumbly cakiness in contrast with the hard dry crunch of more rustic biscotti. The olive oil flavor becomes more pronounced over a few days, so do make them ahead. I created these biscotti for the California Olive Ranch to celebrate the 2009 olive oil harvest. For a transcendent experience, drizzle a little new-crop freshly pressed oil (such as Olio Nuovo), or any favorite extra virgin olive oil, over the biscotti before serving and sprinkle with a few crushed flakes of sea salt. (Photograph on page 82)

Makes 24 to 30 biscotti

INGREDIENTS

1 cup plus 2 tablespoons (5 ounces) unbleached all-purpose flour

⅔ cup (3.67 ounces) cornmeal

⅜ teaspoon baking powder

½ cup extra virgin olive oil

⅔ cup (4.625 ounces) sugar

¼ teaspoon salt

⅛ teaspoon freshly ground white pepper

2 large eggs

Finely grated zest of 1 medium lemon

1⅓ cups (4.5 ounces) walnut halves, coarsely chopped

⅔ cup (3 ounces) moist dried pears in ¼-inch dice

EQUIPMENT

Cookie sheet, lined with parchment paper or foil, or greased

Preheat the oven to 350°F. Position a rack in the center of the oven.

Combine the flour, cornmeal, and baking powder in a medium bowl and whisk together thoroughly.

In a large bowl with an electric mixer, beat the olive oil, sugar, salt, pepper, eggs, and lemon zest on high speed for 3 to 4 minutes, until lightened in color and slightly thickened.

Stir in the flour mixture. The batter will be thick and sticky. Stir in the walnuts and pears. Scrape the batter down the center of the prepared pan and spread it to form a flat rectangle 14 to 15 inches long and 5 inches wide.

Bake for 20 to 25 minutes, until the loaf is golden on top and golden brown at the lower edges. Rotate the pan from front to back halfway through the baking time to ensure even baking. Set the pan on a rack to cool for at least 15 minutes. Leave the oven on, turning it down to 325°F.

Transfer the loaf carefully to a cutting board. If you used a liner, slide a metal spatula under the loaf to detach and remove the liner. Use a thin sharp knife to cut the loaf crosswise into ½-inch slices. Transfer the slices to the unlined cookie sheet, standing them at least ½ inch apart. Bake for 15 to 20 minutes, until the edges and tops of the biscotti turn slightly golden. Rotate the pan from front to back halfway through the baking time. Set the pan on a rack. Cool the cookies completely before stacking or storing. May be kept in an airtight container for at least 2 weeks.

UPGRADES

Cornmeal and Olive Oil Biscotti with Figs and Almonds Replace the lemon zest with the finely grated zest of a medium-large orange, grated directly over the mixing bowl. Substitute ⅔ cup (3.33 ounces) lightly toasted almonds, coarsely chopped, for the walnuts. Add ½ cup (3 ounces) dried figs, stems discarded, diced, with the almonds.

Cornmeal and Olive Oil Biscotti with Pine Nuts, Almonds, and Pears Substitute a generous ½ cup (3 ounces) pine nuts and ⅔ cup (3.33 ounces) lightly toasted almonds, coarsely chopped, for the walnuts.

CORNMEAL AND FRUIT BISCOTTI

These are more like pieces of pleasingly dry toasted cornmeal cake than full-on supercrunchy biscotti. The cornmeal is inherently sweet and lovely with the flavors of any dried fruit.

Makes about 30 small biscotti

INGREDIENTS

1 cup plus 2 tablespoons (5 ounces) unbleached all-purpose flour

1 cup (5.375 ounces) cornmeal

½ teaspoon baking powder

¼ teaspoon salt

4 tablespoons unsalted butter, softened

1 cup (7 ounces) sugar

2 large eggs

1 teaspoon pure vanilla extract

1 teaspoon finely grated lemon zest

1 tablespoon aniseed, crushed in a mortar (optional)

1 cup (5 ounces) raisins; dried cherries, cranberries, or blueberries; or chopped dried apricots

EQUIPMENT

Cookie sheet, lined with parchment paper or foil, or greased

Preheat the oven to 350°F. Position a rack in the center of the oven.

Combine the flour, cornmeal, baking powder, and salt in a medium bowl and mix together thoroughly with a whisk or fork.

Beat the butter and sugar together in a large bowl with an electric mixer until blended. Add the eggs, vanilla, lemon zest, and aniseed, if using, and beat until light and fluffy.

Add the flour mixture, stirring until all of the ingredients are moistened. Mix in the raisins. With wet hands, shape the dough into a 12-by-2-inch log and place it on the lined or greased cookie sheet.

Bake for 35 to 40 minutes, or until lightly browned and cracked on top. Rotate the pan from front to back halfway through the baking time to ensure even baking. Set the pan on a rack to cool for at least 15 minutes. Leave the oven on. Transfer the loaf carefully to a cutting board. If you used a liner, slide a metal spatula under the loaf to detach and remove the liner. Using a long serrated knife, cut the loaf on a diagonal into slices about ⅜ inch wide. If the loaf is too crumbly to cut, let it cool completely before trying again. Transfer the slices to the unlined cookie sheet, standing them at least ½ inch apart. Bake for 15 to 20 mintues, until the cookies are barely beginning to brown at the edges, rotating the pan from front to back halfway through the baking time. Set the pan on a rack. Cool the cookies completely before stacking or storing. May be kept in an airtight container for at least 2 weeks.

UPGRADES

Holiday Biscotti These are colorful and fragrant. | Include the aniseed. Use ½ cup dried cranberries or dried sour cherries and ½ cup chopped dried apricots. Add ½ cup (2.5 ounces) chopped lightly toasted almonds and ½ cup (2 ounces) coarsely chopped pistachios to the batter with the fruit.

WHOLE WHEAT BISCOTTI

Whole wheat pastry flour, finer and more delicate than regular whole wheat flour, will be a revelation to anyone who thinks whole wheat means coarse and chewy. The texture of these biscotti is quite refined, and, of course, I think anything made with whole grains should taste delicious first and healthy as an afterthought (if it comes up at all). If you are after especially nutritious cookies, feel free to add lots of your favorite seeds (flax, hemp, sesame, chia).

Makes 25 to 30 biscotti

INGREDIENTS

2 cups (9 ounces) whole wheat pastry flour

1 teaspoon baking powder

⅔ cup (4.625 ounces) packed dark or light brown sugar

¼ cup vegetable oil or 4 tablespoons unsalted butter, melted

2 large eggs

¼ teaspoon salt

1 teaspoon pure vanilla extract

1 cup (3.5 ounces) walnuts or pecans, or 1 cup (5 ounces) lightly toasted almonds or hazelnuts with skins rubbed off (see page 17), coarsely chopped

EQUIPMENT

Cookie sheet, lined with parchment paper or foil, or greased

Preheat the oven to 325°F. Position a rack in the center of the oven.

Combine the flour and baking powder in a medium bowl and mix together thoroughly with a whisk or fork.

In a large bowl with an electric mixer, beat the brown sugar, oil, eggs, salt, and vanilla for 2 to 3 minutes, until thick and pale.

Add the flour mixture and the nuts and stir until all of the ingredients are moistened. The dough will be thick and sticky. Scrape the dough onto the lined or greased pan and spread it into a 5-by-15-inch rectangle.

Bake for 30 to 35 minutes, until the loaf has puffed and is firm but springy to the touch. Rotate the pan from front to back halfway through the baking time to ensure even baking. Set the pan on a rack to cool for at least 15 minutes. Leave the oven on, turning it down to 300°F.

Transfer the loaf carefully to a cutting board. If you used a liner, slide a metal spatula under the loaf to detach and remove the liner. Using a long serrated knife, cut the loaf crosswise into slices ½ inch wide. Transfer the slices to the unlined cookie sheet, standing them at least ½ inch apart. Bake for 20 to 25 minutes, until the edges of the cookies turn golden, rotating the pan from front to back halfway through the baking time. Set the pan on a rack. Cool the cookies completely before stacking or storing. May be kept in an airtight container for at least 2 weeks.

UPGRADES

Whole Wheat and Oat Flour Biscotti Instead of 2 cups whole wheat pastry flour, use 1 cup (4.5 ounces) unbleached all-purpose flour, ½ cup (1.8 ounces) oat flour, and ½ cup (2.25 ounces) whole wheat pastry flour. The mixture of flours imparts a sweet, mellow flavor and a short, tender texture reminiscent of graham crackers.

BREAKFAST BISCOTTI

Nubbly, crumbly, crunchy. I think of these as oatie biscotie (long o in both words). They smell comfy and deliciously and wholesomely American rather than Italian when they come out of the oven. They are only mildly sweet, and if you *are* having them for breakfast they go well with a little cottage cheese or yogurt and jam. Feel free to add handfuls of hemp seeds, flaxseeds, or sesame seeds for extra flavor— and nutrition too.

Makes about 25 biscotti

INGREDIENTS

⅔ cup (3 ounces) unbleached all-purpose flour

⅔ cup (3 ounces) whole wheat pastry flour

1 teaspoon baking powder

Generous ¼ teaspoon salt

½ to ⅔ cup (3.5 to 4.625 ounces) packed brown sugar

1⅓ cups (4.67 ounces) rolled oats

⅓ cup milk, whole or low-fat

4 tablespoons (2 ounces) melted unsalted butter or 2 ounces safflower or canola oil

2 large eggs, lightly whisked

1 teaspoon pure vanilla extract

1 cup (3.5 ounces) walnut pieces

½ cup (2.5 ounces) dried currants (optional)

1 teaspoon Cinnamon Sugar (page 336)

EQUIPMENT

Cookie sheet, lined with parchment paper or foil, or greased

Preheat the oven to 325°F. Position a rack in the center of the oven.

Combine the flours, baking powder, and salt in a medium bowl and mix thoroughly with a whisk or fork.

In a large bowl, mix the brown sugar and oats. Heat the milk and butter in a small pot or microwave-safe bowl until the milk is hot and the butter is melted. Combine the hot milk with the oat mixture. Let stand for 10 minutes. Whisk in the eggs and vanilla. Stir in the flour mixture. Stir in the nuts and currants, if using. The batter will be very thick and sticky.

Scrape the batter onto the prepared pan. Spread it to form a 5-by-12 inch rectangle about ¾ inch thick. Sprinkle with the cinnamon sugar. Bake for 30 to 35 minutes, until firm and starting to color around the bottom edges. Rotate the pan from front to back halfway through the baking time to ensure even baking. Set the pan on a rack to cool for at least 15 minutes. Leave the oven on, turning it down to 300°F.

Transfer the loaf carefully to a cutting board. If you used a liner, slide a metal spatula under the loaf to detach and remove the liner. Using a sharp serrated knife and a sawing motion, cut the loaf crosswise into ½-inch slices. Transfer the slices to the unlined baking sheet, standing them at least ½ inch apart. Bake for 20 to 25 minutes to toast without overbrowning, rotating the pan from front to back halfway through the baking time. Set the pan on a rack. Cool the biscotti completely before wrapping or storing. May be kept in an airtight container for at least 2 weeks.

UPGRADES

Superwoman's Breakfast Biscotti Everything good for us in here . . . | Substitute 1 cup (3.5 ounces) chopped pecans for the walnuts and ½ cup (2.5 ounces) dried blueberries for the currants. Add 1 generous tablespoon each sunflower seeds, sesame seeds, and hulled hemp seeds and 1 teaspoon flaxseed meal.

ALMOND BISCOTTI

These are adapted from the superb cookies I tasted decades ago in the kitchen of Carole Tibone, who was then the cooking school director at Jungle Jim's in Cincinnati, Ohio. I am partial to this style of biscotti with its porous, hard, crunchy texture. Although they are eminently dippable (into espresso or dessert wine), I love them bone dry, loud, and crunchy. Feel free to make Hazelnut Biscotti by substituting Frangelico liqueur for the amaretto and toasted skinned hazelnuts for the almonds.

Makes about 24 biscotti

INGREDIENTS

2 cups (9 ounces) unbleached all-purpose flour

1 cup (7 ounces) sugar

1¼ teaspoons baking powder

⅛ teaspoon salt

3 large eggs

2 tablespoons amaretto liqueur or 2 tablespoons rum with 1 teaspoon almond extract

1 teaspoon pure vanilla extract

1 tablespoon aniseed, crushed in a mortar to release flavor (optional)

1 cup (5 ounces) whole almonds, toasted (see page 17) and coarsely chopped

EQUIPMENT

Cookie sheet, lined with parchment paper or foil, or greased

Preheat the oven to 300°F. Position a rack in the center of the oven.

Combine the flour, sugar, baking powder, and salt in a medium bowl and mix together thoroughly with a whisk or fork.

Whisk the eggs, amaretto, vanilla, and aniseed, if using, in a large bowl until well blended. Stir in the flour mixture and then the almonds. The dough will be thick and sticky. Scrape the dough into a long log shape lengthwise on the prepared cookie sheet. Wet your hands and shape the dough into a long flat loaf about 12 inches by 4 inches.

Bake for about 50 minutes, until firm and dry, rotating the pan from front to back halfway through the baking time to ensure even baking. Set the pan on a rack to cool for at least 15 minutes. Leave the oven on.

Transfer the loaf carefully to a cutting board. If you used a liner, slide a metal spatula under the loaf to detach and remove the liner. Using a long serrated knife, cut the loaf on a diagonal into slices ½ to ¾ inch wide. Transfer the slices to the unlined baking sheet, standing them at least ½ inch apart. Toast for 40 to 50 minutes, until golden brown, rotating the pan from front to back halfway through the baking time to ensure even baking. Cool the cookies completely before stacking or storing. To retain crispness, put the cookies in an airtight container as soon as they are completely cool. May be stored airtight for several weeks.

UPGRADES

Supercrunch Cinnamon Almond Biscotti The noisiest of all biscotti, these are not for nibbling at the symphony. | Substitute ½ teaspoon baking soda for the baking powder. Add ½ teaspoon ground cinnamon to the flour mixture. Omit the aniseed. Increase the almonds to 2 cups. Spread the dough in a 16-by-6-inch rectangle, about the thickness of the almonds. Moisten the surface with a wet hand. Sprinkle with Cinnamon Sugar (page 336). Bake as directed.

Chocolate Chip Biscotti Omit the liqueur and the aniseed. Substitute ½ cup (3.5 ounces) packed brown sugar for ½ cup of the granulated sugar. Substitute ⅔ cup (2.33 ounces) chopped walnuts and ⅔ cup (4 ounces) chocolate chips for the almonds.

BISCOTTI

Biscotti have become as American as apple pie and infinitely more ubiquitous. Café-goers who invest regularly in single biscotti will be astonished at how easy they are to make and how well they keep. The batter or dough (usually mixed by hand) is shaped into flat "loaves," baked until firm, cooled briefly, and then sliced and returned to the oven to dry out and toast.

How did a twice-baked, dry-as-bones, anise-flavored Italian cookie—so crunchy that it begs to be splashed in sweet wine or strong coffee—acquire American citizenship? At first, probably by losing its anise-flavored accent and welcoming myriad flavorful chunks and chips, from chocolate to cherries, in addition to any nut in the universe or no nuts at all. Now, of course, many Americans even like anise! Not all biscotti are even so hard and dry; I've included a texture to suit everyone, from supercrunchy to something best described as a satisfying slice of crumbly toasted cake.

The texture of biscotti varies with the proportion of ingredients, number of eggs, amount and type of fat (if any), and type of leavening. Harder, crunchier Italian-style biscotti tend to have little or no butter or oil and more eggs. Baking soda, compared with baking powder, makes for browner biscotti and may add some crunch. Each leavening may also affect the flavor of some ingredients (notably chocolate) differently—for better or worse. If you are curious, you can experiment by substituting about ¼ teaspoon of soda for 1 teaspoon of baking powder. Some of my recipes offer a choice.

Biscotti recipes are flexible. You can experiment with inclusions such as nuts (toasted or untoasted), dried or candied fruits, and liqueurs. You may add chocolate chips, even ground coffee beans, or citrus zest. You may exchange brown sugar or maple sugar for equal amounts of granulated sugar. You can fool around with spices such as cinnamon, clove, nutmeg, cardamom, and ginger.

Here are a few bits of biscotti wisdom:

> Batters and doughs for biscotti vary in consistency from sticky doughs that you can shape by hand or spread with a spatula to pourable batters that tend to spread on the cookie sheet.

> You may slice the loaf of biscotti and retoast the cookies after as little as 15 minutes of cooling, or you can wait to perform these steps when it suits you. If the baked loaf is too crumbly or breakable when you slice it, try a different knife (slim and sharp versus serrated) and/or a different stroke (gentle sawing versus controlled guillotine). If all else fails, spray the loaf with water to soften it slightly before cutting.

> Regardless of the directions in the recipes, you can shape the dough or batter to your liking: into a short wide loaf to make long biscotti or into a long narrow loaf to make shorter biscotti. The first baking time will not be affected. You may also slice biscotti as thick or as thin as you like, so long as you adjust the second baking time accordingly.

> Add a little shine to biscotti crust by shaping the dough with wet hands, or moistening it after you spread it with a spatula.

> The easiest way to retoast biscotti is to stand them up . . . but for extra-toasty flavor and crunch, lay them down and retoast them on both sides, about half of the time on each side.

> The driest, crunchiest biscotti will keep for several weeks in an airtight tin.

> Dried fruits are best in the softer, cakier style of biscotti, which are best consumed within two weeks.

CHOCOLATE BISCOTTI

Dry crunchy biscotti with a finer, less open grain and a more tender crunch reminiscent of a good graham cracker. The type of cocoa you use will affect the flavor of the finished cookie. Note, too, that each requires a different leavening. Natural cocoa powder imparts a brighter chocolate flavor, while Dutch-process cocoa adds a slight Oreo cookie flavor. Have it your way.

Makes about 24 biscotti

INGREDIENTS

2 cups (9 ounces) unbleached all-purpose flour

½ cup (1.125 ounces) unsweetened cocoa powder, natural (nonalkalized) or Dutch-process

2 teaspoons instant espresso or coffee powder (optional)

½ teaspoon baking soda if using natural cocoa powder or 2 teaspoons baking powder if using Dutch-process cocoa powder

½ teaspoon salt

8 tablespoons (1 stick) unsalted butter, softened

1 cup (7 ounces) sugar

2 large eggs

2 teaspoons pure vanilla extract

1 cup (3.5 ounces) walnuts, coarsely chopped

EQUIPMENT

Cookie sheet, lined with parchment paper or foil, or greased

Preheat the oven to 300°F. Position a rack in the center of the oven.

Combine the flour, cocoa, espresso powder, if using, baking soda or powder, and salt in a medium bowl and mix together thoroughly with a whisk or fork.

In a mixing bowl, using the back of a large spoon or a mixer, beat the butter and sugar together until soft and creamy. Mix in the eggs and vanilla (switching to a rubber spatula if mixing by hand). Add the flour mixture and stir just until all the ingredients are moistened. Mix in the walnuts. Spread the dough into a long, flat loaf, about 16 by 4 inches, and place on the prepared cookie sheet.

Bake for 30 to 35 minutes, until the loaf is firm but springy to the touch, rotating the pan from front to back halfway through the baking time to ensure even baking. Set the pan on a rack to cool for at least 15 minutes. Leave the oven on.

Transfer the loaf carefully to a cutting board. If you used a liner, slide a metal spatula under the loaf to detach and remove the liner. Using a long serrated knife, cut the loaf crosswise into slices about ½ inch wide. Transfer the slices to the unlined cookie sheet, standing them ½ inch apart. Bake for 30 to 35 minutes, or until the surface of the cookies feels dry and crusty. Place the cookie sheet on a rack. Cool the cookies completely before stacking or storing. May be kept in an airtight container for several weeks.

UPGRADES

Chocolate Orange Biscotti Add 2 to 3 teaspoons finely grated orange zest with the vanilla.

Chocolate Hazelnut Biscotti Substitute 1 cup (5 ounces) hazelnuts, toasted and skinned (see page 17) and then chopped, for the walnuts, and add 1 tablespoon Frangelico liqueur with the vanilla.

Mocha Latte or Mocha Espresso Biscotti Omit the walnuts and substitute 1 cup (6 ounces) milk chocolate or semisweet chocolate chips and 2 tablespoons coarsely ground espresso beans.

Extra-Chocolaty Biscotti Finely chop or process in a food processor (with a handful of the flour mixture) ½ to ⅔ cup (3 to 4 ounces) bittersweet or semisweet chocolate. Add with the flour mixture.

CHOCOLATE BISCOTTI WITH LESS FAT

Good and chocolaty and extra crunchy. Two cookies are 100 calories and less than 2 grams of fat or 2 Weight Watchers points, if you happen to be counting. Make these 2 days ahead, because they improve with time. For darker-colored biscotti with lots of Oreo flavor, try the upgrade.

Makes about 50 small biscotti

INGREDIENTS

⅓ cup (2 ounces) coarsely chopped bittersweet or semisweet chocolate or chocolate chips

2 cups (9 ounces) unbleached all-purpose flour

⅓ cup (1 ounce) unsweetened cocoa powder, natural (nonalkalized) or Dutch-process

½ teaspoon baking soda if using natural cocoa powder or 2 teaspoons baking powder if using Dutch-process cocoa powder

½ teaspoon salt

2 teaspoons instant espresso or coffee powder

2 large eggs

2 large egg whites

1 cup (7 ounces) sugar

1 teaspoon pure vanilla extract

⅔ cup (3.33 ounces) toasted whole almonds or toasted and skinned hazelnuts (see page 17), coarsely chopped

EQUIPMENT

Cookie sheets

Food processor

Preheat the oven to 300°F. Position racks in the upper and lower thirds of the oven. Line one of the cookie sheets with parchment paper or foil, or grease it.

In a food processor, combine the chocolate with the flour, cocoa powder, baking soda or powder, salt, and espresso powder. Pulse until the chocolate is reduced to the size of coarse bread crumbs. Set aside.

In a medium mixing bowl, whisk the eggs and egg whites with the sugar and vanilla until well blended. Stir in the flour mixture and the nuts. The batter will be thick and sticky. Scrape the batter onto the lined or greased pan in 2 skinny strips 16 to 17 inches long and at least 2½ inches apart. Use a spatula to even up the strips.

Put the pan on the lower rack and bake for 35 to 40 minutes, until the loaves are firm but springy to the touch. Rotate the pan from front to back halfway through the baking time to ensure even baking. Set the pan on a rack to cool for at least 15 minutes. Leave the oven on.

Transfer the loaves carefully to a cutting board. If you used a liner, slide a metal spatula under each loaf to detach and remove the liner. Using a sharp serrated knife, cut the loaves on a diagonal into ½-inch slices. Stand the slices on unlined baking sheets at least ½ inch apart. Toast them for 20 to 25 minutes, rotating the pans from top to bottom and front to back halfway through the baking time. Cool the biscotti completely before stacking or storing. May be kept in an airtight container for several weeks.

UPGRADES

Double-Dutch Biscotti Supercrunchy comfort food! The distinct flavor of Dutch-process cocoa is accentuated with baking soda. If you love Oreo cookies, you'll love these. | Use Dutch-process cocoa powder and substitute 1 teaspoon baking soda for the 2 teaspoons baking powder.

CHOCOLATE CHIP BISCOTTI WITH LESS FAT

These taste like supercrunchy chocolate chip cookies, and that's all anyone needs to know! Make them at least 2 days ahead for the best flavor and texture.

Makes 40 to 50 small biscotti

INGREDIENTS

1¾ cups (8 ounces) unbleached all-purpose flour

½ teaspoon baking soda

¼ teaspoon salt

2 large eggs

¼ cup plus 2 tablespoons (2.625 ounces) granulated sugar

¼ cup plus 2 tablespoons (2.625 ounces) packed brown sugar

1 teaspoon pure vanilla extract

½ cup (2 ounces) coarsely chopped walnuts

⅔ cup (4 ounces) bittersweet or semisweet chocolate chunks or chips

EQUIPMENT

Cookie sheets

Preheat the oven to 300°F. Position racks in the upper and lower thirds of the oven. Line one of the cookie sheets with parchment paper or foil, or grease it.

Combine the flour, baking soda, and salt in a small bowl and whisk together thoroughly.

In a medium mixing bowl, whisk the eggs with the sugars and vanilla until well combined. Mix in the flour. Stir in the nuts and chocolate chips. The mixture will be thick and gooey.

Scrape the batter onto the lined or greased pan in 2 skinny strips 16 to 17 inches long and at least 3 inches apart. Use a spatula to even up the strips.

Put the pan on the lower rack and bake for 35 minutes until firm but springy when pressed with your fingers. Rotate the pan from front to back halfway through the baking time to ensure even baking. Set the pan on a rack to cool for at least 15 minutes. Leave the oven on.

Transfer the loaves carefully to a cutting board. If you used a liner, slide a metal spatula under each loaf to detach and remove the liner. Use a sharp serrated knife to slice the loaves on a diagonal into ½-inch slices. Stand the cookies up on the unlined baking sheets at least ½ inch apart. Bake for 20 to 25 minutes, until golden brown, rotating the pans from top to bottom and from front to back halfway through the baking time. Cool the biscotti completely before stacking or storing. The flavor develops and the cookies become more tender after 2 or 3 days, and the biscotti will remain dry and very crunchy after that. May be kept in an airtight container for several weeks.

UPGRADES

Orange Chocolate Chip Biscotti Here I sacrifice the nuts to add lots more chocolate! | Increase the granulated sugar to ¾ cup and omit the brown sugar. Finely grate the zest of ½ medium orange directly over the bowl. Add 2 tablespoons fresh orange juice and ¼ teaspoon orange extract (not orange oil) with the vanilla. Omit the walnuts and increase the chocolate to 1 cup (6.75 ounces).

GREAT GRAHAMS

Graham crackers are *wheat* cookies by definition. Graham flour is coarsely ground whole wheat flour. Real (homemade) grahams are normally hearty and healthy and delicious too. And yet a little oat flour softens that mildly bitter whole wheat edge by adding a compelling nuance of sweet oat flavor and an extra-tender crunch. The result is an extra-good graham that is still 100 percent whole grain. The flavors and textures get even better after a couple of days. Melty toasted marshmallows and good chocolate can always be added to make s'mores, but the naked grahams are superb just so. I'm wild about these.

Makes about thirty-six 2-inch grahams

INGREDIENTS

1¾ cups (8 ounces) graham flour

½ cup plus 1 tablespoon (2 ounces) oat flour

¼ cup (1.75 ounces) sugar, plus additional for sprinkling

½ teaspoon salt

½ teaspoon baking powder

¼ teaspoon baking soda

6 tablespoons cold unsalted butter, cut into ½-inch cubes

3 tablespoons milk

3 tablespoons honey

½ teaspoon pure vanilla extract

EQUIPMENT

Cookie sheet

2 sheets of parchment paper cut to fit the pan

Food processor

In a food processor, combine the flours, the ¼ cup sugar, the salt, baking powder, and baking soda. Pulse to mix thoroughly. Sprinkle the butter cubes over the flour mixture. Pulse until the mixture resembles cornmeal. In a small cup, stir the milk, honey, and vanilla together until the honey is dissolved. Drizzle the honey mixture into the bowl. Process just until the mixture gathers into a single mass.

Shape the dough into a flat 8- or 9-inch-square patty. Wrap and refrigerate it until very firm but supple enough to roll out, 20 to 30 minutes. Or keep it refrigerated for up to 2 days and then let soften slightly at room temperature before rolling.

Preheat the oven to 350°F. Position a rack in the center of the oven.

Roll the dough between the sheets of parchment paper until it is about ⅛ inch thick and as even as possible from the center to the edges. Flip the paper and dough over once or twice to check for deep wrinkles; if necessary, peel the parchment and smooth it over the dough before continuing. Peel off the top sheet of parchment. Sprinkle the dough evenly with 2 to 3 teaspoons sugar. Prick the dough all over with a fork. Slide the dough (and remaining sheet of paper) onto the pan. With a sharp knife, even up the edges of the dough and score it into squares, rectangles, diamonds, or rhomboids as you like. Leave edge scraps in place (for good nibbling and to protect the rest of the grahams from burnt edges).

Bake for 20 to 25 minutes, until the grahams are golden brown with deep brown edges. Rotate the pan from front to back halfway through the baking time to ensure even baking. Set the pan on a rack to cool. Break the grahams along the score lines. Cool the grahams completely before storing. May be kept in an airtight container for at least 3 weeks.

TROUBLESHOOTING

Checking Grahams for Crunch Grahams crisp up *after* they are completely cool unless they are underbaked. If your grahams are not thoroughly crunchy when cool (especially the ones in the center, which might be a little thicker), return them (on a parchment-lined baking sheet) to a preheated 325°F oven for 10 to 15 minutes. Let cool and check for crunch. (If you find it difficult to roll the dough evenly over such a big area—leaving your center grahams underbaked—next time divide the dough into 2 pieces, then roll out and bake 2 smaller sheets. In this case, bake 15 to 20 minutes.)

UPGRADES

Cinnamon Oat Grahams Add 1 tablespoon ground cinnamon to the processor with the flour. If desired, sprinkle the rolled-out dough with Cinnamon Sugar (page 336) before baking.

Nutmeg Oat Grahams Add ¾ teaspoon freshly grated nutmeg to the processor with the flour. If desired, sprinkle the rolled dough with Nutmeg Sugar (page 336) before baking.

Ginger Oat Grahams Add a slightly rounded tablespoon ground ginger to the processor with the flour.

Spicy Oat Grahams Add 1 teaspoon ground cinnamon, 2 teaspoons ground ginger, ½ teaspoon ground cloves, and ¼ teaspoon ground cardamom to the processor with the flour.

Chocolate Oat Grahams (Spicy or Plain) Gentle but addictive chocolate flavor here, and not too sweet. A little salt over the sugar on top (and a little black pepper if you are adventuresome) lifts the flavor. | Reduce the oat flour to ⅓ cup (1.2 ounces) and add ¼ cup (0.8 ounce) unsweetened natural (nonalkalized) cocoa powder to the processor with the flour. Before sprinkling with sugar, sprinkle the dough evenly with a tiny pinch (¹⁄₁₆ teaspoon) of salt. Sprinkle as directed with sugar, or substitute Cardamom Sugar or Cinnamon Sugar (page 336) made without salt. If desired, finely grind a very small amount of black pepper over the dough as well. Bake as directed.

SUGAR CRUNCH COOKIES

Sugar cookies that are very crunchy yet also light and delicate? Over the years, tempted by descriptions like that one, I've tried recipes that call for ammonium carbonate (aka *baker's ammonia*). Each time I'm charmed by the juxtaposition of lightness and crunch and then, half an hour later, distressed by the harsh feeling in the back of my throat. Rather than try again with less ammonia, I've captured the longed-for texture—both airy and crunchy—with baking soda and cream of tartar (basically homemade baking powder) instead. Ammonia now lives at the back of the cupboard (again). See Vanilla Cream Cheese Sandwiches (page 188) to learn how to roll out and cut this dough with cookie cutters.

Makes about sixty 2½-inch cookies

INGREDIENTS

3 cups (13.5 ounces) unbleached all-purpose flour

2 teaspoons cream of tartar

1 teaspoon baking soda

½ teaspoon salt

½ pound (2 sticks) unsalted butter, softened

1½ cups (10.5 ounces) plus 2 tablespoons sugar

2 tablespoons milk

1 tablespoon pure vanilla extract

EQUIPMENT

Cookie sheets, lined with parchment paper or greased

Preheat the oven to 375°F. Position racks in the upper and lower thirds of the oven.

Combine the flour, cream of tartar, baking soda, and salt in a bowl and mix thoroughly with a whisk or fork.

In a medium mixing bowl with an electric mixer, beat the butter with the 1½ cups sugar until smooth and creamy. Beat in the milk and vanilla. Add the flour mixture and stir or beat on low speed just until incorporated. Gather the dough into a ball and wrap in plastic wrap. Refrigerate until firm, at least 30 minutes.

Form level tablespoons of dough into 1-inch balls. Roll the balls in the remaining 2 tablespoons sugar and place 2 inches apart on the lined or greased cookie sheets. Flatten the balls to ¼-inch thickness with the bottom of a glass dipped in sugar.

Bake for 10 to 12 minutes, until the cookies puff and settle down and turn golden. Rotate the cookie sheets from top to bottom and from front to back halfway through the baking time to ensure even baking. For lined pans, set the pans or just the liners on racks to cool; for unlined pans, use a metal spatula to transfer the cookies to racks. Cool the cookies completely before stacking or storing. May be kept in an airtight container for several days.

UPGRADES

Spiced Sugar Crunch Cookies Instead of granulated sugar, roll the dough balls in Cardamom Sugar, Star Anise Sugar, Chinese Five-Spice Sugar, Nutmeg Sugar, or Garam Masala Sugar (page 336).

SNICKER DOODLES

Classic snicker doodles taste like delicately crunchy rounds of cinnamon-topped French toast.

Makes about sixty 2½-inch cookies

INGREDIENTS

3 cups (13.5 ounces) unbleached all-purpose flour

2 teaspoons cream of tartar

1 teaspoon baking soda

½ teaspoon salt

½ pound (2 sticks) unsalted butter, softened

1½ cups (10.5 ounces) plus 2 tablespoons sugar

2 large eggs

2 teaspoons ground cinnamon

EQUIPMENT

Cookie sheets, lined with parchment paper or greased

Preheat the oven to 400°F. Position racks in the upper and lower thirds of the oven.

Combine the flour, cream of tartar, baking soda, and salt in a bowl and mix thoroughly with a whisk or fork.

In a medium mixing bowl with an electric mixer, beat the butter with the 1½ cups sugar until smooth and creamy. Beat in the eggs just until blended. Add the flour mixture and stir or beat on low speed just until incorporated. Gather the dough into a ball and wrap in plastic wrap. Refrigerate until firm, at least 30 minutes.

Mix the remaining 2 tablespoons sugar and the cinnamon in a small bowl. Form level tablespoons of dough into 1-inch balls. Roll the balls in the cinnamon sugar and place 2 inches apart on the lined or greased cookie sheets.

Bake for 10 to 12 minutes, until the cookies puff and begin to settle down. Rotate the cookie sheets from top to bottom and from front to back halfway through the baking time to ensure even baking. For lined pans, set the pans or just the liners on racks to cool; for unlined pans, use a metal spatula to transfer the cookies to racks. Cool the cookies completely before stacking or storing. May be kept in an airtight container for several days.

UPGRADES

Nutmeg Snicker Doodles Substitute 1 teaspoon lightly packed freshly grated nutmeg for the cinnamon.

ANZAC COOKIES

Sweet and satisfying coconut cookies with an appealing crunch, a nubby texture, and a lingering buttery flavor. Authentic cookies by the same name were sturdy and long keeping enough to send to men serving in the Australian New Zealand Army Corps (ANZAC) in Europe during World War I. Versions like this one may be a bit less sturdy, but they keep well, look pretty, and are hard to leave alone.

Makes twenty-four to thirty-two 2¼-inch cookies

INGREDIENTS

1 cup (3.5 ounces) rolled oats

8 tablespoons (1 stick) unsalted butter

¾ cup (5.25 ounces) sugar

1 tablespoon water

2 tablespoons golden syrup or honey

1 cup (4.5 ounces) unbleached all-purpose flour

1 teaspoon cream of tartar

½ teaspoon baking soda

1 cup (3 ounces) unsweetened dried shredded coconut (see page 352)

EQUIPMENT

Cookie sheets, lined with parchment paper or greased

Blender or food processor

Place the oats in a blender or a food processor. Process just until the oats are coarsely ground but not powdered; set aside.

Combine the butter, sugar, water, and golden syrup in a large saucepan and warm over low heat until the butter is melted. Add the flour, cream of tartar, baking soda, coconut, and oats all at once and stir until the flour is completely incorporated. Divide the dough in half and form two 8-by-2-inch logs. Wrap the logs in foil and refrigerate for at least 2 hours or overnight.

Preheat the oven to 325°F. Position racks in the upper and lower thirds of the oven.

Remove the dough from the refrigerator and let it soften at room temperature for 15 minutes. Slice the dough ¼ to ⅜ inch thick with a thin serrated knife, pressing the edges of the cookies together if the dough crumbles a bit, and place the slices at least 1 inch apart on the lined or greased cookie sheets.

Bake for 14 to 17 minutes, or until golden brown all over. Rotate the sheets from top to bottom and from front to back halfway through the baking time to ensure even baking. For lined pans, set the pans or just the liners on racks to cool; for unlined pans, use a metal spatula to transfer the cookies to racks. Cool the cookies completely before stacking or storing. May be kept in an airtight container for at least 2 weeks.

CRUNCHY SEED COOKIES

Noisily crunchy. Light. Addictive.

Makes about sixty 2-inch cookies

INGREDIENTS

2 teaspoons black sesame seeds or poppy seeds

2 teaspoons white sesame seeds

2 teaspoons flaxseeds

2 teaspoons fennel seeds

¼ cup coarse raw sugar, such as Sugar in the Raw or Demerara sugar

2¼ cups (10.125 ounces) unbleached all-purpose flour

1 teaspoon cream of tartar

1 teaspoon baking soda

¼ teaspoon salt

8 tablespoons (1 stick) unsalted butter, very soft

1 cup (7 ounces) granulated sugar

1 large egg

2 tablespoons bourbon

EQUIPMENT

Cookie sheets, lined with parchment paper or greased

Preheat the oven to 375°F. Position racks in the upper and lower thirds of the oven.

Mix the seeds and coarse sugar in a shallow bowl and set aside.

Combine the flour, cream of tartar, baking soda, and salt in a medium bowl and mix together thoroughly with a whisk or fork.

With a large spoon in a medium mixing bowl or with a mixer, mix the butter with the granulated sugar until smooth and well blended but not fluffy. Add the egg and bourbon and mix until smooth. Add the flour mixture and mix until completely incorporated.

To Make Round Cookies Roll heaping teaspoons of dough into 1-inch balls. Press each ball into the seed mixture on both sides, flattening the ball to about ½ inch thick.

To Make Square Cookies On a lightly floured surface, shape all of the dough into an 8-inch-square patty a generous ½ inch thick. Sprinkle the dough with half of the seeds and sugar. Roll lightly over the seeds with a rolling pin to press them in. Turn the dough over. Sprinkle and roll over the remaining seeds. Cut the dough into 8 equal strips in each direction to make a total of 64 equal pieces.

Place the cookies 2 inches apart on the lined or greased pans. Bake for 14 to 16 minutes, until the edges are lightly browned, rotating the pans from top to bottom and from front to back halfway through the baking time to ensure even baking. For lined pans, set the pans or just the liners on racks to cool; for unlined pans, use a metal spatula to transfer the cookies to racks. Cool the cookies completely before stacking or storing. May be kept in an airtight container for at least 2 weeks.

WHOLE WHEAT HAZELNUT COOKIES WITH CURRANTS AND CACAO NIBS

I designed these for a wine and dessert tasting. They were especially enjoyed with a Floodgate vintage port and a Niepoort tawny port. The dough needs time to absorb the flavors of the cacao nibs and vanilla beans, so plan to make the dough 2 days ahead and bake the cookies 1 day ahead.

Makes about forty-eight 2-inch cookies

INGREDIENTS

1 cup (5 ounces) whole hazelnuts

1 cup (4.5 ounces) unbleached all-purpose flour

1 scant cup (4 ounces) whole wheat flour

14 tablespoons (1¾ sticks) unsalted butter, slightly softened

½ cup plus 1 tablespoon (3.875 ounces) sugar

⅜ teaspoon fleur de sel or other coarse salt

Rounded ½ teaspoon ground whole vanilla beans (see page 359) or 1½ teaspoons pure vanilla extract

¼ cup (1 ounce) roasted cacao nibs

Scant ⅔ cup (3.33 ounces) currants

EQUIPMENT

Cookie sheets, lined with parchment paper or greased

Preheat the oven to 350°F. Position a rack in the lower third of the oven. Spread the hazelnuts on a cookie sheet and bake for about 10 minutes, until they are golden brown in the middle when you cut or bite one in half. Cool completely. Rub the nuts together to remove as much of their skins as possible. Chop the nuts between medium and coarse or as you want them.

Combine the flours in a medium bowl and mix together with a whisk or fork.

With the back of a large spoon in a medium mixing bowl, or with a mixer, beat the butter with the sugar, salt, and vanilla for about 1 minute, until smooth and creamy but not fluffy. Mix in the nibs and nuts. Add the flours and mix just until incorporated. Mix in the currants. Scrape the dough into a mass and, if necessary, knead it with your hands a few times to be sure the flour is incorporated evenly. Form the dough into a 12-by-2-inch log. Wrap and refrigerate the dough for at least 2 hours, preferably overnight.

Preheat the oven to 350°F. Position racks in the upper and lower thirds of the oven.

Use a sharp knife to cut the cold dough log into slices ¼ inch thick. Place the cookies at least 1½ inches apart on the lined or greased cookie sheets.

Bake for 12 to 14 minutes, until the cookies are light golden brown at the edges. Rotate the cookie sheets from top to bottom and from front to back halfway through the baking time to ensure even baking. Repeat until all the cookies are baked.

For lined pans, set the pans or just the liners on racks to cool; for unlined pans, use a metal spatula to transfer the cookies to racks. Cool completely before stacking or storing. The cookies are delicious fresh but even better the next day. May be kept in an airtight container for at least 2 weeks.

NIBBY PECAN COOKIES

Roasted cacao nibs and nuts have a natural affinity. Both have rich nutty and fruity flavors and both add a seductive crunch to any cookie. Substitute any nut you can think of for the pecans. For the best taste and texture, make the dough at least a day before baking to allow the cacao bean flavor to permeate the dough, then bake the cookies at least a day ahead of serving for even more flavor.

Makes about forty-eight 2-inch cookies

INGREDIENTS

1 recipe Basic Butter Cookies (page 310)
1 cup (3.5 ounces) toasted pecans (see page 17), chopped
⅓ cup (1.33 ounces) roasted cacao nibs

EQUIPMENT

Cookie sheets, lined with parchment paper or ungreased

Make Basic Butter Cookies as directed, mixing the pecans and nibs into the batter before the flour. Proceed as directed.

NIBBY BUCKWHEAT BUTTER COOKIES

Bits of roasted cocoa beans (called *cacao nibs*) are a perfect complement to the nutty flavor of buckwheat. Since buckwheat flour is low in gluten, it gives cookies a fine sandy texture that is crunchy yet very tender. I like these cookies with blackberry sorbet. They also make superb linzer cookies (page 196) filled with blackberry jam. For the best taste and texture, make the dough at least a day before baking to allow the cacao bean flavor to permeate the dough, then bake the cookies at least a day ahead of serving for even more flavor.

Makes forty-eight 2½-inch cookies

INGREDIENTS

1 recipe Basic Butter Cookies (page 310)
¾ cup (3 ounces) buckwheat flour
⅓ cup (1.33 ounces) roasted cacao nibs

EQUIPMENT

Cookie sheets, lined with parchment paper or ungreased

Make the dough for Basic Butter Cookies, using only 1¼ cups (5.625 ounces) all-purpose flour mixed with the buckwheat flour. Mix the nibs into the batter just before the flour. Proceed as directed.

NUT SLICES

A whole pound of nuts makes these rustic nut cookies more nut than cookie. Textures vary depending on the hardness or softness of the chosen nut and its oil content. The complex flavor of these cookies comes from the use of raw, rather than toasted, nuts. As the cookies bake, the nuts on the surface become more toasted than those inside. The final cookie has a full range of nut flavors, including the subtle fruity notes of raw and lightly toasted nuts that are usually lost when all of the nuts are fully toasted.

The dough is a tad crumbly to slice unless you let it rest for several hours or overnight. Resting the dough also produces a better-tasting cookie. Crunchy to begin with, these cookies soften to a slight chewiness over a few days.

Makes about sixty 2-inch cookies

INGREDIENTS

1⅓ cups (6 ounces) unbleached all-purpose flour

½ teaspoon baking soda

1 pound whole raw unsalted cashews, walnuts, pecans, Brazil nuts, hazelnuts, or almonds

½ cup (3.5 ounces) packed light brown sugar

½ cup (3.5 ounces) granulated sugar

¾ teaspoon salt

8 tablespoons (1 stick) unsalted butter

1 large egg

1 teaspoon pure vanilla extract

EQUIPMENT

Cookie sheets, lined with parchment paper or ungreased

Food processor

Combine the flour and baking soda in a small bowl and mix together thoroughly with a whisk or fork.

Measure and set aside 1 cup of the nuts. Place the remaining nuts in a food processor and add the brown sugar, granulated sugar, and salt. Process for 1 minute, until the nuts are very finely ground and the mixture has a few small clumps. Cut the butter into chunks and add it to the food processor. Add the egg and the vanilla. Process until the mixture forms a mass. Add the flour mixture. Pulse until the flour is mostly incorporated. Add the reserved nuts and pulse just until the flour is no longer visible and the nuts are coarsely chopped. Remove the dough from the processor (it will be slightly crumbly) and press it together. Divide the dough in half and form two 8-by-2-inch logs. Wrap the logs in foil and refrigerate for at least 2 hours or, preferably, overnight.

Preheat the oven to 350°F. Position racks in the upper and lower thirds of the oven.

Slice the chilled dough ¼ to ⅜ inch thick, pressing the edges of the cookies together if the dough crumbles a bit, and place slices at least 1 inch apart on the lined or ungreased pans.

Bake for 12 to 14 minutes, or until golden brown at the edges, rotating the pans from top to bottom and from front to back halfway through the baking time to ensure even baking. For lined pans, set the pans or just the liners on racks to cool; for unlined pans, use a metal spatula to transfer the cookies to racks. Cool the cookies completely before stacking or storing. May be kept in an airtight container for at least 2 weeks.

UPGRADES

Serve Nut Slices with a little bowl of Plain, Vanilla, or Coconut Dulce de Leche (page 337) for slathering, or sandwich the cookies to make Nutty Alfajores (page 193). Or make the dough with hazelnuts and sandwich the cookies with Nutella, and you'll get Double Hazelnut Sandwich Cookies.

AMARETTI

Always a perfect nibble with espresso or dessert wine, these sweet and crunchy Italian cookies with their characteristic bitter almond flavor can also be dunked and layered in glasses with whipped cream or custard or mascarpone and berries. Or sprinkle crushed amaretti over ice cream or stone fruit slices, fresh or grilled. Great pastry chefs sprinkle amaretti crumbs in the bottom of fruit tart crusts to soak up and thicken the juices. Amaretti keep for ages in an airtight container. Might as well make plenty.

Makes about ninety 1½-inch cookies

INGREDIENTS

1⅔ cups (8 ounces) blanched almonds

2 cups (8 ounces) powdered sugar

½ cup egg whites (from about 4 large eggs), at room temperature

¼ teaspoon cream of tartar

2 teaspoons almond extract

½ cup (3.5 ounces) granulated sugar

EQUIPMENT

Cookie sheets, lined with parchment paper

Pastry bag fitted with a ⅝-inch plain round tip (optional)

Preheat the oven to 300°F. Position racks in the lower and upper thirds of the oven.

Combine the almonds and powdered sugar in a food processor. Process until the almonds are finely ground, pulsing to avoid turning the mixture into a paste and scraping the sides as necessary.

In a separate bowl, beat the egg whites with the cream of tartar until soft peaks form when the beaters are lifted. Add the almond extract and continue to beat, gradually adding granulated sugar, until the egg whites are fluffy and very stiff with a dull sheen. Pour the almond mixture over the meringue. Fold with a large rubber spatula just until the dry mixture is fully incorporated (see page 287). Scrape the batter into the pastry bag. Pipe low domes about 1½ inches in diameter and ¾ inches high, 1 inch apart, on the lined cookie sheets. If your domes are pointy, smooth them with a wet finger (or use the method on page 290). Without a pastry bag, use a spoon to scoop tablespoons of batter 1 inch apart onto the pans. While the first two pans are baking, pipe or scoop any remaining batter immediately onto a third lined sheet or onto a parchment liner to be transferred to a baking sheet when the oven is free.

Bake for 30 to 35 minutes, until the cookies are golden. (Or, if you prefer them crunchy on the outside and a little soft and chewy within instead of thoroughly crunchy, bake them for only 12 minutes at 350°F.) Rotate the pans from top to bottom and from front to back halfway through the baking time to ensure even baking. Set the pans or just the liners on racks to cool. Let the cookies cool completely before storing. Repeat with the remaining cookies. May be kept in an airtight container for weeks.

UPGRADES

Spice-Dusted Amaretti Sprinkle unbaked cookies with pinches of Cinnamon Sugar, Garam Masala Sugar, or Nutmeg Sugar (page 336).

TOFFEE BARS

My friend Beryl Radin's aunt Florence gave us this especially rich and happy marriage of American flavors—crunchy, shattering caramel, pecans, and milk chocolate on a thin shortbread crust. The secret is to toast the pecans on the crust before adding the caramel topping. For the most luxurious rendition, chop up a good quality milk chocolate bar in lieu of milk chocolate chips.

Makes 24 bars

INGREDIENTS

FOR THE CRUST

12 tablespoons (1½ sticks) unsalted butter

⅓ cup (2.33 ounces) sugar

1 teaspoon pure vanilla extract

¼ teaspoon salt

2¼ cups (10 ounces) unbleached all-purpose flour

2 cups (7 ounces) pecan halves

FOR THE TOPPING

1 tablespoon water

¾ cup (5.25 ounces) packed light brown sugar

8 tablespoons (1 stick) unsalted butter, cut into 4 chunks

⅔ to 1 cup (4 to 6 ounces) milk chocolate chips or 6 ounces milk chocolate, chopped

EQUIPMENT

A 9-by-13-inch metal pan, the bottom and all 4 sides lined with foil (see page 24)

An additional 9-by-13-inch piece of foil

Preheat the oven to 350°F. Position a rack in the lower third of the oven.

To Make the Crust Cut the butter into chunks and melt it in a large saucepan over medium heat. Remove from the heat and stir in the sugar, vanilla, and salt. Add the flour and mix just until incorporated. Press the dough evenly over the bottom of the pan. Scatter the pecans over the dough without pressing them into it. Lay the extra piece of foil loosely over the nuts to allow them to toast without burning while the crust is baking.

Bake for 20 to 25 minutes, until the crust is lightly browned at the edges. While the crust is baking, make the topping.

To Make the Topping Combine the water and brown sugar in a small saucepan, and whisk until the sugar is moistened. Heat the mixture over medium heat and bring to a boil, stirring occasionally. Whisk in the butter and remove from the heat.

When the crust is ready, whisk the topping until smooth. Remove the foil from the crust and scrape the hot butter mixture over the pecans on the crust. Bake for 12 to 15 minutes, until the topping is dark and bubbling vigorously. Remove the pan from the oven and scatter the chocolate chips evenly over the top. (Or melt and drizzle the chocolate decoratively over the bars after they have cooled.) Cool the bars in the pan on a rack. Lift the ends of the foil liner and transfer to a cutting board. Use a long sharp knife to cut into 24 bars. May be kept in an airtight container for at least 1 week.

WHEAT-FREE TOFFEE BARS

Sweet and crunchy with toasted pecans and brown sugar toffee.

Makes 24 bars

INGREDIENTS

FOR THE CRUST

⅓ cup plus 1 tablespoon (2 ounces) white rice flour, preferably extra-fine (see Note, page 45)

1¼ cups plus 2 tablespoons (5 ounces) oat flour (see Note, page 45)

¼ teaspoon salt

⅛ teaspoon baking soda

⅔ cup (4.625 ounces) sugar

2 ounces (one quarter of an 8-ounce package) cream cheese, cut into chunks

12 tablespoons (1½ sticks) unsalted butter, softened, cut into chunks

1 teaspoon vanilla extract

2 cups (7 ounces) pecan halves

FOR THE TOPPING

1 tablespoon water

¾ cup (5.25 ounces) packed light brown sugar

8 tablespoons (1 stick) unsalted butter, cut into 4 chunks

1 cup milk chocolate chips or 6 ounces milk chocolate, chopped

EQUIPMENT

A 9-by-13-inch metal pan, the bottom and all 4 sides lined with foil (see page 24)

An additional 9-by-13-inch piece of foil

Preheat the oven to 350°F. Position a rack in the lower third of the oven.

To Make the Crust   Combine the flours, salt, and baking soda in a medium bowl, and mix thoroughly with a whisk or fork. In a large bowl, with an electric mixer, beat the sugar with the cream cheese, butter, and vanilla until smooth and creamy. Add the flour mixture and mix just until it is incorporated.

Scrape the dough into the prepared pan and spread to make a thin, even layer. Scatter the pecans over the dough, but don't press them in. Lay the extra piece of foil loosely over the nuts.

Bake for 20 to 25 minutes, until the crust looks lightly browned at the edges but still pale in the center. While the crust is baking, make the topping.

To Make the Topping   Combine the water and brown sugar in a small saucepan and whisk until the sugar is moistened. Bring the mixture to a boil over medium heat, stirring occasionally. Whisk in the butter and remove from the heat.

When the crust is ready, whisk the topping until smooth. Remove the foil from the crust and scrape the hot butter mixture over the pecans on the crust. Bake for 12 to 15 minutes, until the topping is dark and bubbling vigorously. Remove the pan from the oven and scatter the chocolate chips evenly over the top. (Or melt and drizzle the chocolate decoratively over the bars after they have cooled.) Cool the bars in the pan on a rack. Lift the ends of the foil liner and transfer to a cutting board. Use a long sharp knife to cut into 24 bars. May be kept in an airtight container for up to 4 days.

CHUNKY

Chunky is just plain fun. The glory of chunky cookies for the eater is the variety of flavor and texture, the change-up, the surprise, the little explosion of new flavor in each bite. Cookies studded, laced, even loaded with morsels, bits, chunks, and shards are irresistible. Cookie inclusions generally don't affect the chemistry of the dough. So go ahead and fold creative combinations of dried fruit, nuts, chocolate, and even candies into any cookie dough that you like. Choose inclusions with contrasting flavors, textures, and/or sweetness levels. Nibble a little handful of selected inclusions and adjust the proportions before you commit them to your dough. Large pieces of hard crunchy nuts, rich smooth bitter chocolate, or something salty add excitement to sweet, tender melt-in-your-mouth meringues. Little jolts of candied orange peel or ginger add fireworks to rich chocolate cookies. Or choose ingredients that mimic or complement each other.

CHUNKY HAZELNUT MERINGUES

Light, sweet, and tenderly crunchy cookies with hidden pockets of dark chocolate and toasty nuts. Serve them in summer with blackberries and unsweetened whipped cream. Of course you can substitute toasted almonds—or any other nut you like—for the hazels. (Photograph on page 128)

Makes 36 to 40 cookies

INGREDIENTS

5 ounces bittersweet or semisweet chocolate, chopped, or 1 scant cup chocolate chunks or chips

1 cup (5 ounces) toasted and skinned hazelnuts (see page 17), coarsely chopped

3 large egg whites, at room temperature

⅛ teaspoon cream of tartar

⅔ cup (4.625 ounces) sugar

Cinnamon stick (optional)

EQUIPMENT

Cookie sheets, lined with parchment paper

Preheat the oven to 300°F. Position racks in the upper and lower thirds of the oven.

Set aside about one-fifth of the chocolate and the nuts for topping the cookies.

Combine the egg whites and cream of tartar in a clean dry mixer bowl. Beat at medium-high speed with a heavy-duty stand mixer (or high speed with a handheld mixer) until the egg whites are creamy white (instead of translucent) and hold a soft shape when the beaters are lifted. Continue to beat on medium-high speed, adding the sugar a little at a time, taking 1½ to 2 minutes in all. The mixture should stand in very stiff peaks when the beaters are lifted. Use a rubber spatula to fold in the chocolate and nuts just until incorporated.

Drop heaping teaspoons of meringue 1½ inches apart on the lined cookie sheet. Top each meringue with some of the reserved chocolate and nuts. Bake for 10 to 15 minutes, until the meringues begin to turn golden. Rotate the pans from top to bottom and from front to back. Turn the oven down to 200°F and bake for another 1½ hours. Turn off the oven and leave the meringues in it to cool. Let the cookies cool completely before using or storing. If desired, grate a little of the cinnamon stick over each cookie before serving. May be kept in an airtight container for at least 2 months.

UPGRADES

Sweet and Salty Nut Meringues The nuts are salty here, and there are twice as many of them, all left in pretty big pieces, with just enough sweet meringue to hold them together. With or without the chocolate, these could change your mind about meringues in general. Meanwhile, even if your politics are all dark chocolate, you won't want to miss a little rich milk chocolate with those salty nuts. Really. | Omit the chocolate or not. Or use milk chocolate instead of dark. Substitute 2 cups (10 ounces) roasted and salted mixed nuts, very coarsely chopped, for the hazelnuts.

Milk Chocolate and Salted Almond or Cashew Meringues Substitute milk chocolate for the bittersweet chocolate. Substitute 1 to 2 cups salted roasted almonds or cashews for the hazelnuts.

Mocha-Nut Meringue Kisses Combine 1½ teaspoons instant espresso powder with the sugar before adding it to the egg whites. Skip the 10-to-15-minute bake at 300°F. Bake for 2 hours at 200°F and rotate the pans from top to bottom and from front to back after 1 hour.

MY CHOCOLATE CHIP COOKIES

A true American classic, buttery and irresistible, with crisp caramelized edges and rich chewy centers, lots of chocolate and fresh, crunchy nuts. What makes these chocolate chip cookies so good? Melted butter, well-rested dough, cookie sheets without paper liners, and just the right temperature.

Makes about 60 cookies

INGREDIENTS

2¼ cups (10.125 ounces) unbleached all-purpose flour

1 teaspoon baking soda

½ pound (2 sticks) unsalted butter, melted and still warm

¾ cup (5.25 ounces) granulated sugar

¾ cup (5.25 ounces) packed brown sugar

1 teaspoon pure vanilla extract

1 teaspoon salt

2 large eggs

2 cups (12 ounces) chocolate chips or chunks or hand-chopped chocolate

1 cup (3.5 ounces) coarsely chopped walnuts or pecans

EQUIPMENT

Cookie sheets, ungreased or lined with foil, dull side up

Combine the flour and baking soda in a bowl and mix together thoroughly with a whisk or fork.

In a large bowl, combine the melted butter with the sugars, vanilla, and salt. Mix in the eggs. Stir in the flour mixture just until all of the dry ingredients are moistened. Stir in the chocolate chips and nuts. If possible, let the dough stand for 1 or 2 hours, or (better still) overnight.

Preheat the oven to 375°F. Position racks in the upper and lower thirds of the oven.

If necessary, remove the dough from the refrigerator to soften. Scoop rounded tablespoons of dough and place them 3 inches apart on the ungreased or lined cookie sheets. Bake for 9 to 11 minutes, or until the cookies are golden brown at the edges and no longer look wet on top. Rotate the pans from top to bottom and from front to back halfway through the baking time to ensure even baking. Remove from the oven and let the cookies firm up on the pan for 1 to 2 minutes. For unlined pans, use a metal spatula to transfer the cookies to racks to cool; for lined pans, set the pans or just the liners on racks. Cool completely before storing or stacking. May be kept in an airtight container for several days.

UPGRADES

Nibby Nut and Raisin Cookies Substitute ⅔ cup (2.67 ounces) roasted cacao nibs and 1 cup (5 ounces) currants or raisins for the chocolate chips.

Whole Wheat Chocolate Chip Cookies Whole wheat pastry flour is made with soft wheat, so it contains less protein than regular whole wheat flour. It contributes the lovely flavor of the grain without compromising the buttery tenderness that we want in a chocolate chip cookie. | Substitute an equal measure of whole wheat pastry flour for the all-purpose flour and increase the nuts to 1½ cups (5.25 ounces).

Whole Wheat Walnut or Pecan Cookies I especially love this version with twice the nuts and no chips at all. | Substitute an equal measure of whole wheat pastry flour for the all-purpose flour. Omit the chocolate chips and increase the nuts to 2½ or 3 cups (8.75 or 10.5 ounces). Add a handful of healthy seeds such as sesame, hulled hemp seeds, flax meal (ground flaxseed), or any combination if you like.

WHEAT-FREE CHOCOLATE CHIP COOKIES

Don't save these for a special audience. My notes said it best: the results were kind of good—actually, *very* good. The combination of oat and brown rice flours with a little potato starch tastes surprisingly like butterscotch—quite nice! These cookies have a beautiful butterscotch color as well, with a lovely buttery crunch at the edges and a delicate cakey interior. Also noted: these are even better after resting the dough overnight. Read about measuring non-wheat flours on page 153.

Makes about sixty 3½-inch cookies

INGREDIENTS

1 cup plus 3 tablespoons (4.375 ounces) oat flour (see page 354)

1 cup (4.375 ounces) brown rice flour (see page 355)

¼ cup plus 2 tablespoons (2.25 ounces) potato starch (see page 354)

½ teaspoon salt

½ teaspoon baking soda

¾ teaspoon xanthan gum (see page 359)

½ pound (2 sticks) unsalted butter, melted

¾ cup (5.25 ounces) granulated sugar

¾ cup (5.25 ounces) packed dark brown sugar

1 teaspoon pure vanilla extract

2 large eggs

2 cups (12 ounces) chocolate chips or chunks or hand-chopped chocolate

1 cup (4 ounces) coarsely chopped walnuts or pecans

EQUIPMENT

Cookie sheets, lined with foil, dull side up, or greased

Combine the flours, potato starch, salt, baking soda, and xanthan gum in a medium bowl and mix thoroughly with a whisk or fork.

In a large bowl, mix the melted butter, sugars, and vanilla. Whisk in the eggs. Stir in the flour mixture. With a rubber spatula, mix the batter briskly for about 45 seconds (to activate the binding power of the xanthan gum—the more you mix, the chewier and less crunchy the cookies will be). Stir in the chocolate chips and nuts. If possible, let the dough stand for 1 to 2 hours or (better still) cover and refrigerate overnight.

Preheat the oven to 375°F. Position racks in the upper and lower thirds of the oven.

Scoop 2 tablespoons of dough and place 2 inches apart on the lined or greased cookie sheets. Bake until the cookies are golden brown, 12 to 14 minutes. Rotate the pans from top to bottom and from front to back halfway through the baking time to ensure even baking. For lined pans, set the pans or just the liners on racks to cool; for unlined pans, use a metal spatula to transfer the cookies to racks. Cool the cookies completely before stacking or storing. May be kept in an airtight container for several days.

UPGRADES

Wheat-Free Pecan Spice Cookies Add 2 teaspoons ground cinnamon, ½ teaspoon ground nutmeg, ½ teaspoon ground cloves, and ½ teaspoon ground ginger with the sugar. Omit the chocolate chips and substitute 2 cups (7 ounces) lightly toasted pecan pieces for the walnuts.

Wheat-Free Nibby Nut and Raisin Cookies Omit the chocolate chips. Add 1 cup (5 ounces) raisins and ⅔ cup (2.67 ounces) roasted cacao nibs with the walnuts.

Dairy-Free and Wheat-Free Chocolate Chip Cookies Omit the salt in the recipe (or in either upgrade) and substitute dairy-free margarine (salted) for the butter.

HAZELNUT GIANDUJA CHUNK COOKIES

Elegant flavors in a rustic-looking cookie. Crunchy nuts and pockets of smooth chocolate interrupt an otherwise melt-in-your-mouth cookie.

Makes about forty-eight 1½-inch cookies

INGREDIENTS

16 tablespoons (2 sticks) unsalted butter, softened

½ cup (3.5 ounces) granulated sugar

2 teaspoons pure vanilla extract

½ teaspoon salt

2 cups (9 ounces) unbleached all-purpose flour

¾ cup coarsely chopped gianduja or milk chocolate

¾ cup (3.75 ounces) coarsely chopped toasted hazelnuts (see page 17)

½ cup powdered sugar

EQUIPMENT

Cookie sheets, lined with parchment or ungreased

In a large bowl, with a large spoon or a handheld mixer, mix the butter, granulated sugar, vanilla, and salt just until blended. Stir in the flour just until moistened. Stir in the gianduja and the nuts. Cover and refrigerate for at least 2 hours, and preferably overnight.

Preheat the oven to 325°F. Position racks in the upper and lower thirds of the oven.

Using a fork, pull off irregular lumps of dough—each should measure slightly more than a level tablespoon of dough. Or pinch the dough off with your fingers. Do not smooth or round the pieces. Place the pieces 2 inches apart on the lined or ungreased cookie sheets. Bake for 18 to 20 minutes, until lightly colored on top and golden brown on the bottom. Rotate the pans from top to bottom and from front to back halfway through the baking time to ensure even baking.

While baking, put the powdered sugar in a small sieve. When the cookies are done, let them cool on the pan for 5 minutes, and then sieve powdered sugar over the top of each one. For lined pans, set the pans or just the liners on racks to cool; for unlined pans, use a metal spatula to transfer the cookies to racks. Let the cookies cool completely before stacking or storing. May be stored in an airtight container for at least 2 weeks. Before serving, sieve additional powdered sugar over the cookies if necessary.

MACADAMIA AND WHITE CHOCOLATE CHUNK COOKIES

A little sweet with a little salty and lots of satisfying crunch. I like the challenge of making white chocolate more interesting. A handful of oats and lots of salted and roasted macadamias do the job.

Makes about 36 cookies

INGREDIENTS

¾ cup (2.5 ounces) rolled oats

¾ cup (3.375 ounces) unbleached all-purpose flour

½ teaspoon baking soda

¼ teaspoon salt

8 tablespoons (1 stick) unsalted butter, melted and still warm

⅓ cup (2.33 ounces) granulated sugar

⅓ cup (2.33 ounces) packed brown sugar

½ teaspoon pure vanilla extract

1 large egg

1 cup (4.5 ounces) dry-roasted salted macadamia nuts, coarsely chopped

1 cup (6 ounces) white chocolate chips, or (better still) 6 ounces chopped white chocolate

EQUIPMENT

Cookie sheets, ungreased or lined with foil, dull side up

Food processor or blender

Pulverize the oats in the processor or blender until fine. Add the flour, baking soda, and salt and pulse to combine. Set aside.

In a large bowl, combine the melted butter with the sugars and vanilla. Whisk in the egg. Stir in the flour mixture just until all of the dry ingredients are moistened. Let the mixture cool for a few minutes if it is at all warm. Stir in the nuts and chocolate chips. Cover and refrigerate for at least 2 hours, and preferably overnight.

Preheat the oven to 325°F. Position racks in the upper and lower thirds of the oven.

Remove the dough from the refrigerator to soften. Scoop rounded tablespoons of dough and place about 2 inches apart on the ungreased or lined pans. Bake until the cookies are deep golden brown, 13 to 15 minutes. Rotate the pans from top to bottom and from front to back halfway through the baking time to ensure even baking. For unlined pans, use a metal spatula to transfer the cookies to racks to cool; for lined pans, set the pans or just the liners on racks. Cool the cookies completely before storing or stacking. May be kept in an airtight container for several days.

BITTERSWEET DECADENCE COOKIES

Richer than sin, with an irresistible jolt of unrelenting bittersweet chocolate, these cookies are slightly crunchy on the outside with chunky but divinely gooey centers. For the best gooey texture and balanced flavor, pay attention to the amount of chocolate vis-à-vis the specific cacao percentages called for in the first part of the ingredient list and the sugar adjustment. For the chocolate chunks, I like to chop my own from a bar of bittersweet with 70% or up to 82% cacao for a deeply dramatic contrast to the flavor and sweetness of the batter. This ultrachocolaty batter begins to stiffen almost as soon as you mix it. Your cookies will look best if you scoop them ASAP, while the batter is still soft.

Makes 30 to 36 cookies

INGREDIENTS

¼ cup (1.125 ounces) unbleached all-purpose flour

¼ teaspoon baking powder

⅛ teaspoon salt

8 ounces bittersweet or semisweet chocolate with up to 60% cacao or 7 ounces chocolate
    with 61% to 64% cacao, chopped

2 tablespoons unsalted butter

2 large eggs

½ cup (3.5 ounces) sugar (plus 1 tablespoon [0.375 ounce] if using chocolate with 61% to 64% cacao)

1 teaspoon pure vanilla extract

6 ounces semisweet or bittersweet chocolate with any percentage cacao you like, chopped into
    generous-size chunks, or purchased chocolate chunks

2 cups (7 ounces) walnut or pecan halves or large pieces

EQUIPMENT

Cookie sheets, lined with parchment paper

Preheat the oven to 350°F. Position racks in the upper and lower thirds of the oven.

Combine the flour, baking powder, and salt in a small bowl and mix together thoroughly with a whisk.

Place the 8 ounces of chocolate and the butter in a large heatproof bowl set directly in a wide skillet of barely simmering water. Stir frequently just until melted and smooth. Remove the chocolate from the skillet and set it aside. Leave the heat on under the skillet.

In another large heatproof bowl, whisk the eggs, sugar, and vanilla together thoroughly. Set the bowl in the skillet and stir until the mixture is lukewarm to the touch. Stir the egg mixture into the warm (not hot) chocolate. Stir in the flour mixture, then the chocolate chunks and nuts.

Scoop slightly rounded tablespoons of batter and place 1½ inches apart onto the lined cookie sheets. Bake for 12 to 14 minutes, until the surface of the cookie looks dry and set and the centers are still gooey. Rotate the sheets from top to bottom and from front to back halfway through the baking time to ensure even baking. Set the pans or just the liners on racks to cool. Let the cookies cool completely before storing or stacking. May be kept in an airtight container for up to 3 days.

NOTE

To Make the Dough Ahead Refrigerate or freeze scoops of batter until hard. Place them in an airtight bag and refrigerate for up to 3 days, or place in a second freezer bag or airtight container and freeze for up to 3 months. When ready to bake, thaw frozen scoops in the refrigerator. Place scoops on lined pans, bring to room temperature, and bake as directed.

UPGRADES

Bittersweet Orange Decadence Cookies San Francisco pastry chef Deirdre Davis had the brilliant idea of adding a handful of her exquisite homemade candied orange peel. *Voilà!* The big trick is to fold the peel in at the end, with just a few strokes, so that the flavor of the peel does not blend with the batter. Instead, you want little explosions of chewy orange flavor with crunchy walnuts enveloped in bittersweet chocolate. Make these if you can get very good quality candied peel or if you make your own peel—or if you know someone who does. These are extra chunky but still a little gooey. | Increase the nuts to 2½ cups (8.75 ounces). Fold in ½ cup (2.25 ounces) diced good quality or homemade candied orange peel after the nuts.

CHUNKY PEANUT BUTTER CLOUDS

Tender melting peanut butter meringues burst with toasted hazelnuts or almonds and shards of milk chocolate. Crunchy, then soft . . . dissolving on the tongue.

Makes 30 to 36 cookies

INGREDIENTS

1 recipe Peanut Butter Clouds (page 296)

⅔ cup (3.3 ounces) toasted and skinned hazelnuts or toasted almonds (see page 17)

4 ounces milk chocolate, coarsely chopped, or ⅔ cup (4 ounces) milk chocolate chips

EQUIPMENT

Cookie sheets, lined with parchment paper

Preheat the oven to 200°F. Position racks in the upper and lower thirds of the oven.

Prepare the batter as directed in the recipe on page 296, but fold only two or three strokes after adding the peanut butter. Pour the nuts and chocolate over the batter and continue to fold until they are dispersed and the peanut butter is mostly blended; a few uneven streaks of white meringue are okay. Shape and bake as directed.

CHOCOLATE CHUNK COOKIES WITH CHERRIES AND PECANS

The same dough that makes crisp chocolate wafers becomes chunky, crusty-edged cookies with moist, cakey interiors loaded with chewy tart cherries, rich nuggets of chocolate, and plenty of toasty pecans.

Makes about forty-eight 2-inch cookies

INGREDIENTS

1 recipe Chocolate Wafers 3.0 (page 68)

6 ounces bittersweet or semisweet chocolate (any cacao percentage you like), cut into small chunks, or 1 cup (6 ounces) bittersweet or semisweet chocolate chips or chunks

1⅓ cups (5.25 ounces) chopped toasted pecans (see page 17)

1 cup (6 ounces) dried sour cherries

EQUIPMENT

Cookie sheets, lined with parchment paper or greased

Food processor

Preheat the oven to 350°F. Position racks in the upper and lower thirds of the oven.

Make the dough as directed in the recipe on page 68. Transfer it to a large bowl and mix in the chocolate pieces, pecans, and cherries.

Drop level tablespoons of dough 2 inches apart on the prepared cookie sheets. Bake for 10 to 12 minutes, until the cookies look dry but are soft (not squishy) when pressed lightly with a finger. Rotate pans from top to bottom and back to front halfway through the baking time. Set the lined pans or just the liners on racks to cool; for unlined pans, use a metal spatula to transfer the cookies to racks. Cool the cookies completely before stacking or storing. May be kept in an airtight container for up to 2 weeks.

CHEWY

Chewy conjures up childhood Tootsie Rolls and stretchy bubble gum, burnished turkey skin at Thanksgiving, or sweet salty bacon for breakfast. The desire for chewy is surely primal. Ancient humans—before fire and cooking—chewed for hours to extract vital nutrients from plants. Now chewy provides as much (more?) pleasure as nourishment. Chewy makes us work, but just a little, for that sweet slow release of flavor. Cookie lovers craving chewy will find herein cookies decidedly or delicately resistant to the tooth, from New Classic Coconut Macaroons and Honey Hemp Bars (quite chewy!) to My Ginger Cookies (aka Screaming Ginger Cookies) with their soft centers and crackly chewy edges, as well as Spicy Carrot Masala Macaroons (practically dainty). Meanwhile, Pebbly Beach Fruit Squares marry a crunchy sugar cookie with scads of toothsome dried fruit, and Black Bottom Pecan Praline Bars pair chewy brown sugar cookie dough with creamy chocolate.

PEBBLY BEACH FRUIT SQUARES

These crunchy-crisp *and* chewy cookies with sparkling bumpy tops started out to be simple raisin cookies. Indeed, you can pair lemon zest, cinnamon, or anise with dark or golden raisins. But you can also make the cookies with prunes, apricots, cherries, dates, cranberries, or candied ginger. Verbatim from our testing notes: anise is best with the prunes but smells divine in the oven, no matter what fruit we use. Try a ginger/cranberry combo for the holidays (and note that the cookies are sturdy enough to ship). If dried fruit is especially hard or chewy, it will only get harder after baking. To avoid this, soak pieces in a small bowl with just enough cold water (or fruit juices or wine) to cover for 20 minutes (longer will dilute and oversoften the fruit). Drain and pat pieces very dry before using. (Photograph on page 146)

Makes thirty-two 2½-inch square cookies

INGREDIENTS

1¾ cups plus 2 tablespoons (8.5 ounces) unbleached all-purpose flour

½ teaspoon baking powder

¼ teaspoon salt

8 tablespoons (1 stick) unsalted butter

¾ cup (5.25 ounces) granulated sugar

1 large egg

1 teaspoon pure vanilla extract

1 teaspoon finely grated lemon zest or ground cinnamon or anise

1 cup moist dried fruit (one kind or a combination): dark or golden raisins; dried sour cherries;
    dried cranberries; coarsely chopped dates, dried apricots, or prunes; finely chopped candied ginger

¼ cup (1.75 ounces) turbinado or other coarse sugar

EQUIPMENT

Cookie sheets, lined with parchment paper or greased

Combine the flour, baking powder, and salt in a bowl and mix together thoroughly with a whisk or fork.

With a large spoon in a medium mixing bowl or with a mixer, beat the butter with the granulated sugar until smooth and well blended but not fluffy. Add the egg, vanilla, and lemon zest and beat until smooth. Add the flour mixture and mix until completely incorporated.

Divide the dough in half and form each into a rectangle. Wrap the patties in plastic wrap and refrigerate for at least 2 hours or overnight.

Preheat the oven to 350°F. Position racks in the upper and lower thirds of the oven.

Remove the dough from the refrigerator and let sit for 15 minutes to soften slightly. On a sheet of parchment paper or plastic wrap, roll one piece of dough into a rectangle 8½ inches by 16½ inches. With a short side facing you, scatter half of the dried fruit on the bottom half of the dough. Fold the top half of the dough over the fruit, using the paper as a handle. Peel the paper from the top of the dough. (If it sticks, chill the dough for a few minutes until the paper peels easily.) Dust the top of the dough lightly with flour. Flip the dough onto a lightly floured cutting board and peel off the remaining paper. Sprinkle with half of the coarse sugar and pat lightly to make sure the sugar adheres. Use a heavy knife to trim the edges. Cut into 4 strips and then cut each strip into 4 pieces to make 16 squares. Place the cookies 2 inches apart on the lined or greased pans. Repeat with the remaining dough, fruit, and sugar.

Bake for 12 to 15 minutes, or until the edges are lightly browned. Rotate the pans from top to bottom and from front to back halfway through the baking time to ensure even baking. For lined pans, set the pans or just the liners on racks to cool; for unlined pans, use a metal spatula to transfer the cookies to racks. Cool the cookies completely before stacking or storing. May be kept in an airtight container for a week.

UPGRADES

Wheat-Free Fruit Squares Substitute the dough from Wheat-Free Butter Cookies (page 44). Roll the well-chilled dough out on plastic wrap. Fill and cut as directed. Bake at 325°F on parchment-lined sheets for 17 to 20 minutes, or until the bottoms are rich brown while the tops remain pale.

OATMEAL COOKIES

Melted butter and moistened oats are the keys to the satisfying texture of these great cookies. Overnight chilling allows the oats to absorb the dough's moisture. The cookies have a great toasted oat flavor, caramelized crunchy brown edges, and flavorful chewy centers. Perfection!

Makes forty 3¼-inch cookies or eighty 2½-inch cookies

INGREDIENTS

2 cups (6.67 ounces) rolled oats

¼ cup water

1¼ cups (5.625 ounces) unbleached all-purpose flour

½ teaspoon baking soda

1 teaspoon ground cinnamon

¼ teaspoon freshly grated nutmeg

½ pound (2 sticks) unsalted butter

¾ cup (5.25 ounces) packed light brown sugar

½ cup (3.5 ounces) granulated sugar

1 teaspoon pure vanilla extract

½ teaspoon salt

1 large egg

1 cup (3.5 ounces) walnuts, chopped

1 cup (5 ounces) raisins

EQUIPMENT

Cookie sheets, ungreased or lined with foil, dull side up

Place the oats in a small bowl and sprinkle with the water. Combine the flour, baking soda, cinnamon, and nutmeg in a medium bowl and mix together thoroughly with a whisk or fork.

Cut the butter into chunks and melt in a large saucepan over medium heat. Remove from the heat and stir in the sugars, vanilla, and salt. Add the egg and stir briskly. Stir in the flour mixture just until all of the dry ingredients are moistened. Stir in the walnuts, raisins, and oats. Let the dough stand for at least 1 but preferably 2 hours or (better still) cover and refrigerate overnight.

Preheat the oven to 350°F. Position racks in the upper and lower thirds of the oven.

For large cookies, scoop about 2 level tablespoons of dough and place the cookies about 3 inches apart on the ungreased or lined pans. For small cookies, scoop 1 level tablespoon of dough. Bake for 12 to 15 minutes for large cookies, 10 to 12 minutes for small cookies, or until the cookies are golden brown on top. Rotate the pans from top to bottom and from front to back halfway through the baking time to ensure even baking. For unlined pans, use a metal spatula to transfer the cookies to racks to cool; for lined pans, set the pans or just the liners on racks. Cool the cookies completely before storing or stacking. May be kept in an airtight container for several days.

UPGRADES

Bridget's Oat Raisin Coconut Cookies Hearty and satisfying, these cookies were adapted from a recipe given to me many years ago, from the Bovine Bakery in Point Reyes Station, California. | Substitute ¾ cup (2.25 ounces) unsweetened dried shredded coconut (see page 352) for the walnuts.

WHEAT-FREE DOUBLE-OATMEAL COOKIES

If you love oats as I do, the idea of oatmeal cookies with both rolled oats and oat flour (instead of the usual wheat flour) should tempt you, regardless of whether you can eat wheat or not. I like these so much that I may never look back. Xanthan gum is the magic ingredient (it's also, by the way, a natural ingredient) that acts like gluten, adding chewiness to cookies made with flours that don't naturally contain gluten. You can even adjust the chewiness of your cookie by mixing the batter more or mixing it less. Even chewy cookies are improved by crunchy edges, and that's what the dull side of the foil provides.

Makes about thirty-two 3½-inch cookies

INGREDIENTS

1 cup plus 3 tablespoons (4.375 ounces) oat flour (see Notes)

2 cups (6.625 ounces) rolled oats

½ teaspoon salt

1 teaspoon baking soda

¾ teaspoon xanthan gum (see page 359)

½ pound (2 sticks) unsalted butter, melted

¾ cup (5.25 ounces) granulated sugar

¾ cup (5.25 ounces) packed light brown sugar

1 teaspoon ground cinnamon

¼ teaspoon freshly grated nutmeg

1 teaspoon pure vanilla extract

2 large eggs

Generous 1 cup (4 ounces) coarsely chopped or broken walnut pieces

1 cup (5 ounces) raisins

EQUIPMENT

Cookie sheets, lined with foil, dull side up, or greased

Combine the oat flour, rolled oats, salt, baking soda, and xanthan gum in a medium bowl and combine with a whisk or fork.

In a large bowl, mix the melted butter, sugars, cinnamon, nutmeg, and vanilla. Whisk in the eggs. Stir in the oat mixture and mix the batter briskly for about 1 minute (to activate the binding power of the xanthan gum—the more you mix, the chewier and less crunchy the cookies will be). Stir in the nuts and raisins. Let the dough stand for at least 1 but preferably 2 hours or (better still) cover and refrigerate overnight.

Preheat the oven to 325°F. Position racks in the upper and lower thirds of the oven.

Scoop 2 tablespoons of the dough and place 2 inches apart on the lined or greased cookie sheets. Bake for 16 to 20 minutes, until the cookies are deep golden brown. Rotate the sheets from top to bottom and from front to back halfway through the baking time to ensure even baking. For lined pans, set the pans or just the liners on racks to cool; for unlined pans, use a metal spatula to transfer the cookies to racks. Cool the cookies completely before stacking or storing. May be kept in an airtight container for several days.

NOTES

To be totally wheat-free, oats and oat flour must never have come in contact with wheat or equipment used to process wheat. These products will be specifically labeled "gluten-free." See Resources (page 362) to order online.

Weights of non-wheat flours and starches vary wildly—even more than regular wheat flour—and a lot depends on the smallest differences in one's measuring style. Such variations can drastically alter results, even making a good cookie quite dreadful. Weighing is the surest way to get the same results that I got. But if you must use measuring cups instead of a scale do it like this: Set your measuring cup on a sheet of wax paper. Spoon the flour or starch lightly from the bag into the measuring cup until the cup is heaping. Sweep a knife across the rim of the cup to level it without tapping or packing. (Pick up the wax paper and fold it in half to pour excess flour back into the bag.)

MY GINGER COOKIES

Also known as Screaming Ginger Cookies. With crunchy edges and a chewy center, beautifully crackled on top, spicy, and loaded with diced crystallized ginger, this is my favorite spice cookie. You can tone down the heat by omitting the fresh and cutting down on the candied ginger and still end up with a great cookie.

Makes fifty-six 2¼-inch cookies

INGREDIENTS

2 cups (9 ounces) unbleached all-purpose flour

2 teaspoons baking soda

2 teaspoons ground ginger

1½ teaspoons ground cinnamon

½ teaspoon ground allspice

¼ teaspoon salt

8 tablespoons (1 stick) unsalted butter, melted and still warm

¼ cup unsulfured mild or full-flavored molasses

½ cup (3.5 ounces) granulated sugar

⅓ cup (2.33 ounces) packed brown sugar or light muscovado sugar

2 tablespoons finely minced or grated fresh ginger

1 large egg

¾ cup (4 ounces) ginger chips or crystallized ginger, cut into ¼-inch dice

About ½ cup (3.5 ounces) Demerara or turbinado sugar or ¼ cup (1.75 ounces) granulated sugar
    for rolling

EQUIPMENT

Cookie sheets, lined with parchment paper or ungreased

Preheat the oven to 350°F. Position racks in the upper and lower thirds of the oven.

Combine the flour, baking soda, ground ginger, cinnamon, allspice, and salt in a medium bowl and mix thoroughly with a whisk or fork.

Combine the warm butter, molasses, sugars, fresh ginger, and egg in a large bowl and mix thoroughly. Add the flour mixture and ginger chips and stir until incorporated. The dough will be soft.

Form the dough into 1-inch balls (0.5 ounce dough for each). Roll the balls in the Demerara sugar and place them 2 inches apart on the lined or ungreased cookie sheets. Bake for 10 to 12 minutes, or until the cookies puff up and crack on the surface and then begin to deflate in the oven. Rotate the sheets from top to bottom and from back to front halfway through the baking time to ensure even baking. For chewier cookies, remove them from the oven when at least half or more of the cookies have begun to deflate; for crunchier edges with chewy centers, bake for a minute or so longer.

For lined pans, set the pans or just the liners on racks to cool; for unlined pans, use a metal spatula to transfer the cookies to racks. Cool the cookies completely before storing. May be kept in an airtight container for several days.

UPGRADES

Gentler Ginger Cookies Turn down the heat by omitting the fresh ginger and decreasing the candied ginger to ½ cup. Still a great ginger cookie!

Wheat-Free Ginger Cookies These are superb and also gluten free if you use gluten-free oat flour! | Make My Ginger Cookies or Gentler Ginger Cookies, substituting 2 cups (7.25 ounces) oat flour and ½ cup (2.5 ounces) extra-fine white rice flour for the all-purpose flour. Substitute 2 large egg whites for the whole egg. After the flour mixture is completely mixed in, stir briskly for another 40 strokes to aerate the dough slightly.

HONEY HEMP BARS

This is my chewy, crunchy homage to the irresistible hemp and pecan bars I used to buy (and devour) from my young friend Zachary Wilson back in the 1990s, before he set hemp and underground baking aside to become a teacher. The shiny amber bars embedded with colorful good-for-you seeds, nuts, fruit, and cereal are terrifically tasty, even a little addictive. A healthy on-the-run snack for sure, but if you cut them into dainty squares, they make an exquisite confection to savor with your best oolong tea.

Makes 16 to 20 bars

INGREDIENTS

1⅔ cups (0.875 ounce) puffed rice or millet cereal

½ cup (2.33 ounces) hemp seeds

½ cup (1.875 ounces) pecan or walnut halves, medium-finely chopped

2 tablespoons black (or white or tan) sesame seeds

⅓ cup (1.67 ounces) raw pumpkin seeds

2 teaspoons flax meal (ground flaxseed)

2 tablespoons dried currants

Scant ½ cup (5 ounces) honey

1 tablespoon date paste or mashed dates

Rounded ⅛ teaspoon salt

½ teaspoon pure vanilla extract

EQUIPMENT

An 8-inch square metal baking pan, the bottom and all 4 sides lined with parchment paper
   (see page 24)

Preheat the oven to 300°F. Position a rack in the lower third of the oven.

In a large bowl, toss the cereal, hemp seeds, nuts, sesame seeds, pumpkin seeds, flax meal, and currants to mix.

In a small saucepan, warm the honey, date paste, salt, and vanilla, stirring and mashing until the date paste is dissolved and/or evenly dispersed. Pour the honey mixture over the dry ingredients and fold until all of the ingredients are moistened and sticky. It may seem at first that there is not enough honey; just continue to fold.

Scrape the mixture into the lined pan and spread it evenly with a fork. Using the back of the fork tines, press the mixture very firmly all over to compact and adhere the ingredients.

Bake for 30 to 40 minutes, until the top is barely golden (if in doubt, take it out so that the honey does not get scorched). Cool in the pan on a rack. Lift the ends of the parchment to remove the bars from the pan. Gently peel off the parchment. Use a heavy sharp knife to cut bars or squares. May be kept in an airtight container for 2 weeks or more.

UPGRADES

Try goji or golden berries, diced dried apricots, or bits of any tasty and colorful fruit in lieu of the currants.

ALMOND MACAROONS

Chewy dense cookies with a texture like almond paste, in stark contrast with the almost ethereal French Macarons (page 276) or the light but supercrunchy Amaretti (page 122).

Makes fifty-five 2-inch cookies

INGREDIENTS

1⅓ cups (7 ounces) whole or 1⅔ cups slivered (7 ounces) blanched almonds

1½ cups (10.5 ounces) sugar

1½ teaspoons almond extract

3 to 4 large egg whites (see Tech Support, opposite)

EQUIPMENT

Cookie sheets, lined with parchment paper

Food processor

In a food processor, combine the almonds and sugar. Process until the almonds are very fine and the mixture is beginning to pack together around the sides of the bowl, at least 3 minutes. Add the almond extract and 2 of the egg whites and process for several seconds. With the processor on, gradually add enough of the remaining egg whites to form a ball of dough around the blade. Continue to add egg white, with the processor running, until the batter no longer forms a ball and has the consistency of very thick, sticky mashed potatoes. Drop rounded teaspoons (equivalent to 2 level teaspoons) 2 inches apart on the lined cookie sheets. Smooth the top of each cookie with a moistened pastry brush or your fingertips. Let the cookies stand for 30 minutes before baking them.

Preheat the oven to 300°F. Position racks in the upper and lower thirds of the oven.

Bake the cookies for 20 to 25 minutes, or until the edges of the cookies barely begin to color. Rotate the pans from top to bottom and from front to back halfway through the baking time to ensure even baking. Set the pans or just the liners on racks to cool. Cool the cookies completely before detaching them from the parchment. May be kept in an airtight container for 2 to 3 days.

TECH SUPPORT

How to add a little bit of egg white at a time . . . It's almost impossible to pour a little bit of egg white into a bowl; the entire egg white usually slithers in as well. But some recipes call for just enough egg white to achieve a certain consistency—and too much will result in a runny batter. Here's how to add little bits of egg white at a time: In a small cup, beat the egg white(s) briefly with a fork to break up the viscous mass. Press your index finger firmly across the lip of the cup like a dam. As you pour, raise your finger just enough to let a thin stream pass and lower your finger to shut off the stream.

UPGRADES

Chocolate Macaroons Increase the sugar by ¼ cup. Add ¼ cup (0.8 ounce) unsweetened cocoa powder to the almonds and sugar. Reduce the almond extract to ⅛ teaspoon or omit it.

Chestnut Macaroons Substitute ⅓ cup (1.5 ounces) chestnut flour for ⅓ cup of the almonds. Substitute 1 tablespoon rum and/or 1 teaspoon pure vanilla extract for the almond extract.

PANNELETS

My version of these golden orange yam and coconut cookies from Spain is delicate and flavorful.

Makes 36 to 40 cookies

INGREDIENTS

1 cup (8 ounces) mashed or pureed baked orange-fleshed yam (see Note), such as jewel or garnet

2 cups (6 ounces) unsweetened dried shredded coconut, toasted (see page 16)

1⅓ cups (9.3 ounces) sugar

2 large egg whites

⅜ teaspoon salt

1 teaspoon finely grated lemon zest

1 cup (5 ounces) whole almonds, with or without skin

Sugar or Cardamom Sugar (page 336) or turbinado sugar for rolling

EQUIPMENT

Cookie sheets, lined with parchment paper or greased

Food processor

In a medium bowl, whisk the yam, toasted coconut, sugar, egg whites, salt, and lemon zest together.

In a food processor, pulse the almonds to an uneven meal ranging in texture from very fine (mostly) to finely chopped. Stir the almonds into the batter. The dough will be very soft and sticky. Chill for at least 1 hour and up to 2 days to allow the coconut to absorb moisture from the yams.

Preheat the oven to 325°F. Position racks in the upper and lower thirds of the oven. Scoop level tablespoons of the soft dough and roll into balls about 1¼ inches. Roll the balls in sugar (or, if using turbinado sugar, roll only the top half of each ball in the sugar to avoid oversweetening). Place 1½ inches apart on the lined or greased cookie sheets.

Bake for 18 to 24 minutes, until the cookies are slightly crusty on the surface (though still very tender and moist inside) and deep golden brown on the bottom. Rotate the pans from top to bottom and from front to back halfway through the baking time to ensure even baking. For lined pans, set the pans or just the liners on racks to cool; for unlined pans, use a metal spatula to transfer the cookies to racks. Cool the cookies completely before storing. May be kept in an airtight container for up to 4 or 5 days.

NOTE

Wash, prick, and cook a large yam on high in the microwave, turning it a couple times until easily pierced with a fork, about 10 minutes. Or bake until tender in a 400°F oven, 45 to 60 minutes.

UPGRADES

Cardamom Pannelets Omit the lemon zest. Add 1½ teaspoons ground cardamom, 2 teaspoons grated orange zest, and 2 teaspoons orange flower water to the yam mixture.

Masala Pannelets A little Spanish/Asian fusion cookie and very good. | Omit the lemon zest. Add 2 teaspoons garam masala to the yam mixture. Roll in plain sugar or Cinnamon Sugar (page 336).

SPICY CARROT MASALA MACAROONS

Carrots are not just for cake. These chewy little sweet and spicy cookies are exotic and pretty with fine shreds of carrot and a little warming heat from the pepper in the spice blend. Garam masala is found in the spice section of the supermarket, though of course Indian cooks often blend their own. If Indian flavors are unfamiliar to you, imagine an adventuresome twist on pumpkin pie spice.

Makes thirty-six 1½-inch cookies

INGREDIENTS

¾ cup (3.75 ounces) whole almonds, with or without skins

2 large egg whites

1 cup (7 ounces) sugar

1 teaspoon garam masala, pumpkin pie spice, or ground cinnamon

¼ teaspoon salt

1⅓ cups (5.625 ounces) lightly packed finely to medium-finely shredded carrot

¾ cup (2.25 ounces) unsweetened dried shredded coconut (see page 352)

A rounded ¼ teaspoon finely grated lemon zest

EQUIPMENT

Cookie sheets, lined with parchment paper

Food processor

Preheat the oven to 325°F. Position racks in the upper and lower thirds of the oven.

In a food processor, pulse the almonds to an uneven meal ranging in texture from very fine (mostly) to finely chopped. Set aside.

In a medium stainless-steel bowl, whisk the egg whites with a fork until frothy. Stir in the sugar, garam masala, and salt. Add the carrot, coconut, almonds, and lemon zest and stir until all of the ingredients are moistened. Set aside for 10 minutes to dissolve the sugar and hydrate the coconut.

Set the bowl directly in a wide skillet of barely simmering water and stir the mixture with a silicone spatula, scraping the bottom to prevent burning, until the mixture is very hot to the touch and any liquid at the bottom of the bowl has thickened slightly and turned from translucent to opaque, 5 to 7 minutes.

Drop heaping teaspoons 1 inch apart on the lined cookie sheets. If you like, form tall beehive-shaped cookies with your fingers. Bake for 20 to 25 minutes, until the tips of the carrot shreds begin to color and the bottoms of the cookies are deep golden brown (without removing a cookie, turn a corner of the parchment over to see the color). Rotate the pans from top to bottom and from front to back halfway through the baking time to ensure even baking. Set the pans or just the liners on racks to cool. Let the cookies cool completely before storing. To remove the cookies from the parchment, hold one cookie at a time while gently peeling the parchment away from it. The cookies keep for 3 to 4 days, loosely covered to prevent sogginess, rather than airtight. Do not freeze.

NEW CLASSIC COCONUT MACAROONS 2.0

Always a fan of golden brown sweet toasty coconut macaroons with moist chewy centers, I was excited to reinvent them using wide shaved flakes of unsweetened dried coconut instead of the usual sweetened (alas, always artificially preserved) shreds. They turned out more stunningly beautiful than ever, and the flavor is pure coconut. Default to the classic recipe, using the sweetened shreds, and keep the same sugar measure (trust me). Either way, don't miss the sensational version with a nuance of lime zest and cinnamon. (Photographs on pages 8 and 169)

Makes twenty-two 2¼-inch cookies

INGREDIENTS

4 large egg whites

3½ cups (5.25 ounces) unsweetened dried flaked (not shredded) coconut, also called coconut chips, or
    3 cups (9 ounces) sweetened dried shredded coconut (see page 352)

¾ cup (5.25 ounces) sugar

2 teaspoons pure vanilla extract

Slightly rounded ¼ teaspoon salt

EQUIPMENT

Cookie sheets, lined with parchment paper

Combine all of the ingredients in a large heatproof mixing bowl, preferably stainless steel because the mixture will heat faster than in glass. Set the bowl directly in a wide skillet of barely simmering water and stir the mixture with a silicone spatula, scraping the bottom to prevent burning, until the mixture is very hot to the touch and the egg whites have thickened slightly and turned from translucent to opaque, 5 to 7 minutes. Set the batter aside for 30 minutes to let the coconut absorb more of the goop.

Preheat the oven to 350°F. Position racks in the upper and lower thirds of the oven.

Using 2 tablespoons of batter, make attractive heaps 2 inches apart on the lined cookie sheets. Bake for about 5 minutes, just until the coconut tips begin to color, rotating the pans from top to bottom and from front to back halfway through the baking time to ensure even baking. Lower the temperature to 325°F and bake for 10 to 15 minutes, until the cookies are a beautiful cream and gold with deeper brown edges, and again rotating the pans from top to bottom and from front to back halfway through the baking time. If the coconut tips are browning too fast, you can lower the heat to 300°F. Set the pans or just the liners on racks to cool. Let cool completely before gently peeling the parchment away from each cookie. The cookies are best on the day they are baked—the exterior is crisp and chewy and the interior soft and moist. Although the crispy edges will soften, the cookies remain delicious stored in an airtight container for 4 to 5 days.

UPGRADES

Chocolate-Topped Coconut Macaroons Do this for any version of Coconut Macaroons: while the cookies are still hot, top each with a little piece of your favorite milk or dark chocolate. Or drizzle a little melted chocolate over each cookie.

Coconut Macaroons with Lime Zest and Cinnamon Stir 1½ to 2 teaspoons freshly grated lime zest into the batter before scooping it. Using a fine grater or Microplane zester, grate a little cinnamon stick over the cookies just before serving.

Coconut Banana Macaroons Crush unsweetened freeze-dried banana slices to make a scant 2 tablespoons of banana powder. Add the powder to the ingredients before mixing and heating.

Coconut Pineapple Macaroons Crush freeze-dried unsweetened pineapple to make a scant 2 tablespoons of pineapple powder. Add the powder to the ingredients before mixing and heating. Or stir in 3 to 4 tablespoons finely diced or slivered sweetened dried pineapple before resting the batter.

Nutty Coconut Macaroons with Chocolate and Sour Cherries Make the batter as described and let it rest. Meanwhile, preheat the oven to 325°F. Scatter ⅔ cup (2.33 ounces) pecan halves on a cookie sheet and toast them until lightly colored and fragrant, 8 to 10 minutes. Remove the nuts and raise the oven temperature to 350°F. Set the nuts aside to cool. Break or chop them coarsely. When the batter has rested, stir in 2 ounces chopped dark chocolate (semisweet or bittersweet) or ⅓ cup (2 ounces) bittersweet or semisweet chocolate chips, ¼ cup (1.25 ounces) coarsely chopped dried sour cherries, and the toasted nuts. Scoop and bake the cookies at 350°F, as described.

Chocolate Latkes No potatoes, just lots of chocolate and coconut for a crunchy/chewy exterior that is soft and brownielike within. If you bake them for Passover, call them Chocolate Coconut Macaroons instead of latkes. Either way, they make a fabulous "plated" dessert with a little dollop of sour cream (or unsweetened whipped cream) and a scatter of fresh raspberries. | Use 3 cups (9 ounces) sweetened dried shredded coconut. Decrease the sugar to 2 tablespoons and add 3½ ounces chopped semisweet or bittersweet chocolate (with up to 62% cacao). Heat as directed, until the mixture is hot and very sticky.

Scoop rounded tablespoons of the mixture and place about 2 inches apart on the lined cookie sheets. Flatten each cookie slightly with your fingers to resemble miniature potato pancakes. Bake for 13 to 15 minutes, until the cookies feel dry on the surface and the edges and the protruding coconut shreds are dark golden brown (despite the chocolate color) and the interior still looks like melted chocolate.

FRUIT AND NUT BARS

Easy. Lots of dried fruit and nuts, with just enough batter to hold everything together. The results are chewy, crunchy, and delicious but also healthy. Create endless variations by substituting combinations of dried cranberries or cherries, dried pears, whole almonds or hazelnuts.

Makes sixteen 2-inch bars

INGREDIENTS

¼ cup plus 2 tablespoons (1.625 ounces) unbleached all-purpose flour

⅛ teaspoon baking soda

⅛ teaspoon baking powder

¼ teaspoon salt

¼ cup plus 2 tablespoons (2.625 ounces) packed light or dark brown sugar

2 cups (7 ounces) walnut pieces

1½ cups (9 ounces) dates, pitted and cut into quarters

1 cup (5 ounces) lightly packed dried apricot halves, each cut in half

1 large egg

½ teaspoon pure vanilla extract

EQUIPMENT

An 8-inch square pan, the bottom and all 4 sides lined with foil (see page 24)

Preheat the oven to 325°F. Position a rack in the center of the oven.

Combine the flour, baking soda, baking powder, and salt in a large bowl and mix together thoroughly with a whisk or fork. Add the brown sugar, walnuts, dates, and apricots. Use your fingers to mix the ingredients until the nuts and fruits are coated with the flour mixture, separating any sticky fruit pieces.

Beat the egg with the vanilla in a small bowl until light colored and thick. Scrape the egg into the large bowl and mix with your hands until all of the fruit and nut pieces are thinly coated with batter. Spread the mixture in the pan, pressing to even it out.

Bake for 35 to 40 minutes, or until the thin batter coating is golden brown and has pulled away from the sides of the pan. Cool in the pan on a rack. Lift the ends of the foil and transfer the bars to a cutting board. Use a sharp knife to cut 16 squares. May be kept in an airtight container for at least 2 weeks at room temperature, longer in the refrigerator.

UPGRADES

You can trade the dates and walnuts and apricots for similar amounts of other dried fruits and nuts to make an infinite variety of customized bars.

Even Healthier Fruit and Nut Bars Substitute ¼ cup plus 2 tablespoons whole wheat pastry flour for the all-purpose flour. Cut the sugar by 2 or 3 tablespoons.

SPICY LINZER BARS

Sweet and spicy. These jam-filled bars, rich with butter and ground nuts, are nothing more than my own rustic version of the classic Austrian linzertorte, recast as finger-food. Divine with vanilla ice cream or vanilla whipped cream. Loves a cup of black coffee.

Makes 25 squares

INGREDIENTS

¾ cup (3.75 ounces) whole almonds, or a mixture of almonds and toasted skinned hazelnuts
    (see page 17)

1 cup (4.5 ounces) unbleached all-purpose flour

¾ cup (5.25 ounces) granulated sugar

¼ teaspoon salt

1½ teaspoons ground cinnamon

Scant ½ teaspoon ground cloves

11 tablespoons unsalted butter, cut into chunks, slightly softened

1 large egg yolk

Grated zest of ½ lemon, preferably organic or unsprayed

Grated zest of ½ orange, preferably organic or unsprayed

Scant ¼ teaspoon almond extract

¾ cup (8.25 ounces) raspberry, blackberry, or apricot preserves

Powdered sugar for dusting (optional)

EQUIPMENT

A 9-inch square metal baking pan, the bottom and all 4 sides lined with foil (see page 24)

Food processor

Grease only the sides of the foil (to prevent the jam from sticking).

Combine the almonds, flour, sugar, salt, cinnamon, and cloves in a food processor and pulse until the almonds are finely ground. Add the butter, egg yolk, grated zests, and almond extract. Pulse just until blended.

Make the lattice first: Pinch off about 1 tablespoon of dough. On a floured surface, with well-floured hands, roll the piece of dough into a pencil-thin rope (the lattice expands in the oven, so it must be very thin to start with) about 9 inches long. If the rope is too delicate to lift, roll it onto a sheet of wax paper. Repeat with 9 more pieces of dough, rolling each piece onto the wax paper. Slide the paper with the lattice strips onto a tray and freeze until needed.

Press the remaining dough evenly and smoothly over the bottom of the pan. Refrigerate for at least 1 hour.

Preheat the oven to 350°F. Position a rack in the lower third of the oven.

Spread the preserves evenly over the dough. Place 5 lattice strips over the jam, parallel with one another, at even intervals. Lay the remaining 5 strips on top and perpendicular to the first five.

Bake 45 to 50 minutes, until deep golden brown. After 30 minutes, check to see whether the dough has puffed up from the pan. If necessary, lift the edge of the pan an inch or so and let it drop to settle the dough. If the dough is getting too brown too early, tent it loosely with foil to finish. Remove the foil tent. Cool in the pan on a rack.

When the linzer sheet is completely cool, lift the edges of the foil to remove it from the pan. Peel away the sides of the foil (with the help of a sharp knife if the jam sticks). Slide a metal spatula under the linzer to detach it from the foil. Cut into 25 or more squares. Serve sprinkled with powdered sugar if desired. Linzer squares are most delicious served within 3 to 4 days, but they are still remarkably good after a week (or more!) stored in an airtight container.

BLONDIES

This iconic American bar with crusty edges and chewy insides is updated for modern taste buds: a tad less sugar and baking powder. A little booze is nice. Try the spice-dusted versions too.

Makes 16 blondies

INGREDIENTS

1 cup (4.5 ounces) unbleached all-purpose flour

½ teaspoon baking powder

¼ teaspoon salt

8 tablespoons (1 stick) unsalted butter

¾ cup plus 2 tablespoons (6.125 ounces) packed light brown sugar

1 large egg

½ teaspoon pure vanilla extract

1 tablespoon dark rum or bourbon (optional)

⅔ cup (2.33 ounces) broken or coarsely chopped walnut pieces

½ cup (3 ounces) semisweet chocolate chips

EQUIPMENT

An 8-inch square pan, the bottom and all 4 sides lined with foil (see page 24)

Preheat the oven to 350°F. Position a rack in the lower third of the oven.

Combine the flour, baking powder, and salt in a small bowl and mix together thoroughly with a whisk or fork.

Melt the butter in a small saucepan. Remove the pan from the heat and stir in the brown sugar. Use a wooden spoon to beat in the egg, vanilla, and rum, if using. Stir in the flour mixture followed by half of the walnuts. Spread the batter in the pan. Sprinkle the remaining walnuts and the chocolate chips evenly over the top.

Bake for 20 to 25 minutes, or until the nuts look toasted, the top is golden brown, and the edges have pulled away from the sides of the pan. Cool in the pan on a rack. Lift the ends of the foil and transfer to a cutting board. Use a long sharp knife to cut into squares. May be kept in an airtight container for 3 to 4 days.

UPGRADES

Nutmeg or Cinnamon Blondies Just before serving, grate a little nutmeg or cinnamon stick over the bars.

Peanut Butter Blondies For kids of all ages . . . | Reduce the amount of brown sugar to ⅔ cup. Add ⅓ cup (3 ounces) well-stirred natural peanut butter (chunky or smooth) with the brown sugar. Substitute ½ cup (2 ounces) roasted salted peanuts for the walnuts.

Peanut Butter Hazelnut Blondies Reduce the amount of brown sugar to ⅔ cup. Add ⅓ cup (3 ounces) well-stirred natural peanut butter (chunky or smooth) with the brown sugar. Substitute toasted skinned hazelnuts (see page 17) for the walnuts. Before baking, sprinkle the top very lightly with tiny pinches of flaky sea salt.

LACY COCONUT-TOPPED BROWNIES

Bittersweet brownies with a chewy golden brown coconut macaroon topping. Classic candy bar combo . . . only better.

Makes 25 brownies

INGREDIENTS

FOR THE TOPPING

1 large egg white

Scant 1¼ cups (1.75 ounces) unsweetened dried flaked (not shredded) coconut, also called coconut chips, or 1 cup (3 ounces) sweetened dried shredded coconut (see page 352)

¼ cup (1.75 ounces) sugar

¾ teaspoon pure vanilla extract

Large pinch of salt (1/16 teaspoon)

FOR THE BROWNIE LAYER

8 tablespoons (1 stick) unsalted butter

4 ounces unsweetened chocolate (see Tech Support for chocolate options), coarsely chopped

1 cup plus 2 tablespoons (7.875 ounces) sugar

1 teaspoon pure vanilla extract

¼ teaspoon salt

2 large eggs, cold

½ cup (3.5 ounces) unbleached all-purpose flour

EQUIPMENT

A 9-inch square pan, the bottom and all 4 sides lined with foil (see page 24)

To Make the Macaroon Topping Combine all of the topping ingredients in a medium heatproof mixing bowl, preferably stainless steel because the mixture will heat faster than in glass. Set the bowl directly in a wide skillet of barely simmering water and stir the mixture with a silicone spatula, scraping the bottom to prevent burning, until the mixture is very hot to the touch and the egg whites have thickened slightly and turned from translucent to opaque, 3 to 5 minutes. Leave the water in the skillet. Set the batter aside for 30 minutes to let the coconut absorb more of the goop while you make the brownie batter.

Preheat the oven to 350°F. Position a rack in the lower third of the oven.

To Make the Brownie Layer Place the butter and chocolate in a medium heatproof bowl and set it in the skillet of barely simmering water. Stir frequently until melted and smooth and hot enough that you want to remove your finger fairly quickly after dipping it in to test.

Remove the bowl from the water. Stir in the sugar, vanilla, and salt with a wooden spoon. Add the eggs and stir well. Stir in the flour and beat vigorously with the wooden spoon until the batter is smooth and glossy and begins to come away from the sides of the pan. Scrape the batter into the pan and spread it evenly.

Use your fingers to drop the macaroon mixture in a lacy layer over the brownie batter. Bake for about 25 minutes, until the brownies puff at the edges and the shreds of coconut look deep golden brown and crusty. Let cool completely in the pan on a rack. Lift the ends of the foil liner and transfer the brownies to a cutting board. Cut into 25 squares. May be kept in an airtight container for up to 3 days.

TECH SUPPORT

Substituting Chocolate Instead of 4 ounces of unsweetened chocolate, you can use 6½ ounces bittersweet chocolate with 70% cacao if you reduce the sugar to ¾ cup plus 2 tablespoons (6.125 ounces) and reduce the butter to 7 tablespoons.

BLACK BOTTOM PECAN PRALINE BARS

A thin layer of bittersweet brownie on the bottom with a sweet and chewy pecan and brown sugar topping.

Makes 24 to 30 bars

INGREDIENTS

FOR THE BROWNIE LAYER

8 tablespoons (1 stick) unsalted butter

4 ounces unsweetened chocolate (see Tech Support for chocolate options), coarsely chopped

1 cup plus 2 tablespoons (7.875 ounces) sugar

1 teaspoon pure vanilla extract

¼ teaspoon salt

2 large eggs, cold

½ cup (2.25 ounces) unbleached all-purpose flour

FOR THE TOPPING

½ cup (2.25 ounces) unbleached all-purpose flour

½ teaspoon baking soda

8 tablespoons (1 stick) unsalted butter, melted

¾ cup (5.25 ounces) packed brown sugar

½ teaspoon salt

2 large egg yolks

1 teaspoon pure vanilla extract

2½ cups (8.75 ounces) coarsely chopped pecans or walnuts

EQUIPMENT

A 9-by-13-inch metal baking pan, the bottom and all 4 sides lined with foil (see page 24)

Preheat the oven to 350°F. Position a rack in the lower third of the oven.

To Make the Brownie Layer Place the butter and chocolate in a medium heatproof bowl set directly in a wide skillet of barely simmering water. Stir frequently until melted and smooth and hot enough that you want to remove your finger fairly quickly after dipping it in to test.

Remove the bowl from the water. Stir in the sugar, vanilla, and salt with a wooden spoon. Add the eggs and stir well. Stir in the flour and beat vigorously with the wooden spoon until the batter is smooth and glossy and begins to come away from the sides of the pan. Scrape the batter into the pan. Set aside.

To Make the Topping Combine the flour and baking soda in a bowl and mix together thoroughly with a whisk or fork.

Combine the melted butter, brown sugar, and salt in a bowl. Stir in the egg yolks and vanilla, then the flour mixture, and finally the nuts. Drop spoonfuls of batter all over the top of the brownie layer (it will spread and cover the brownies entirely during baking).

Bake for 20 to 25 minutes, until the edges of the topping are well browned and cracked. Rotate the pan from front to back halfway through the baking time to ensure even baking. Let cool completely on a rack. Lift the ends of the foil and transfer the brownies to a cutting board. Cut into 24 or 30 squares. May be kept in an airtight container for 2 or 3 days.

TECH SUPPORT

Substituting Chocolate Instead of 4 ounces of unsweetened chocolate, you can use 6½ ounces bittersweet chocolate with 70% cacao. In that case, reduce the sugar to ¾ cup plus 2 tablespoons (6.125 ounces) and reduce the butter to 7 tablespoons.

GOOEY

FROM VERY TANGY LEMON BARS 2.0 (left) TO ROCKY ROAD BROWNIES

Gooey is a sensual experience that transcends the mere "sweet and sticky" offered by *Merriam-Webster*. Gooey is creamy and suave, moist, oozy, slick, or velvet on the tongue. It's goopy—in a good way. It's often just a little too much (in the best possible way) of a good thing: the extra-thick satiny lemon layer on a luscious lemon bar; thick, lush chocolate pudding heaped on just enough crust to allow it to be picked up; nearly flourless brownies that melt like chocolate mousse on the palate; oozing dulce de leche pushing out from the sides of an Alfajore; cheesecake with a goopy caramel swirl through it. Gooey involves a little tongue now and again—quick or lingering licks to catch a drip or shore up the sides of a bulging bar or sandwich cookie about to lose filling. For some, gooey is the nirvana of texture—the ultimate and luxurious tongue in cheek.

VERY TANGY LEMON BARS 2.0

An esteemed New England cooking magazine once pronounced my lemon bars too sour, though my cooking students and guests continue to declare them the best ever. Perhaps it's a New England versus California thing. I mention this so you will know what you are getting into here: very special (and very tangy) citrus bars with a tender, crunchy crust. (Photograph on page 180)

Makes 16 large (2-inch) bars or 25 smaller bars

INGREDIENTS

FOR THE CRUST

7 tablespoons unsalted butter, melted

2 tablespoons sugar

¾ teaspoon pure vanilla extract

¼ teaspoon salt

1 cup (4.5 ounces) unbleached all-purpose flour

FOR THE TOPPING

1 cup plus 2 tablespoons (7.875 ounces) granulated sugar

3 tablespoons unbleached all-purpose flour

3 large eggs

1½ teaspoons finely grated lemon zest (see Note), preferably from an organic or unsprayed fruit

½ cup strained fresh lemon juice (see Note), preferably from an organic or unsprayed fruit

Powdered sugar for dusting (optional)

EQUIPMENT

An 8-inch square metal baking pan, the bottom and all 4 sides lined with foil (see page 24)

Preheat the oven to 350°F. Position a rack in the lower third of the oven.

To Make the Crust In a medium bowl, combine the melted butter with the sugar, vanilla, and salt. Add the flour and mix just until incorporated. Press the dough evenly over the bottom of the pan.

Bake for 25 to 30 minutes, or until the crust is fully baked, well browned at the edges, and golden brown in the center.

To Make the Topping While the crust is baking, stir together the sugar and flour in a large bowl until well mixed. Whisk in the eggs. Stir in the lemon zest and juice.

When the crust is ready, turn the oven down to 300°F. Slide the rack with the pan out and pour the filling onto the hot crust. Bake for 20 to 25 minutes longer, or until the topping barely jiggles in the center when the pan is tapped. Set on a rack to cool completely in the pan.

Lift up the foil liner and transfer the bars to a cutting board. If the surface is covered with a thin layer of moist foam (not unusual), you can blot it gently to reveal the zest by laying a square of paper towel on the surface and gently sweeping your fingers over it to absorb excess moisture. Remove the paper and repeat with a fresh piece if necessary. Use a long sharp knife to cut into sixteen 2-inch or 25 daintier bars. Sift powdered sugar over the bars just before serving, if desired. May be stored in an airtight container in the refrigerator for several days or more. After 3 days the crust softens, but the bars still taste quite good for up to a week.

NOTE

Meyer lemons are less tart and more floral than most other lemons. If you want to use them, reduce the sugar in the topping to ½ cup plus 2 tablespoons (4.375 ounces).

LIGHTER LEMON BARS

Tart lemon filling sits atop a crunchy cornmeal cookie, instead of rich shortbread crust. Superbly tart and tangy, which is just the way I like them.

Makes 16 large (2-inch) bars or 25 smaller bars

INGREDIENTS

FOR THE CRUST

⅔ cup (3 ounces) unbleached all-purpose flour

¼ cup (1.375 ounces) yellow cornmeal

Pinch of salt

⅛ teaspoon baking soda

2 tablespoons unsalted butter, softened

⅓ cup (2.33 ounces) sugar

1 large egg yolk

1 tablespoon nonfat yogurt

¼ teaspoon pure vanilla extract

FOR THE TOPPING

⅔ cup (4.625 ounces) granulated sugar

2 large eggs

1 large egg white

Grated zest of 1 large lemon, preferably from an organic or unsprayed fruit

½ cup strained lemon juice, preferably from an organic or unsprayed fruit

¼ cup (1.125 ounces) unbleached all-purpose flour

Powdered sugar for dusting (optional)

EQUIPMENT

An 8-inch square metal baking pan, the bottom and all 4 sides lined with foil (see page 24)

Preheat the oven to 350°F. Position a rack in the lower third of the oven.

To Make the Crust Combine the flour, cornmeal, salt, and baking soda in a small bowl and mix together thoroughly with a whisk or fork.

In a medium mixing bowl with an electric mixer, beat the butter until creamy. Add the sugar and beat at high speed for about 1 minute, or until the mixture begins to form a mass. Beat in the egg yolk, yogurt, and vanilla. Add the flour mixture and beat on low speed just until combined. Scrape the bowl and beater. Knead the mixture briefly with your hands to be sure all of the flour is incorporated.

Press the dough evenly into the pan. Prick it all over with a fork. If the pan is lightweight, place it on a baking sheet to prevent the crust from burning on the bottom. Bake for 20 to 25 minutes, until the surface is deep golden brown.

To Make the Topping While the crust is baking, whisk the sugar with the eggs and the egg white until well blended. Grate the lemon zest directly into the bowl. Whisk in the lemon juice. Whisk in the flour.

When the crust is brown, turn the oven temperature down to 300°F. Slide the rack with the pan out and pour the topping over the hot crust. Bake for 15 to 20 minutes, until it barely jiggles when you shake the pan gently back and forth. Cool on a rack. Chill before cutting into squares.

Serve cold (my favorite) or at room temperature, dusted with powdered sugar. May be stored in an airtight container in the refrigerator for 2 or 3 days.

APRICOT LEMON BARS WITH HAZELNUT CRUST

A little twist on my lovely lemon bar. Vary these by changing the hazelnuts for walnuts or toasted almonds or whatever nuts you like.

Makes 16 large (2-inch) bars or 25 smaller bars

INGREDIENTS

FOR THE CRUST

¾ cup plus 2 tablespoons (4 ounces) unbleached all-purpose flour

¼ cup (1.75 ounces) sugar

¼ teaspoon salt

¼ cup (1.25 ounces) toasted and skinned hazelnuts (see page 17)

8 tablespoons (1 stick) unsalted butter, melted

¾ teaspoon pure vanilla extract

FOR THE TOPPING

¼ cup (1.75 ounces) granulated sugar

2 tablespoons unbleached all-purpose flour

2 large eggs

½ cup (5.5 ounces) apricot preserves

⅓ cup strained fresh lemon juice

2 to 3 tablespoons powdered sugar for dusting (optional)

EQUIPMENT

An 8-inch square metal baking pan, the bottom and all 4 sides lined with foil (see page 24)

Preheat the oven to 350°F. Position a rack in the lower third of the oven.

To Make the Crust Place the flour, sugar, salt, and nuts in a food processor. Pulse until the nuts are finely ground. Add the melted butter and vanilla and pulse just until the dry ingredients look damp and the mixture begins to clump around the blade. Remove the dough and knead it a couple of times to be sure it is evenly mixed.

Press the dough evenly over the bottom of the pan. Bake for 25 to 30 minutes, or until the crust is fully baked, well browned at the edges, and golden brown in the center.

To Make the Topping While the crust is baking, stir together the sugar and flour in a large bowl until well mixed. Whisk in the eggs. Stir in the preserves, breaking up any extra-large pieces. Mix in the lemon juice. When the crust is ready, turn the oven down to 300°F. Slide the rack with the pan out and pour the filling onto the hot crust.

Bake for 20 to 25 minutes longer, or until the topping no longer jiggles when the pan is tapped. Set on a rack to cool completely in the pan.

Lift up the foil liner and transfer the bars to a cutting board. Use a long sharp knife to cut into sixteen 2-inch or 25 daintier bars. Sift powdered sugar over the bars just before serving, if desired. May be stored in an airtight container in the refrigerator for several days or more. After 3 days the crust softens, but the bars still taste quite good for up to a week.

VANILLA CREAM CHEESE SANDWICHES

Cookies à la minute? Sweet, extra-crunchy vanilla cookies are filled, just before serving, with cream cheese, mascarpone, or creamy Greek-style yogurt, then drizzled with a little honey. Nibble them out of hand or plate them (with a scatter of seasonal berries?) like tartlets for an appealing little dessert or teatime indulgence. I can't help admitting that plain yogurt is more exciting with the sweet cookie and sticky honey than the more decadent mascarpone. You have to love it when the least expensive and least fattening choice actually tastes the best!

Makes 24 to 30 sandwiches

INGREDIENTS

3 cups (13.5 ounces) unbleached all-purpose flour

2 teaspoons cream of tartar

1 teaspoon baking soda

½ teaspoon salt

½ pound (2 sticks) unsalted butter, softened

1½ cups (10.5 ounces) sugar

2 tablespoons milk

1 tablespoon pure vanilla extract

Vanilla Sugar (page 336) for sprinkling

1 pound cream cheese, mascarpone, or Greek-style yogurt
   (or regular yogurt, drained for several hours to remove extra liquid)

Honey for drizzling (optional)

EQUIPMENT

Cookie sheets, lined with parchment paper or greased

A 3-inch round cookie cutter

A 1½-inch round cookie cutter

Combine the flour, cream of tartar, baking soda, and salt in a bowl and mix together thoroughly with a whisk or fork.

In a large mixing bowl with an electric mixer, beat the butter with the sugar until smooth and creamy. Beat in the milk and vanilla. Add the flour mixture and stir or beat on low speed just until incorporated. The dough will be very soft.

Divide the dough into 2 pieces. Gently roll the first piece ⅛ inch thick between sheets of wax paper. Slide the whole business onto a cookie sheet. Repeat with the second piece of dough, sliding it onto the cookie sheet on top of the first piece. Refrigerate the dough for at least 2 hours or overnight.

Preheat the oven to 350°F. Position racks in the upper and lower thirds of the oven.

Remove 1 sheet of dough from the fridge. Peel off the top piece of wax paper and sprinkle the dough with a little flour. Put the wax paper loosely back over the dough and flip the dough and both sheets of wax paper over. Peel off the top sheet of wax paper. Cut out 3-inch rounds of dough. Cut 1½-inch circles from half of the rounds and remove them with a fork or knife point. (Combine and save scraps and small rounds.) Transfer the cookies to the lined or greased cookie sheets. Sprinkle the cookies with holes in them with pinches of vanilla sugar. Bake for 10 to 12 minutes, until golden, rotating the sheets from top to bottom and from front to back halfway through the baking time to ensure even baking.

For lined pans, set the pans or just the liners on racks to cool; for unlined pans, use a metal spatula to transfer the cookies to racks. Cool the cookies completely before stacking, filling, or storing. Repeat with the remaining rolled-out dough until all the cookies are baked. Combine all the scraps, roll, chill, cut, and bake as described.

The cookies may be stored, in an airtight container for several days.

Just before serving, mix the cream cheese, if using, with a rubber spatula until creamy and easy to spread. Spread the solid cookies liberally with the cheese or yogurt. Top with the remaining cookies. Drizzle with honey, if desired.

UPGRADES

Spiced Sugar Sandwiches Substitute any of the Spiced Sugars on page 336 for the Vanilla Sugar.

Chocolate and Vanilla Sandwiches Substitute Fast Fudge Frosting (page 343) for the cream cheese. Omit the honey.

Honey Vanilla Buttercream Sandwiches Substitute Honey Vanilla Buttercream (page 339) for the cream cheese. Omit the honey drizzle.

ALFAJORES

Alfajores (al-fah-HOR-ays) are *the* fancy sandwich cookies of Spain and Latin America. But they are not just one cookie. There are myriad regional variations that feature different cookies and different fillings and flavors; some are dipped or coated with chocolate, and some have extra layers. The most compelling involve dulce de leche, the gooey Latin-style caramel.

Commercial Alfajores are sold individually wrapped in foil or cellophane. These are soft and cakey because the filling softens the cookie. When you make your own Alfajores, you get better cookies and better dulce de leche. You get to eat the sandwiches fresh, while the cookies are still crisp or crunchy and the caramel oozes from between them. And you get to eat more of them later, after the cookies have softened and merged delectably with the dulce.

Makes thirty-two 2-inch or 48 miniature sandwich cookies

INGREDIENTS

2¼ cups (10.125 ounces) unbleached all-purpose flour

1 teaspoon cream of tartar

1 teaspoon baking soda

¼ teaspoon salt

8 tablespoons (1 stick) unsalted butter, very soft

1 cup (7 ounces) sugar

1 large egg

2 tablespoons brandy or rum

1 cup Dulce de Leche, plain, vanilla, or coconut (page 337)

EQUIPMENT

Cookie sheets, lined with parchment paper or ungreased

Preheat the oven to 325°F. Position racks in the upper and lower thirds of the oven.

Combine the flour, cream of tartar, baking soda, and salt in a medium bowl and mix together thoroughly with a whisk or fork.

With a large spoon in a medium mixing bowl or with a mixer, mix the butter with the sugar until smooth and well blended but not fluffy. Add the egg and brandy and mix until smooth. Add the flour mixture and mix until completely incorporated.

Shape heaping teaspoons of dough into 1-inch balls. (Or, on a lightly floured surface, shape dough into a square and cut into 8 strips and then cut each strip into 8 pieces to make a total of 64 equal pieces. Roll each piece into a 1-inch ball.) For miniature cookies, shape level teaspoons of dough into 96 smaller balls. Place the cookies 2 inches apart on the lined or ungreased pans and flatten to about ½ inch thick. Bake for 14 to 16 minutes for larger cookies or 12 to 15 minutes for miniature cookies, until the edges are lightly browned. Rotate the pans from top to bottom and from front to back halfway through the baking time. For lined pans, set the pans or just the liners on racks to cool; for unlined pans, use a metal spatula to transfer the cookies to racks. Cool the cookies completely before storing or filling.

Sandwich the cookies with a generous dab of dulce de leche. The cookies will soften as they stand. They are good crunchy or soft. May be stored in an airtight container for at least 1 week.

UPGRADES

Orange Alfajores Substitute orange juice or orange liqueur (Triple Sec, Cointreau, or Grand Marnier) and 1 teaspoon finely grated orange zest for the brandy.

Coconut Alfajores Fill cookies with Coconut Dulce de Leche; roll the gooey edges in toasted unsweetened or sweetened shredded coconut.

Nutty Alfajores Substitute Almond Sablés (page 318) or Nut Slices (page 120). These are exquisitely rich but somehow balanced. Consider bite-sized sandwiches. They create an aura of virtue *and* prevent filling from squishing out from between crunchy cookies.

LINZER COOKIES

Hearts or stars or scalloped squares—use your imagination with shapes and try different kinds of preserves. Personal favorites are blackberry, raspberry, and apricot. My version of these classic sandwich cookies borrows flavors from the traditional linzertorte: almonds and/or hazelnuts with cinnamon, cloves, and a touch of citrus.

Makes about twenty 3½-inch cookies

INGREDIENTS

2¼ cups (10.125 ounces) unbleached all-purpose flour

1 cup (5 ounces) almonds and/or hazelnuts

½ cup (3.5 ounces) granulated sugar

¼ teaspoon salt

2½ teaspoons ground cinnamon

¼ teaspoon ground cloves

½ pound (2 sticks) unsalted butter

¼ teaspoon almond extract

1 teaspoon grated lemon zest or ¼ teaspoon lemon extract

1 teaspoon grated orange zest or ¼ teaspoon orange extract

Strained or pureed good quality preserves or fruit spread

Powdered sugar for dusting

EQUIPMENT

Cookie sheets, lined with parchment paper or ungreased

Food processor

Large and small cookie cutters of the same or a different shape, such as a 3-inch square and
   a 1¼-inch square

Combine the flour, nuts, granulated sugar, salt, cinnamon, and cloves in a food processor. Pulse until the nuts are finely ground. Add the butter (cut into several pieces if firm). Pulse until the mixture looks damp and crumbly. Add the almond extract and the lemon and orange zests or extracts and pulse until the mixture begins to clump up around the blade. Remove the dough, press it into a ball, and knead it a few times to be sure all of the dry ingredients are blended into the dough.

Form the dough into 2 flat patties. Wrap and refrigerate the dough for at least 2 hours and preferably overnight or up to 3 days. The dough may be frozen for up to 3 months.

Preheat the oven to 325°F. Position racks in the upper and lower thirds of the oven.

To Roll and Cut Cookies Remove 1 patty from the refrigerator and let it sit at room temperature until supple enough to roll but still quite firm. It will continue to soften as you work. Roll the dough to a thickness of ⅛ inch between sheets of wax paper or between heavy plastic sheets cut from a plastic bag. Turn the dough over once or twice while you are rolling it out to check for deep wrinkles; if necessary, peel off and smooth the paper or plastic over the dough before continuing to roll it. When the dough is thin enough, peel off the top sheet of paper or plastic and keep it in front of you. Invert the dough onto that sheet and peel off the second sheet. Cut as many large shapes as possible. Dip the edges of the cookie cutters in flour as necessary to prevent sticking. Cut a smaller shape from the center of half of the large shapes. Use the point of a paring knife to lift and remove scraps as you transfer the cookies to the lined or ungreased pans. Place large cookies at least 1½ inches apart on the cookie sheets. If the dough gets too soft at any time—while rolling, cutting, removing scraps between cookies, or transferring cookies—slide a cookie sheet underneath the paper or plastic and refrigerate the dough for a few minutes, until firm. Repeat with the second piece of dough. Gently press all of the dough scraps together (don't overwork them with too much kneading) and reroll.

Bake for 13 to 15 minutes, or until the cookies are just beginning to color at the edges. Rotate the pans from top to bottom and from front to back halfway through the baking time to ensure even baking. (The small shapes may be baked for 8 to 10 minutes on a separate cookie sheet to make miniature cookies, or the dough may be combined with other dough scraps to be rerolled and cut.)

Let the cookies firm up on the pan for 1 to 2 minutes. For lined pans, set the pans or just the liners on racks to cool; for unlined pans, use a metal spatula to transfer the cookies to racks. Cool the cookies completely before stacking or storing. The cookies are delicious fresh but even better the next day. May be kept in an airtight container for a month or more.

To assemble, shortly before serving, spread each solid cookie with a thin layer of preserves. Sift powdered sugar over the cookies with cutouts. Place a sugared cutout cookie on top of each preserve-covered cookie. Leftover cookies can be stored in an airtight container, but the moisture from the preserves will soften them.

UPGRADES

Nibby Buckwheat Linzer Hearts Dark berry preserves are sensational with buckwheat, walnuts, and roasted cacao nibs. The combination makes a dressy cookie for a special occasion. | Substitute the dough for Nibby Buckwheat Butter Cookies (page 119) for the linzer dough, adding 1 cup (4 ounces) finely chopped walnuts along with the nibs. Cut out the cookies using a 3½-inch heart-shaped cookie cutter and a 1½- or 2-inch heart-shaped cookie cutter. Fill with ½ cup good quality blackberry or black raspberry preserves.

MENEINAS

I fell hard for these meneinas (pronounced meh-NAY-na), fragrant date- and walnut-filled cakes scented with orange blossoms and tangerine zest—and immediately started to imagine new fillings. This cherished family recipe from Alexandria, Egypt, was given to me by Los Angeles teacher and artist Jeannette Nemon-Fischman. Nice do-ahead bonus: meneinas become even more flavorful and compelling after a day or two. You can substitute Pear Filling (page 340), Spiced Fig Filling (page 340), Apricot Vanilla Filling with Cinnamon and Almonds (page 341), or Sour Cherry Filling with Black Pepper (page 341). The dough can be flavored with rose water instead of orange flower water; this is especially nice with apricot filling.

Makes 30 to 36 cookies about 1¾ inches in diameter

INGREDIENTS

3 cups (13.5 ounces) unbleached all-purpose flour

2 teaspoons baking powder

½ pound (2 sticks) unsalted butter, softened

2 tablespoons granulated sugar

2 tablespoons milk

1 tablespoon orange flower water

Date and Walnut Filling (page 339), or other filling

Powdered sugar for coating the cookies

EQUIPMENT

Cookie sheets, lined with parchment paper or greased

To Make the Dough Combine the flour and baking powder in a medium bowl and mix together thoroughly with a whisk or fork.

In another medium bowl with a handheld or stand mixer, beat the butter and sugar until soft and creamy. Gradually add the milk and orange flower water, beating until blended. Add the flour mixture all at once. Beat on low speed just until all of the flour is incorporated; the dough need not form a single mass as long as there is no loose flour. Gather the dough into a smooth ball with your hands. Use immediately or wrap and refrigerate for up to 2 days.

To Form and Fill the Cookies Pinch off or scoop a level tablespoon of the filling and roll it into a ball. Set the ball on a plate. Repeat with the remaining filling.

Pinch off a piece of dough slightly larger than the filling (a slightly rounded tablespoon) and roll it into a ball. Push a deep depression into the dough with a knuckle and widen it to form a little bowl. Press a ball of filling into the bowl. Pressing gently with your fingers, ease the dough up all around the filling to completely enclose it. Set the cookie, seam side down, on a lined or greased cookie sheet. Repeat with the remaining dough and filling, placing cookies 2 inches apart. Press the sides of the cookies all around to form the traditional beehive shape—or leave them round. Let the cookies rest for at least 30 minutes before baking.

Preheat the oven to 350°F. Position racks in the upper and lower thirds of the oven.

Bake for 20 to 25 minutes, until the cookies are slightly golden (the bottoms will be golden brown). Rotate the pans from top to bottom and from front to back halfway through the baking time to ensure even baking. Sift powdered sugar onto a plate. Cool the cookies for 5 minutes, then transfer them one by one and coat with the powdered sugar. Cool the cookies completely before storing. May be kept in an airtight container for at least a week.

PECAN POLVORONES WITH MUSCOVADO FILLING

Polvorones are exquisitely tender Spanish or Latin American shortbread cookies. Mine are shaped as for thumbprint cookies and filled with a gorgeous muscovado sugar sauce. Or you can fill them with Chocolate Butter Filling (page 344), Chocolate Ganache (page 343), Nutella, or, at the last minute, any Dulce de Leche (page 337) or Lemon Curd (page 337).

Makes forty-eight 2-inch cookies

INGREDIENTS

FOR THE COOKIES

1½ cups (5.25 ounces) pecans or walnut halves or pieces

⅓ cup (2.33 ounces) sugar

½ teaspoon salt

½ pound (2 sticks) unsalted butter, slightly softened and cut into chunks

2 teaspoons pure vanilla extract

1 large egg yolk (optional)

2 cups (9 ounces) unbleached all-purpose flour

FOR THE FILLING

⅔ cup (4.625 ounces) firmly packed dark muscovado sugar

⅓ cup heavy cream

Scant ⅛ teaspoon salt

EQUIPMENT

Cookie sheets, lined with parchment paper or ungreased

Food processor

To Make the Cookies Pulse the nuts in a food processor until most are finely ground and the largest pieces are about ¼ inch. Transfer to a bowl and set aside.

Wipe the processor bowl with a paper towel to remove excess oil from the nuts. Add the sugar and salt and process until fine and powdery. Add the butter, vanilla, and egg yolk, if using, and pulse until the mixture is smooth. Add the flour and pulse until the dough starts to clump together. Add the nuts and pulse just until combined. Transfer the dough to a bowl and knead it by hand briefly to make sure it is evenly mixed.

Shape the dough into 1-inch balls (0.5 ounce each) and place them slightly apart on a plate or tray big enough to hold all the balls yet small enough to fit in your refrigerator. Press the handle of a wooden spoon dipped in flour (or your finger) into each ball to form a depression. Cover and chill the cookies for at least 2 hours, and preferably overnight.

Preheat the oven to 325°F. Position racks in the upper and lower thirds of the oven.

Remove the cookies from the refrigerator and place them 1 inch apart on the lined or ungreased cookie sheets. Bake for 20 to 22 minutes, until the cookies are lightly colored on top and light golden brown on the bottom. Rotate the pans from top to bottom and from front to back halfway through the baking time to ensure even baking. For lined pans, set the pans or just the liners on racks to cool; for unlined pans, use a metal spatula to transfer the cookies to racks.

To Make the Filling While the cookies are cooling, combine the muscovado sugar with the cream and salt in a small saucepan. Bring to a boil over low heat, stirring, until the sugar is dissolved. Boil gently for about 2 minutes without stirring. Cool the sauce briefly.

Spoon a little filling into the depression in each cookie. Allow the filling to cool completely. May be stored in an airtight container for at least a week.

CHOCOLATE-FILLED HAMANTASCHEN

Here, Haman's hat brims with gooey bittersweet chocolate rather than prunes, poppy seeds, or apricots. Please don't save these for a Jewish holiday . . . great cookies should be shared anytime by everyone.

Makes 36 cookies

INGREDIENTS

6 tablespoons (¾ stick) unsalted butter

4 ounces unsweetened chocolate, coarsely chopped

¾ cup (5.25 ounces) sugar

1 teaspoon pure vanilla extract

¼ teaspoon salt

2 large eggs, cold

2 tablespoons unbleached all-purpose flour

1 recipe Vanilla Sugar Cookies (page 38)

EQUIPMENT

Cookie sheets, lined with parchment paper or foil

A 3-inch round cookie cutter

Melt the butter with the chocolate in a heatproof bowl set directly in a wide skillet of barely simmering water. Stir frequently until the mixture is melted and smooth.

Remove the chocolate from the heat. Stir in the sugar, vanilla, and salt. Add the eggs one at a time, stirring in the first until incorporated before adding the second. Stir in the flour and beat with a spoon until the mixture is smooth and glossy and comes away from the sides of the pan, about 1 minute. Scrape into a small bowl, cover, and refrigerate until needed.

Make the dough as directed in the recipe on page 38.

Preheat the oven to 350°F. Position racks in the upper and lower thirds of the oven.

Cut out 3-inch cookies and place them ½ inch apart on the lined pans. Scoop and place a level teaspoonful of filling in the center of each cookie. Bring 3 sides of each cookie up to partially cover the filling. If the dough gets too soft to handle, slide the pans into the refrigerator for a few minutes to firm it up. Pinch the edges of the cookie to seal the corners.

Bake for 12 minutes, or until pale golden at the edges. Rotate the cookie sheets from top to bottom and from front to back halfway through the baking time to ensure even baking. Repeat until all of the cookies are baked.

Set the pans or just the liners on racks to cool. Cool the cookies completely before stacking or storing. Although best on the day they are made, the cookies keep for 3 to 4 days in an airtight container.

CHOCOLATE ESPRESSO COOKIES

Inspired by a recipe from Maida Heatter, these cookies are a defining statement about modern chocolate for the sophisticated palate. Rich and gooey and only slightly sweet, they are laced with tiny chunks of the finest unsweetened chocolate. If you do not have unsweetened chocolate that is superb enough to nibble, use any unsweetened chocolate for the batter plus hand-chopped or purchased bittersweet chunks for the chunks—the higher the cacao percentage, the better (if you ask me).

Makes 50 small or 25 large cookies

INGREDIENTS

10 ounces finest-quality unsweetened chocolate, or 6 ounces ordinary unsweetened chocolate plus
    4 ounces bittersweet chocolate (with any cacao percentage you like)

⅓ cup (1.5 ounces) unbleached all-purpose flour

¼ teaspoon baking powder

¼ teaspoon salt

4 tablespoons unsalted butter

2 large eggs, at room temperature

1⅓ cups (9.33 ounces) sugar

1½ teaspoons freshly and finely ground coffee

1 teaspoon pure vanilla extract

½ cup (1.75 ounces) walnut pieces (optional)

EQUIPMENT

Cookie sheets, lined with parchment paper or greased

Chop 6 ounces of unsweetened chocolate and set aside for melting. Cut the remaining 4 ounces of unsweetened or bittersweet chocolate into small chunks (larger than chocolate chips) and set aside.

Combine the flour, baking powder, and salt in a small bowl and mix together thoroughly with a whisk or fork.

Melt the butter with the 6 ounces of chopped chocolate in a heatproof bowl set directly in a wide skillet of barely simmering water, stirring occasionally, until melted and smooth. Remove from the heat and set aside.

Beat the eggs with the sugar, coffee, and vanilla with an electric mixer until pale and thick, about 5 minutes. Stir in the chocolate mixture with a rubber spatula. Stir in the flour mixture followed by the chocolate chunks and, if using, the nuts. Cover and refrigerate until firm, about an hour or up to 4 days.

Preheat the oven to 350°F. Position racks in the upper and lower thirds of the oven.

Drop level tablespoons of batter for small cookies or heaping tablespoons (equivalent of 2 level tablespoons) for large cookies 2 inches apart on the lined or greased pans. Bake until the cookies are puffed, dry, and crackled on the surface but soft and gooey within, 8 to 10 minutes for small cookies, 10 to 12 minutes for large cookies. Rotate the cookie sheets from top to bottom and from front to back halfway through the baking time to ensure even baking. For lined pans, set the pans or just the liners on racks to cool; for unlined pans, use a metal spatula to transfer the cookies to racks. Let cool completely before storing or stacking. May be kept in an airtight container for 2 days.

UPGRADES

Chocolate Espresso Cookies with Toasted Almonds Replace the walnuts with toasted almonds (see page 17).

LESS-IS-MORE OVERNIGHT BROWNIES

Great brownies with less fat? These will fool you. To make them taste and feel as rich and gooey as they can be, remember that even the richest brownies dry out when overbaked. But with less fat, you must absolutely, positively remove the brownies from the oven when the toothpick is still a little gooey. Combining cocoa with sizzling hot butter brings out the deepest chocolate flavor. But the really big trick is to let the pan of batter rest in the fridge overnight, or even for just a few hours, before baking. The rest hydrates the cocoa and flour and brings all of the flavors into sharper focus. It also makes the top glossier and creates a fine, thin crust to offset the soft, gooey interior. In a big hurry? OK, you can skip the overnight and just bake the brownies—they were excellent even before I tried the overnight technique.

Makes sixteen 2-inch brownies

INGREDIENTS

1 scant cup (4 ounces) unbleached all-purpose flour

¼ teaspoon baking powder

¼ teaspoon salt

4½ tablespoons (2.25 ounces) unsalted butter

½ cup plus 1 tablespoon (1.75 ounces) unsweetened natural cocoa powder

1¼ cups (8.75 ounces) sugar

1 large egg

2 large egg whites

2 teaspoons pure vanilla extract

EQUIPMENT

An 8-inch square pan, the bottom and all 4 sides lined with foil (see page 24)

If not resting the batter, preheat the oven to 350°F. Position a rack in the lower third of the oven.

Combine the flour, baking powder, and salt in a small bowl and mix together thoroughly with a whisk or fork.

In a medium saucepan, heat the butter until melted and sizzling hot. Remove from the heat and stir in the cocoa. Stir in the sugar. The mixture will look like a mass of very dark brown sugar. Add the egg, egg whites, and vanilla. Stir briskly, about 40 strokes, until smooth. Add the flour mixture. Stir until just incorporated. Then stir briskly for 40 to 50 strokes. Scrape the batter into the pan and spread it evenly. The batter will be very shallow in the pan.

If you have time to rest the batter, cover and refrigerate the pan for a few hours or overnight. Remove the pan from the fridge about 30 minutes before baking. Preheat the oven now.

Bake for 15 to 18 minutes, or until a toothpick inserted in the center comes out with a little batter— thickened and gooey, not thin and liquid—still clinging to it. Do not overbake. Cool on a rack. Lift the ends of the foil and transfer the brownies to a cutting board. Cut into 16 squares. If you have not overbaked the brownies, they will remain moist and delicious for at least 2 days in an airtight container.

UPGRADES

For a different kind of flavor, you can decrease the sugar to ¾ cup and add ⅓ cup (2.33 ounces) packed brown sugar and/or add 1 teaspoon instant espresso powder dissolved in 1 teaspoon water to the batter with the vanilla.

GOOEY TURTLE BARS

For the sweet tooth: salty and sweet, crunchy and creamy all together in one decadent bar. Divine-but-easy-to-make soft vanilla caramel atop a buttery shortbread crust with loads of toasted pecan halves and chocolate shards. Sinful but celebratory. Might as well make a big batch. This shortcut caramel with sweetened condensed milk is fairly foolproof if you follow the directions and use a silicone spatula to keep the sides of the pot clean. Salt fans will want to top these with extra tiny pinches of flaky salt. Be my guest.

Makes thirty-five 1¾-inch bars

INGREDIENTS

1 recipe Shortbread Crust (see page 346)

1¾ cups (12.25 ounces) packed brown sugar

¼ cup honey or light corn syrup

⅜ teaspoon salt (½ teaspoon for coarse or flaky sea salt)

¼ cup water

4 tablespoons unsalted butter

One 14-ounce can sweetened condensed milk

1 tablespoon pure vanilla extract

2 cups (7 ounces) whole pecan halves, toasted (see page 17)

6 ounces milk chocolate or semisweet chocolate, coarsely chopped, or 1 cup milk chocolate or
semisweet chocolate chips

EQUIPMENT

A 9-by-13-inch metal baking pan, the bottom and all 4 sides lined with foil (see page 24)

Silicone spatula

Candy thermometer

Preheat the oven to 325°F. Position a rack in the lower third of the oven.

Prepare the shortbread crust as directed.

To Make the Topping In a heavy 2- to 3-quart saucepan (about 8 inches in diameter), combine the brown sugar, honey, salt, and water. Set on medium heat and drop in the chunk of butter. Stir constantly with a heatproof spatula, scraping the corners and bottom of the pan as the butter melts. From time to time, scrape the mixture off the spatula against the top edge of the pan and scrape the sides of the pan clean. Bring the mixture to a medium boil and continue stirring and scraping the pan for about 3 minutes, dissolving the sugar. Stir in the condensed milk and return to a boil, stirring constantly, scraping the sides, corners, and bottom of the pan. Adjust the heat so the mixture boils actively but not too furiously. Continue stirring and cooking until the mixture registers 235°F. Total cooking time will be close to 15 minutes. Remove the pan from the heat and stir in the vanilla. Scrape the hot caramel over the warm crust.

Tilt the pan to level the caramel. Scatter the toasted pecans and chopped chocolate over the surface and set aside until the caramel is cool and the chocolate is set.

Lift the ends of the foil liner and transfer to a cutting board. Peel the foil away from the edges on all 4 sides. Slide a knife or spatula under the crust to detach the foil. Holding the bars in place, slide the foil out from under it. Use a long sharp knife to cut 35 bars. May be kept in an airtight container for at least 1 week.

UPGRADES

Wheat-Free Gooey Turtle Bars Substitute a fully baked 9-by-13-inch Wheat-Free Shortbread Crust (page 346) for the crust. Proceed as directed.

DAIRY-FREE CARAMEL ROCKY ROAD SQUARES

Warm, gooey chocolate cake squares laced with extra chunks of chocolate, caramels, chewy marshmallows, and nut pieces. Easy enough for a child to make.

Makes sixteen 2¼-inch squares

INGREDIENTS

1⅔ cups (7.5 ounces) unbleached all-purpose flour

1 cup plus 2 tablespoons (7.875 ounces) sugar

¼ cup plus 2 tablespoons (1.2 ounces) natural (nonalkalized) cocoa powder

1 teaspoon baking soda

¼ teaspoon salt

1 cup cold water

¼ cup flavorless vegetable oil

1 tablespoon distilled vinegar

2 teaspoons pure vanilla extract

6 ounces dairy-free semisweet or bittersweet chocolate, chopped into shards or pieces (not too small), or purchased chocolate chunks or chips, the larger the better

1 cup (3.5 ounces) broken or very coarsely chopped walnut or pecan pieces

3 ounces purchased vegan caramels, cut into ½-inch pieces

12 marshmallows, quartered

EQUIPMENT

A 9-inch square pan, the bottom and all 4 sides lined with foil (see page 24)

Preheat the oven to 350°F. Position a rack in the lower third of the oven.

Combine the flour, sugar, cocoa, baking soda, and salt in a large bowl and mix together thoroughly with a whisk or fork.

In a small bowl, mix the water, oil, vinegar, and vanilla. Pour the liquid over the flour mixture. Mix with a wooden spoon or rubber spatula just until smooth. Add half of the chocolate, half of the walnuts, and all the caramel, and stir to incorporate.

Scrape the batter into the pan and spread it evenly. Distribute the marshmallow quarters all over the brownies and poke them into the batter, leaving the tips exposed. Sprinkle the remaining chocolate and nuts around the marshmallows.

Bake for 20 to 25 minutes, or until the batter no longer sways or jiggles when you nudge the side of the pan. Cool on a rack. Lift the edges of the foil to transfer the squares to a cutting board. Slide a slim metal spatula under the cake to release it from the foil. Cut into squares. Serve warm or at room temperature. May be kept in an airtight container for up to 3 days.

TECH SUPPORT

Large pieces of hand-chopped chocolate are more decadent (and gooey) than purchased chips or chunks, and regular-size marshmallows cut into quarters are much better than small marshmallows, which taste mostly of the starch that coats them.

ROCKY ROAD BARS

These are gooey *and* chewy—definitely a recipe to make with kids. But try it on friends who think they are too sophisticated to appreciate chocolate with marshmallows and nuts on a graham cracker crust. Use an oiled knife to cut the marshmallows. This is a little more work than buying miniature marshmallows, but the results will be more delicious.

Makes sixteen 2-inch bars

INGREDIENTS

6 tablespoons (¾ stick) unsalted butter, melted

1½ cups (5 ounces) fine graham cracker crumbs (made from about 9 double graham crackers)

¼ cup (1.75 ounces) sugar

1 cup (3.5 ounces) walnut halves or large pieces

12 regular marshmallows (3.25 ounces), quartered

1 cup (6 ounces) milk chocolate or semisweet chocolate chips

EQUIPMENT

An 8-inch square pan, the bottom and all 4 sides lined with foil (see page 24)

Preheat the oven to 350°F. Position racks in the upper and lower thirds of the oven.

Mix the butter with the graham cracker crumbs and sugar until all of the crumbs are moistened. Turn the mixture into the lined pan and spread it evenly, pressing very firmly all over the bottom to form a crust. Scatter half of the nut pieces evenly over the crust.

Bake on the lower oven rack for 10 minutes, or until the crust begins to turn golden brown. Remove from the oven and scatter the marshmallows, chocolate chips, and remaining walnuts evenly over the crust. Turn the oven temperature up to 375°F, return the pan to the oven on the upper rack, and bake for 10 to 12 minutes, until the marshmallows are golden brown and merged with one another. Set on a rack to cool completely. Lift the ends of the foil liner and transfer the bars to a cutting board. Use a long sharp knife to cut into sixteen 2-inch bars. May be kept in an airtight container for 4 to 5 days.

UPGRADES

You can use chocolate graham crackers, plain chocolate wafers, or purchased gingersnaps instead of the graham crackers. You can add ¼ teaspoon ground cinnamon to the crust mixture. You can swap pecans or any other nuts for the walnuts. You could grate some cinnamon stick or nutmeg on top or sprinkle with tiny pinches of cardamom . . .

Wheat-Free Rocky Road Bars Instead of the crumb crust, substitute half a recipe of Wheat-Free Shortbread Crust (page 346) baked in an 8-inch square pan. When it's done, sprinkle the crust with half of the quartered marshmallows; then add half the walnuts and chocolate chips. Repeat with the remaining marshmallows, walnuts,and chocolate chips. Turn the oven up to 375°F and bake for 10 to 12 minutes on the upper rack until the marshmallows are golden brown and merged with one another.

CHOCOLATE PUDDING BARS

The best way to eat pudding without a spoon. Extra chocolaty, creamy smooth, and slightly bittersweet pudding on just enough crust to keep the pudding off your fingers.

Makes 20 small bars or 16 rounds (as photographed)

INGREDIENTS

FOR THE CRUST

7 tablespoons butter, melted and still warm

¼ cup (1.75 ounces) packed brown sugar

½ teaspoon pure vanilla extract

⅜ teaspoon salt

1 cup (4.5 ounces) unbleached all-purpose flour

2 ounces semisweet or bittersweet chocolate, chopped, or purchased chocolate chips or chunks

FOR THE FILLING

¼ cup (1.75 ounces) sugar

⅓ cup (1 ounce) unsweetened cocoa powder (I prefer natural)

2 tablespoons cornstarch

⅛ teaspoon salt

1½ cups whole milk

½ cup heavy cream

5 ounces semisweet or bittersweet chocolate with up to 62% cacao, finely chopped

1 teaspoon pure vanilla extract

1 tablespoon dark rum (optional)

EQUIPMENT

A 9-inch square metal baking pan, the bottom and all 4 sides lined with foil (see page 24)

Preheat the oven to 350°F. Position a rack in the lower third of the oven.

To Make the Crust In a medium bowl, combine the melted butter with the brown sugar, vanilla, and salt. Add the flour and mix just until blended. Don't worry if the dough seems too soft or oily; this is normal. Press the dough evenly and smoothly over the bottom of the lined pan. Bake for 15 to 20 minutes, until the crust is deep golden brown at the edges. Remove the pan from the oven and immediately sprinkle the chopped chocolate over the hot crust. Let stand for 2 to 3 minutes to melt the chocolate. Use a pastry brush or rubber spatula to spread the chocolate over the surface of the crust in a thin but thorough layer. Let the crust cool and then refrigerate it until the chocolate is set.

To Make the Filling In a heavy medium-large saucepan, whisk the sugar, cocoa, cornstarch, and salt to blend. Add about 3 tablespoons of the milk and whisk to form a smooth paste. Whisk in the remaining milk and the cream. Heat the mixture over medium heat, stirring constantly with a flat-ended heatproof spatula or wooden spoon and scraping the bottom, sides, and corners of the pan until the pudding thickens and begins to bubble at the edges, 5 or 6 minutes. Add the chocolate, vanilla, and rum and stir a bit faster to smooth out the pudding, cook the starch, and melt the chocolate, about 1½ minutes. Scrape the hot pudding onto the crust and level it with one or two strokes of the spatula. Let the pudding cool, undisturbed (without mixing, jiggling, or spooning out a taste), at room temperature for 1 hour. Refrigerate the pan, uncovered, until the pudding is completely cool. Cover it and chill for at least several hours or overnight. Use the edges of the foil to lift the bars from the pan and transfer to a cutting board.

Cut into 20 bars or use round biscuit cutters for rounds, as illustrated opposite. Store leftovers in the refrigerator, as you would pudding.

UPGRADES
Wheat-Free Chocolate Pudding Bars Substitute half a recipe of Wheat-Free Shortbread Crust (page 346) baked in a 9-inch square pan. Proceed as directed.

NEW BITTERSWEET BROWNIES

Voilà! Bittersweet brownies with a texture between very moist cake and rich chocolate mousse. One secret is whipping the eggs with the sugar and salt. On a plate, with a fork and a dollop of cream, these are definitely dessert.

Makes 16 brownies

INGREDIENTS

8 ounces bittersweet chocolate (70% cacao), coarsely chopped

6 tablespoons unsalted butter, cut into several pieces

3 eggs

1 cup (7 ounces) sugar

Scant ¼ teaspoon salt

1 teaspoon pure vanilla extract

⅓ cup plus 1 tablespoon (1.75 ounces) unbleached all-purpose flour

EQUIPMENT

An 8-inch square metal baking pan, the bottom and all 4 sides lined with foil (see page 24)

Preheat the oven to 350°F. Position a rack in the lower third of the oven.

Place the chocolate and butter in a heatproof bowl set directly in a wide skillet of barely simmering water. Stir frequently until the mixture is melted and smooth and quite warm. Set aside. In a medium bowl, with an electric mixer on high speed, beat the eggs, sugar, salt, and vanilla until the eggs are thick and light colored, about 2 minutes. Whisk the warm chocolate into the egg mixture. Fold in the flour. Scrape the batter into the lined pan and spread evenly. Bake for 25 to 30 minutes, until a toothpick inserted in the center comes out free of gooey batter. Cool in the pan on a rack. Lift the edges of the foil liner and transfer to a cutting board. Use a long sharp knife to cut into 16 or more squares. May be kept in an airtight container for up to 3 days.

UPGRADES

Spice-Dusted Bittersweet Brownies   After grating nutmeg for a recipe, I stopped to taste a brownie, still warm from the oven. The aroma of nutmeg from my fingers came on just seconds before the taste of intense bittersweet chocolate. The nutmeg enhanced the chocolate flavor without destroying its clarity, as it might have done had the nutmeg actually been mixed into the batter. The effect was memorable. Could one ask guests to handle nutmeg before eating brownies? Or simply dust the brownies with spice for the same effect?

Just before serving, grate a little nutmeg or cinnamon stick over the brownies. Or sprinkle with pinches of ground cardamom or any type of ground chile.

STEVE RITUAL BROWNIES

Iconic brownies. These are a little crusty on the surface and marvelously creamy within, with vibrant chocolate flavor. The ingredient proportions are absolutely classic—found in dozens of cookbooks—but the method, originally devised by my friend Steve Klein, is pure genius.

The brownies are baked at a high temperature for a short time, and then cooled fast in an ice bath. Steve claims to have developed the ritual slowly and thoughtfully, rigorously applying the scientific method over many months. His wife, also my friend, seems to think it had more to do with college boys rescuing brownies from a too-hot oven. No matter, she and I tested the ritual ourselves (rigorously) and found that it improves any brownie recipe that includes at least ½ cup of flour for an 8-inch brownie pan—even purchased brownie mixes. (Recipes with less flour and more than 5 ounces of chocolate are already gooey and rich enough.)

Makes 16 brownies

INGREDIENTS

8 tablespoons (1 stick) unsalted butter

4 ounces unsweetened chocolate

1¼ cups (8.75 ounces) sugar

1 teaspoon pure vanilla extract

¼ teaspoon salt

2 large eggs

½ cup (2.25 ounces) unbleached all-purpose flour

⅔ cup (2.33 ounces) walnut or pecan pieces (optional)

EQUIPMENT

An 8-inch square metal pan, the bottom and all 4 sides lined with foil (see page 24)

Preheat the oven to 400°F. Position a rack in the lower third of the oven.

Melt the butter with the chocolate in a medium heatproof bowl set directly in a wide skillet of barely simmering water. Stir frequently until the mixture is melted and smooth and fairly hot to the touch.

Remove the bowl from the water bath. Stir in the sugar, vanilla, and salt. Add 1 egg, stirring until it is incorporated. Repeat with the second egg. Stir in the flour and beat vigorously with a wooden spoon until the batter is smooth and glossy and comes away from the sides of the bowl. Stir in the nuts, if using. Scrape the batter into the pan.

Bake for 20 minutes, or until the brownies just begin to pull away from the sides of the pan. The surface of the brownies will look dry, but a toothpick inserted in the center will still be quite gooey.

While the brownies are baking, prepare the crucial Steve Ritual Ice Bath: fill a roasting pan or large baking pan with ice cubes and water about ¾ inch deep.

When the brownies are ready, remove the pan from the oven and set it immediately in the ice bath, taking care not to splash water on the brownies. Cool the brownies in the ice bath.

When cool, lift the edges of the foil and transfer the brownies to a cutting board. Cut into 16 squares. May be kept in an airtight container for 2 to 3 days.

COCOA BROWNIES

The best brownies are not always made with a bar of chocolate. Cocoa brownies have divinely soft centers and slightly chewy, almost candylike tops. Natural (nonalkalized) cocoa produces brownies with the most complex, fruity, and nuanced chocolate flavor and a relatively light reddish brown chocolate color. Dutch-process (alkalized) cocoa yields darker-colored brownies with the flavor—reminiscent of childhood—of Oreo cookies or old-fashioned chocolate pudding. The choice is yours.

Makes sixteen 2-inch or 25 smaller brownies

INGREDIENTS

11 tablespoons unsalted butter

1¼ cups (8.75 ounces) sugar

1 scant cup (3 ounces) unsweetened cocoa powder, natural or Dutch-process

¼ teaspoon salt

1 teaspoon pure vanilla extract

2 large eggs, cold

⅓ cup plus 1 tablespoon (1.75 ounces) unbleached all-purpose flour

EQUIPMENT

An 8-inch square pan, the bottom and all 4 sides lined with foil (see page 24)

Preheat the oven to 325°F. Position a rack in the lower third of the oven.

Melt the butter in a medium heatproof bowl set directly in a wide skillet of barely simmering water. Add the sugar, cocoa, and salt. Stir until the ingredients are blended and the mixture is hot. Remove the bowl from the skillet and set aside briefly until the mixture is only warm, not hot. Mix in the vanilla. Add the eggs, one at a time, mixing vigorously with a spatula after each addition. When the mixture looks thick, shiny, and well blended, add all of the flour at once and stir until you cannot see it any longer. Then mix vigorously for 40 strokes with a wooden spoon or rubber spatula. Spread evenly in the lined pan.

Bake for 20 to 25 minutes, until a toothpick plunged into the center emerges slightly dirty looking. Cool on a rack. Lift the edges of the foil liner and transfer the brownies to a cutting board. Cut into 16 or 25 squares. May be kept in an airtight container for 2 or 3 days.

ROCKY ROAD BROWNIES

Over-the-top bars embody the spirit of gooey. The secret is to start with a lighter brownie and lace it with big pieces of chocolate and nuts as well as marshmallows and/or caramels. Make a big statement by serving them warm. Feel free to sprinkle with sea salt, ground cardamom, or grated cinnamon stick.

Makes sixteen 2¼-inch brownies

INGREDIENTS

1 recipe Light Cakey Brownies (page 304)

12 marshmallows, quartered; or 4 ounces chewy caramels, cut into ½-inch cubes (I used Werther's); or a combination of 9 or 10 marshmallows and 3 ounces caramels

3 ounces milk chocolate or semisweet or bittersweet chocolate, chopped into shards or pieces (not too small), or purchased chocolate chunks or chips, the larger the better

1 cup (3.5 ounces) broken or very coarsely chopped walnut or pecan pieces

EQUIPMENT

A 9-inch square metal baking pan, the bottom and all 4 sides lined with foil (see page 24)

Preheat the to 350°F. Position a rack in the lower third of the oven.

Mix the brownie batter as directed on page 304.

Scrape the batter into the pan and level it. Distribute the marshmallow pieces and/or caramels all over the brownies. Poke the marshmallow pieces into the batter, leaving the tips exposed. Sprinkle the chocolate and nuts around the marshmallows and/or caramels. Bake for 20 to 25 minutes, until a toothpick inserted in a cakey part of the brownies comes out with a few moist crumbs.

Cool on a rack. Lift the edges of the foil to transfer the brownies to a cutting board. Slide a slim metal spatula under the brownies. Cut into squares. Serve warm or at room temperature.

ROBERT'S BROWNIES MY WAY

I resist the term *fudgy*—it is inadequate for these exceptional brownies. They are densely creamy and intensely bittersweet beneath a paper-thin nuance of crust on top.

The late Robert Steinberg (cofounder of Scharffen Berger Chocolate) created the recipe for the company's first chocolate, Scharffen Berger Bittersweet 70% Chocolate. I published the recipe in *Alice Medrich's Cookies and Brownies* in 1997, and it appeared again in *The Essence of Chocolate* by John Scharffenberger and Robert Steinberg in 2006. It remains a go-to modern recipe for *very* chocolaty brownies that are not excessively sweet.

Makes sixteen 2-inch brownies

INGREDIENTS

6 tablespoons unsalted butter

8 ounces bittersweet chocolate with 70% cacao

1 scant cup (6.5 ounces) sugar

¼ teaspoon salt

½ teaspoon pure vanilla extract (optional)

2 large eggs, cold

⅓ cup plus 1 tablespoon (1.75 ounces) unbleached all-purpose flour

1 cup (3.5 ounces) walnut or pecan pieces (optional)

EQUIPMENT

An 8-inch square pan, the bottom and all 4 sides lined with foil (see page 24)

Preheat the oven to 350°F. Position a rack in the lower third of the oven.

Melt the butter with the chocolate in a medium heatproof bowl set directly in a wide skillet of barely simmering water. Stir frequently until the mixture is melted and smooth and fairly hot to the touch. Remove the bowl from the water. Stir in the sugar, salt, and vanilla, if using. Add 1 egg, stirring until it is incorporated. Repeat with the second egg. Stir in the flour and beat with a wooden spoon or spatula until the batter is smooth and glossy and comes away from the sides of the pan; it is critical that the batter pull itself together, so don't stop mixing until it does. Stir in the nuts, if using. Scrape the batter into the pan.

Spread the batter evenly but with lots of raised swirls and ridges—these look great and get slightly crusty in the oven. Bake for 30 to 35 minutes, until a toothpick inserted in the center comes out with a few moist crumbs, not totally gooey.

Cool on a rack. Lift the foil ends to transfer the brownies to a cutting board. Cut into 16 squares. May be kept in an airtight container for 2 to 3 days.

UPGRADES

Robert's Brownies Transposed I often make the brownies using chocolate with 60% to 62% cacao, altering the sugar and butter in the recipe to accommodate the change. (Photograph on page 2) | Substitute 11 ounces of semisweet or bittersweet chocolate with 60% to 62% cacao. Reduce the butter to 4 tablespoons and the sugar to ⅔ cup (4.625 ounces).

BROWNIES

So many brownies, so little time. In the decades since I made brownies as a child, brownies have changed dramatically. We use less flour and more chocolate and relatively less sugar. Brownies have become moist, dense, gooey, and *über*-chocolaty. Some people use the word *fudgy*, but I don't think that such a sugar-saturated word adequately describes the best brownies. My best brownies actually have a melting creaminess beneath a nuanced glossy crust on top, so that the teeth meet a nanosecond of resistance before sinking into the smooth chocolate abyss.

I've included brownies made with different kinds of chocolate as well as with cocoa, as each yields a different kind of texture and flavor. You'll also find the (by now) famous Steve Ritual Brownies (page 220), which involve baking brownies at a very high temperature and then plunging them into an ice bath to cool fast, and Less-Is-More Overnight Brownies (page 206) with a superb trick to make them taste far richer than they are.

Mixing creamy ultrachocolate brownies these days is not for the faint of heart! The more chocolate and less flour in the batter, the more prone it is to separating or curdling. If you don't stir vigorously enough or long enough for the batter to emulsify—it should visibly become smoother and start to pull away from the sides of the bowl as you mix—your brownies will ooze fat (you will see the fat sizzling in the pan) in the oven and the finished product will be both grainy and greasy when cool. So you must not give up on vigorous mixing until you see that transformation in the bowl. Although everyone swears by hand-mixed brownies, mixing thick batter vigorously for more than a minute or two takes a little arm strength, so by all means feel free to use a handheld electric mixer. I always use the mixer when I double or triple a batch.

There are more tricks. Contrary to what you might think, the melted chocolate and butter should be very hot to the touch and need not be cooled before the other ingredients are added. This tactic produces great chocolate flavor and a glossy surface. I also swear by adding eggs cold (where called for), as this helps cool and emulsify the batter a little more quickly, so you won't have to wear out your elbow with vigorous mixing.

Finally, an altogether new scheme for a new kind of brownie: beat the eggs and sugar with the salt until light and fluffy before you do anything else. An electric mixer is necessary, and the results are more like a dense mousse.

So many brownies, so little time.

ESPRESSO SWIRL BROWNIES

A jolt of strong espresso flavor, barely sweetened, makes a suave, creamy complement to bittersweet bars.

Makes 16 brownies

INGREDIENTS

1 recipe Steve Ritual Brownies (page 220) without the nuts

1 tablespoon instant coffee or espresso powder

1 tablespoon water

8 ounces cream cheese, softened

⅓ cup (2.33 ounces) sugar

1 teaspoon pure vanilla extract

1 large egg

EQUIPMENT

A 9-inch square pan, the bottom and all 4 sides lined with foil (see page 24)

Preheat the oven to 400°F. Position a rack in the lower third of the oven.

Mix the batter for Steve Ritual Brownies. Spread all but ½ cup of the batter in the prepared pan. Set aside.

Combine the coffee powder with the water in a small bowl. In a medium bowl, mix the cream cheese with the sugar and vanilla until smooth. Stir in the egg and the coffee mixture until well blended. Spread the cream cheese mixture over the batter in the pan. Spoon dollops of the reserved brownie batter on top. Without scraping the bottom of the pan, draw a table knife through the dollops to swirl and marble the chocolate and espresso batter without thoroughly mixing them.

Bake for 20 to 25 minutes, or until the brownies just begin to pull away from the sides of the pan.

While the brownies are baking, prepare the crucial Steve Ritual Ice Bath: fill a roasting pan or large baking pan with ice cubes and water about ¾ inch deep.

When the brownies are ready, remove the pan from the oven and immediately set it in the ice bath, taking care not to splash water on the brownies. Cool the brownies in the ice bath. Refrigerate and chill thoroughly, about 2 hours, before cutting.

Lift the edges of the foil to transfer the brownies to a cutting board. Cut into 16 squares. May be kept in an airtight container in the refrigerator for 3 to 4 days.

UPGRADES

Espresso Swirl Brownies Redux The same creamy espresso swirl in a cakier brownie offers a little texture change-up. | Preheat the oven to 350°F instead of 400°F. Make Cakey Brownie batter (page 302) instead of Steve Ritual Brownie batter. Omit the ice bath.

MACADAMIA SHORTBREAD BROWNIES

Nuts beneath the crust—rather than mixed into it—transform macadamias (which can otherwise taste rich and boring) into an extra crunchy and fantastically rich nutty counterpoint to the brownies on top. You can substitute hazelnuts or almonds for the macs, or use 2 tablespoons sesame seeds.

Makes 25 brownies

INGREDIENTS

FOR THE CRUST

5½ tablespoons (2.75 ounces) unsalted butter, melted

2 tablespoons sugar

¼ teaspoons pure vanilla extract

Pinch of salt

¾ cup (3.375 ounces) unbleached all-purpose flour

½ cup (2.5 ounces) untoasted macadamia nuts, salted or unsalted, medium-finely chopped

FOR THE BROWNIE LAYER

6½ ounces bittersweet chocolate with 70% cacao

7 tablespoons unsalted butter

1 cup (7 ounces) sugar

1 teaspoon pure vanilla extract

¼ teaspoon salt

2 large eggs, cold

½ cup (2.25 ounces) unbleached all-purpose flour

EQUIPMENT

A 9-inch square pan, the bottom and all 4 sides lined with foil (see page 24)

Preheat the oven to 350°F. Position a rack in the lower third of the oven.

To Make the Crust Combine the melted butter with the sugar, vanilla, and salt in a bowl. Stir in the flour to make a very soft dough (it will firm up).

On a piece of foil or wax paper, pat the dough into an even square layer slightly smaller than the bottom of the baking pan. Sprinkle the dough evenly with the nuts and press them in. Slide the dough and foil into the freezer to firm up while you make the brownie layer.

To Make the Brownie Layer Place the chocolate and butter in a medium heatproof bowl set directly in a wide skillet of barely simmering water. Stir frequently until the chocolate is melted and the mixture is smooth and hot enough that you want to remove your finger fairly quickly after dipping it in to test.

Remove the bowl from the skillet. Stir in the sugar, vanilla, and salt with a wooden spoon or rubber spatula. Add 1 egg, stirring until it is incorporated. Repeat with the second egg. Stir in the flour and beat with the wooden spoon or rubber spatula until the batter is smooth and glossy and beginning to come away from the sides of the bowl, 1 or 2 minutes or more. Set aside.

Remove the dough from the freezer (it should be stiff). Invert it, nut side down, into the bottom of the lined pan and remove the top foil. Let the dough soften for a few minutes, then press it evenly against the bottom of the pan, making sure it reaches the edges of the pan and into the corners.

Bake the crust for 15 to 20 minutes, until it is nicely brown all over.

Spread the brownie batter evenly over the hot crust and bake for 20 to 25 minutes, until the edges puff and begin to show fine cracks. Let cool completely in the pan on a rack.

Remove the brownies from the pan by lifting the ends of the foil and transfer to a cutting board. Cut into 25 squares with a heavy knife. May be kept in an airtight container for up to 3 days.

MAYA'S NO-NO-NANAIMO BARS

Named after the city in British Columbia, the traditional Nanaimo bar is a no-bake layered affair with a crumb crust and layers of sweet vanilla filling crowned with chocolate. These here—with a coconut pecan crust, vanilla cream cheese filling, and dark chocolate ganache—are for people who like the idea of the Nanaimo bar but wish it were different: less sweet, more grown-up, a bit modern. Oh, and these are baked. Thus, no claims to authenticity . . . only a very good bar created by a very good friend, Portland food maven Maya Klein.

Makes 16 large (2¼-inch) bars or 25 smaller bars

INGREDIENTS

1½ cups (5 ounces) chocolate cookie crumbs (from 9 chocolate graham crackers)

½ cup (1.5 ounces) unsweetened dried shredded coconut (see page 352)

½ cup (2 ounces) finely chopped pecans

8 tablespoons (1 stick) unsalted butter, melted

½ cup plus 2 tablespoons (4.375 ounces) granulated sugar

8 ounces cream cheese, at room temperature

2 tablespoons (0.875 ounce) packed brown sugar

½ teaspoon pure vanilla extract

1 large egg

½ cup heavy cream

7 ounces semisweet or bittersweet chocolate with 55% to 60% cacao

EQUIPMENT

A 9-inch square metal baking pan, the bottom and all 4 sides lined with foil (see page 24)

Preheat the oven to 350°F.

Mix the crumbs, coconut, pecans, butter, and ¼ cup of the granulated sugar and pat it very firmly into the lined pan. Bake the crust for 10 to 12 minutes, or until it looks slightly darker at the edges and smells toasted.

While the crust is baking, mix the filling. In a large bowl, beat the softened cream cheese, brown sugar, and ¼ cup of the remaining granulated sugar until smooth. Beat in the vanilla and then the egg. When the crust is baked, dollop the filling onto the hot crust and spread gently with the back of a spoon. Bake the bars until the edges are slightly puffed, about 10 minutes. Cool on a rack for 30 minutes. Chill for at least 2 hours.

Dissolve the remaining 2 tablespoons granulated sugar in the cream. Bring ½ inch of water to a simmer in a medium skillet. Coarsely chop the chocolate and combine with the cream in a medium metal bowl. Place the bowl directly in the skillet of hot water and turn off the heat. Let rest for 5 minutes and whisk until smooth. Set aside until needed.

Pour the warm ganache onto the bars, spread, and chill for at least 30 minutes before serving. Lift the bars out of the pan by using the edges of the foil liner. Cut into 16 or 25 squares, wiping the knife between cuts. May be stored in an airtight container in the refrigerator for 3 to 4 days.

CARAMEL CHEESECAKE BARS

Creamy and gooey! Rich vanilla cheesecake, slightly tangy, laced with sweet salted caramel. The flavor and texture of cheesecake only gets better, so make these a day or two ahead if you can.

Makes thirty-six 1½-by-2-inch bars

INGREDIENTS

1 recipe Shortbread Crust (page 346)

½ cup (6 ounces) caramel sauce, purchased or homemade

⅛ teaspoon salt

1½ pounds cream cheese, at room temperature

¼ cup (1.75 ounces) sugar

1½ teaspoons pure vanilla extract

2 large eggs, at room temperature

EQUIPMENT

A 9-by-13-inch metal baking pan or an 8-by-12-inch quarter sheet pan, the bottom and all 4 sides lined with foil (see page 24)

Prepare the shortbread crust.

Preheat the oven to 325°F.

Stir the caramel sauce together with the salt. Set aside.

In a medium mixing bowl, with an electric mixer, beat the cream cheese just until smooth, about 30 seconds. Scrape the bowl and beaters. Add the sugar and vanilla and beat just until smooth and creamy, 1 to 2 minutes. Add 1 egg and beat just until incorporated. Scrape the bowl and beaters. Beat in the

second egg. Stir 2 tablespoons of the batter into the caramel sauce. Pour the remaining batter over the prepared crust and smooth the top.

Spoon pools of the caramel mixture over the filling, leaving plenty of plain filling showing. If the caramel does not settle into the batter, jiggle the pan gently until the surface is level. Marble the caramel with a toothpick by stirring gently—being careful not to scrape the crust—in small loopy circles until the colors are marbled but not blended. Bake for 20 to 25 minutes, until the filling is puffed at the edges but still jiggles like Jell-O when the pan is nudged.

Set the pan on a cooling rack. When the bars are completely cool, cover and refrigerate the bars until set, at least 4 hours, but preferably 24 hours before serving. To serve, lift the edges of the foil liner and transfer to a cutting board. Use a long sharp knife to cut into bars 1½ by 2 inches. May be kept in an airtight container, refrigerated, for up to 4 days.

UPGRADES

Peanut Caramel Cheesecake Bars (Photograph on page 237) | Use only a scant ½ cup of caramel sauce. Mix ⅓ cup (3 ounces) well-stirred creamy natural peanut butter* into the sauce with the salt. Do not add any of the cheesecake batter to the caramel mixture. If the mixture is too thick or stiff to flow (slightly) from a spoon, warm it briefly in a pan of hot water or for a few seconds in the microwave. Use as directed.

Almond or Hazelnut Caramel or Honey Cheesecake Bars Use only a scant ½ cup of caramel sauce or substitute honey. Mix ⅓ cup (3 ounces) well-stirred roasted almond or hazelnut butter* into the sauce with the salt. Do not add any of the cheesecake batter to the caramel or honey mixture. Add a bit of extra salt to taste if the nut butters are unsalted. If the mixture is too thick or stiff to flow (slightly) from a spoon, warm it briefly in a pan of hot water or for a few seconds in the microwave. Use as directed.

Wheat-Free Caramel Cheesecake Bars Substitute a fully baked 9-by-13- or 8-by-12-inch Wheat-Free Shortbread Crust (page 346) for the crust. Proceed as directed.

---

*A natural nut butter (peanut, almond, or hazelnut), without sugar or emulsifier, must be stirred before using in order to blend in any separated nut oils. Nevertheless, it is a better choice for this recipe than emulsified or no-stir nut butters.

STICKY PECAN BITES

Rich, tender, cakey, with a bit of caramely brown sugar goop. Think bite-sized sticky buns without the time-consuming yeast dough. These little cheaters are made with a quick stirred-together cream biscuit concoction. Too simple for words.

Makes 24 rolls

INGREDIENTS

24 pecan halves

1 cup (4.5 ounces) unbleached all-purpose flour

1 teaspoon baking powder

¼ teaspoon salt, plus additional for sprinkling

¾ cup heavy cream

½ cup (3.5 ounces) packed brown or muscovado sugar

½ teaspoon ground cinnamon

2 tablespoons unsalted butter, very soft

EQUIPMENT

1 miniature muffin pan with 24 cups, or 2 miniature muffin pans with 12 cups each

Preheat the oven to 400°F. Position a rack in the lower third of the oven. Lightly grease the muffin cups unless they are nonstick pans.

Place a pecan half in each cup, top side down. Combine the flour, baking powder, and ¼ teaspoon salt in a medium bowl and mix together thoroughly with a whisk or fork. Make a well in the center. Pour the cream into the well. Use a rubber spatula to fold and stir the flour mixture and cream together just until the dry ingredients are entirely moistened and a soft dough is formed; it should not look perfectly smooth. Let the dough rest for 2 to 3 minutes to firm up. Meanwhile, mix the sugar with the cinnamon.

On a lightly floured surface, with a floured rolling pin, roll the dough to a rectangle 12 by 7 inches and ¼ inch thick. Spread the dough with the soft butter, and sprinkle with a pinch of salt and the brown sugar. Starting at one short end, roll the dough tightly. Gently stretch the dough to lengthen the roll. Cut the roll crosswise into 24 equal pieces. Place each piece in a muffin cup, cut side up.

Bake for 12 to 15 minutes, until well browned. Rotate the pan(s) from front to back halfway through the baking time to ensure even baking. Immediately turn the cookies out onto a sheet of parchment on a heatproof surface. Serve on the day you make them.

UPGRADES

Cinna-minis Omit the pecans and increase the cinnamon to 1 teaspoon.

Chocolate Roll-Ups Omit the pecans, cinnamon, and butter. Spread the dough with a mixture of ½ cup sour cream and ¼ cup packed brown sugar. Sprinkle evenly with 1¾ ounces finely chopped semisweet or bittersweet chocolate with 55% to 62% cacao.

FLAKY

FROM CARDAMOM CARAMEL PALMIERS (left) TO BROWNIE BOW TIES

In the world of baked goods, flaky implies quality: Who ever heard of a terrible flaky pastry? Or, if a pastry is flaky, how terrible could it be? Flaky is phyllo dough, puff pastry, or even the lowly rugelach—when prepared properly. Flaky is buttery and shattering. It makes us lean over the plate at a tea party—or the sidewalk outside the patisserie—to protect shirtfronts or Parisian walking shoes from falling fragments. | Flaky suggests the awesome skill of pastry chefs or storied Hungarian grandmothers. Actually, flakiness is produced by layering fat with flour and just enough moisture to steam, or by otherwise mixing so that ingredients are kept at once separate *and* together. Flaky doughs are never perfectly blended—they are variegated, rough, or layered. The best of all, flaky cookies are often crunchy or gooey as well. Regardless of their mystique, the dozen-plus flaky cookies in this section are remarkably easy to make.

CARDAMOM CARAMEL PALMIERS

Both flaky and crunchy, this is a much quicker and easier version of a very classic and elegant pastry, normally made without the cardamom, which a purist may choose to omit! Using a stand mixer yields flakier pastry, but I've also provided a food processor method. (Photograph on page 242)

Makes about 48 cookies

INGREDIENTS

FOR THE DOUGH

2½ cups (11.25 ounces) unbleached all-purpose flour

2 tablespoons sugar

¼ teaspoon salt

½ pound (2 sticks) unsalted butter, cold

8 ounces cream cheese, cold

FOR THE FILLING

1 cup (7 ounces) sugar

1 teaspoon ground cardamom

2 pinches of salt

EQUIPMENT

Cookie sheets, ungreased or lined with foil, dull side up

Stand mixer with paddle attachment or food processor

If Using a Stand Mixer to Make the Dough Combine the flour, sugar, and salt in the mixer bowl. Using the paddle attachment, mix briefly to distribute the ingredients. Cut each stick of butter into 8 pieces and add them to the bowl. Mix on low speed until most of the mixture resembles very coarse bread crumbs with a few larger pieces of butter the size of hazelnuts. Cut the cream cheese into 1-inch cubes and add them to the bowl. Mix on medium-low speed until the mixture is damp and shaggy looking and holds together when pressed with your fingers, 30 to 60 seconds. Dump the dough onto the work surface, scraping the bowl. Knead two or three times to incorporate any loose pieces. There should be large streaks of cream cheese.

If Using a Food Processor to Make the Dough Combine the flour, sugar, and salt in a food processor and pulse a few times to mix. Cut the butter into ¾-inch cubes and add to the flour mixture. Pulse until the butter pieces range in size from coarse bread crumbs to hazelnuts. Cut the cream cheese into 1-inch cubes and add to the mixture. Pulse until the dough looks damp and shaggy and holds together when pressed with your fingers. Dump the dough onto the work surface, scraping the bowl. Knead two or three times to incorporate any loose pieces. There should be large streaks of cream cheese.

Divide the dough into 2 equal pieces and shape each into a 4-by-5-inch rectangular patty about 1 inch thick. Wrap and chill the dough until firm, at least 2 hours and up to 3 days.

Remove the dough from the refrigerator. If necessary, let the dough sit at room temperature until pliable enough to roll, but not too soft.

To Make the Filling Mix the sugar with the cardamom. Transfer 2 tablespoons of the mixture to a small cup and mix thoroughly with the salt. Set aside.

Divide the remaining cardamom sugar equally between 2 bowls; you will use one bowl for each piece of dough you roll out.

Sprinkle the work surface liberally with some of the cardamom sugar from one of the bowls. Set 1 piece of dough on the sugared surface and sprinkle it with more cardamom sugar. Turn the dough frequently and resugar it and the work surface liberally as you roll the dough into a 24-by-8-inch rectangle that's less than ⅛ inch thick. Use the cardamom sugar generously to prevent sticking and to ensure that the cookies will caramelize properly in the oven. Trim the edges of the rectangle evenly.

Mark the center of the dough with a small indentation. Starting at one short edge, fold about 2½ inches of dough almost one-third of the distance to the center mark. Without stretching or pulling, loosely fold the dough over two more times, leaving a scant ¼-inch space at the center mark. Likewise, fold the other end of the dough toward the center 3 times, leaving a tiny space at the center. The dough should now resemble a tall, narrow open book. Fold one side of the dough over the other side, as if closing the book. You should have an 8-layer strip of dough about 2½ inches wide and 8 inches long.

Sprinkle the remaining cardamom sugar under and on top of the dough. Roll gently from one end of the dough to the other to compress the layers and lengthen the strip to about 9 inches. Wrap the dough loosely in wax paper (not plastic wrap, which might cause moisture to form on the outside of the dough and will dissolve the sugar). Refrigerate the dough for at least 30 minutes and up to 4 hours. Meanwhile, repeat with the second piece of dough and the second bowl of cardamom sugar.

Preheat the oven to 375°F. Position racks in the upper and lower thirds of the oven.

Remove 1 piece of dough from the refrigerator, unwrap it, and use a sharp knife to trim the ends evenly. Cut ⅓-inch slices (I mark the dough at 1-inch intervals and cut 3 slices from each inch) and arrange them 1½ inches apart on the ungreased or lined cookie sheets. Bake for 8 to 10 minutes, until the undersides are deep golden brown. Rotate the pans from top to bottom and from front to back halfway through the baking time to ensure even baking.

Remove the pans from the oven. Turn the cookies over. Sprinkle each one with a pinch or two of the salted cardamom sugar, reserving half of the sugar for the second round of baking. Return the sheets to the oven and bake for another 3 to 5 minutes, until the cookies are deep golden brown. Rotate the pans and watch the cookies carefully at this stage to prevent burning. If the cookies brown at different rates, remove the dark ones and let the lighter ones continue to bake. For lined pans, set the pans or just the liners on racks to cool; for unlined pans, use a metal spatula to transfer the cookies to racks. Making sure the cookie sheets are completely cool, repeat with the second piece of dough. Cool the cookies completely before storing. May be kept in an airtight container for up to 4 days.

UPGRADES

Cinnamon Caramel Palmiers Substitute 2 teaspoons ground cinnamon for the 1 teaspoon cardamom.

RUGELACH

Rugelach are miniature flaky pastries masquerading as cookies. Simple and fun to make, they can be filled with anything you can dream up, though the classic sugar, cinnamon, nuts, and currants combo is hard to beat. As children, my mother taught us to make primitive rugelach by rolling up cinnamon-sugar-sprinkled scraps of leftover pie dough. Which is just to say you can even get by without nuts or currants! Making the dough in a stand mixer yields the best results, or use the food processor method on page 245.

Makes 48 cookies

INGREDIENTS

FOR THE DOUGH

2½ cups (11.25 ounces) unbleached all-purpose flour

2 tablespoons sugar

¼ teaspoon salt, plus additional for sprinkling

½ pound (2 sticks) unsalted butter, cold

8 ounces cream cheese, cold

FOR THE FILLING

2 tablespoons granulated sugar

½ cup (3.5 ounces) packed brown sugar

1 teaspoon ground cinnamon

1 cup (3.75 ounces) finely chopped walnuts

½ cup (2.5 ounces) currants

EQUIPMENT

Cookie sheets, lined with parchment paper or foil

Stand mixer with paddle attachment or food processor

To Make the Dough Combine the flour, sugar, and ¼ teaspoon salt in the bowl of a stand mixer. Using the paddle attachment, mix briefly to distribute the ingredients. Cut each stick of butter into 8 pieces and add them to the bowl. Mix on low speed until most of the mixture resembles very coarse bread crumbs with a few larger pieces of butter the size of hazelnuts. Cut the cream cheese into 1-inch cubes and add them to the bowl. Mix on medium-low speed until the mixture is damp and shaggy looking and holds together when pressed with your fingers, 30 to 60 seconds. Dump the dough onto the work surface, scraping the bowl. Knead two or three times to incorporate any loose pieces. There should be large streaks of cream cheese.

Divide the dough into 4 pieces. Press each piece into a flat patty about 4 inches in diameter. Wrap and refrigerate until firm, at least 2 hours and up to 3 days.

Preheat the oven to 350°F. Position racks in the upper and lower thirds of the oven.

To Make the Filling Combine the sugars, cinnamon, walnuts, and currants in a medium bowl and mix together thoroughly with a whisk or fork. Remove 1 piece of dough from the refrigerator. If necessary, let it stand at room temperature until pliable enough to roll, but not too soft. Roll into a 12-inch circle a scant ⅛ inch thick between sheets of wax paper. Peel the top sheet of wax paper from the dough and place it on the counter or a cutting board. Flip the dough over onto the paper and peel off the second sheet. Sprinkle a quarter of the filling over the dough, and then sprinkle with a tiny pinch of salt. Roll over the filling with a rolling pin to press it gently into the dough. Cut the dough like a pie into 12 equal wedges. Roll the wide outside edge up around the filling toward the point. Place the roll, with the dough point underneath to prevent it from unrolling, on the lined cookie sheets. Repeat with the remaining wedges, placing cookies 1½ inches apart. If at any time the dough becomes too soft to roll, return it to the refrigerator to firm up. Roll, cut, and fill the remaining pieces of dough.

Bake for about 25 minutes, until the cookies are light golden brown at the edges. Rotate the pans from top to bottom and from front to back halfway through the baking time to ensure even baking. Set the pans or just the liners on racks to cool. Cool the rugelach completely before storing or stacking. Rugelach are always most exquisite on the day they are baked, but they remain delicious, stored in an airtight container, for about 5 days.

UPGRADES

Apricot Nut Rugelach Process 1 cup apricot jam or preserves in a food processor if there are large pieces of fruit. Mix with ½ teaspoon ground cinnamon. Roll out the dough as described. In place of the filling, spread each piece with one-quarter of the jam mixture and then sprinkle with ¼ cup finely chopped walnuts. Sprinkle with salt, roll up, and bake as described.

Chocolate Hazelnut Rugelach Combine ½ cup (3.5 ounces) sugar, 1 teaspoon pure vanilla extract, 1 cup (4 ounces) finely chopped toasted and skinned hazelnuts (see page 16), and 1 cup (6 ounces) miniature chocolate chips. Use in place of the filling. Sprinkle with salt, roll up, and bake as directed.

Date Nut Rugelach Stuff each of 48 whole pitted dates with a walnut or pecan half. Instead of using the filling, roll the rugelach wedges around the stuffed dates.

Cacao Nib Rugelach Substitute ½ cup (2.5 ounces) finely chopped cacao nibs for the walnuts. Sprinkle with salt, roll up, and bake as directed.

Whole Wheat Rugelach Whole wheat rugelach are best with fillings that are simple and sweet: jam, semisweet or bittersweet chocolate that doesn't exceed 60% cacao, Nutella, or just cinnamon sugar. In rugelach, cacao nibs, high-percentage chocolate, and nuts, all of which have an otherwise pleasing bitterness, seem to exaggerate the bitter notes in the whole wheat flour. | Substitute 2½ cups (11.25 ounces) of whole wheat pastry flour for the all-purpose flour.

WHEAT-FREE RUGELACH

Rugelach were a challenge. I wanted flakiness and good flavor, at least a little bit of color (wheat-free pastries often look pale and unappetizing), and I didn't want the little devils to fall apart in handling, as wheat-free pastries are wont to do. The dough method may seem odd. Cream cheese, xanthan gum, sugar, and water are mixed until wet and stretchy, before the flour is added. A combination of oat flour and white rice flour gave me a good flavor. I needed the xanthan gum to hold the dough together, and the water to hydrate the flours and starches so they wouldn't taste raw in the finished cookie. Meanwhile, I also needed bits of unmixed butter in the dough for flakiness.

The dough is more fragile and quirky than the classic flaky cream cheese dough it is modeled on, so I changed method for shaping the cookies to eliminate any frustration: instead of forming cookies individually from little wedges of dough, large pieces of dough are rolled between pieces of plastic wrap, then rolled up with filling into long logs, using the handy plastic wrap as an aid to rolling. Finally the logs are cut into individual pieces. Easy! Ordinary plastic wrap is the best thing here; it peels away from the dough more easily, without sticking, than wax paper, parchment paper, or thicker plastic sheets. Problems solved.

The final key to success with these cookies—and I think with other wheat-free (or gluten-free) cookies— is to bake them as long as possible without burning them, so that the starches are fully cooked and a bit caramelized. The best test for doneness is to look for a deep brown (but not burnt) color on the bottom of the cookies.

When samples were gobbled up by my wheat-eating family, I figured I'd met the challenge.

WHEAT-FREE RUGELACH

These cookies are a little bit flaky and tenderly crumbly at the same time. People who know and love rugelach may not even notice a difference. The flaky cream cheese dough used for these rugelach can also be substituted for the dough in Pecan Tassies (page 258) or Cardamom Caramel Palmiers (page 244), so this recipe is the key to several little pastries and cookies. Xanthan gum is available in the baking aisle of better grocery stores, gourmet stores, and online (see Resources, page 362).

Makes 52 cookies

INGREDIENTS

FOR THE CREAM CHEESE DOUGH

1⅜ cups (7 ounces) white rice flour, preferably extra-fine (see Note, page 153, and page 355)

1¾ cups (6.375 ounces) oat flour (see Note, page 153, and page 354)

8 ounces cream cheese

2 tablespoons sugar

2 teaspoons xanthan gum (see page 359)

½ teaspoon baking soda

¼ teaspoon salt

¼ cup water

½ pound (2 sticks) unsalted butter, cold

FOR THE FILLING

2 tablespoons granulated sugar, plus additional for sprinkling

½ cup (3.5 ounces) packed brown sugar

1 teaspoon ground cinnamon

1 cup (4 ounces) finely chopped walnuts

½ cup (2.5 ounces) dried currants

Salt

EQUIPMENT

Cookie sheets, lined with parchment paper or foil
Box grater

To Make the Dough Combine the flours in a bowl and mix together thoroughly with a whisk or fork.

In a large bowl with a handheld mixer or in the bowl of a stand mixer with the paddle attachment, mix the cream cheese, sugar, xanthan gum, baking soda, salt, and water for about 2 minutes on medium speed. The mixture will look wet and stretchy.

Add the flour mixture and beat on low speed until the mixture resembles coarse bread crumbs (it will not be smooth). Using the largest holes on a box (or other) grater, grate the butter into the bowl. Mix on low speed to break the butter shreds into bits and distribute them. The mixture will resemble loose crumbs, sticking together only when pinched. If necessary, sprinkle and mix in another tablespoon of water. Do not try to form a cohesive dough. Divide the mixture into quarters. Dump one-quarter in the center of a sheet of plastic wrap. Bring the sides of the wrap up around the mixture on all sides, pressing firmly to form a 5-inch square patty. Wrap the patty tightly. Repeat with the remaining 3 portions of dough. Refrigerate the patties until firm, at least 2 hours and up to 3 days.

Preheat the oven to 350°F. Position racks in the upper and lower thirds of the oven.

To Make the Filling Mix together the sugars, cinnamon, walnuts, and currants in a medium bowl.

Remove 1 piece of dough from the refrigerator. If necessary, let it stand until pliable enough to roll, but not too soft. Roll between sheets of plastic wrap into a 14-by-18-inch rectangle a scant ⅛ inch thick. Peel off the top sheet of plastic from the dough. Sprinkle a quarter of the filling over the dough, and then sprinkle with a tiny pinch of salt. Roll over the filling with a rolling pin to press it gently into the dough.

Roll the dough into a long log: Starting from one long edge, lift the plastic wrap to fold ½ inch of dough onto itself. (If the dough sticks to the plastic, refrigerate the whole business for 10 minutes before proceeding.) Continue to roll the dough using the plastic wrap. Finish with the seam on the bottom, or centered on top (if you like the ragged edge as I do). Sprinkle the log with pinches of sugar. Trim the ends. Cut into 1-inch slices. Using a small spatula, place the pieces 1½ inches apart on the lined cookie sheets. Repeat with the remaining pieces of dough.

Bake for 18 to 20 minutes, until the cookies are golden brown at the edges and deep brown on the bottom. Rotate the sheets from top to bottom and from front to back halfway through the baking time to ensure even baking. Set the pans or just the liners on racks to cool. Let the rugelach cool completely before storing or stacking. Rugelach are always most exquisite on the day they are baked, but they remain delicious, stored in an airtight container, for about 5 days.

UPGRADES

Apricot Nut Wheat-Free Rugelach Use the filling for Apricot Nut Rugelach (page 250).

Chocolate Hazelnut Wheat-Free Rugelach Use the filling for Chocolate Hazelnut Rugelach (page 250).

Date Nut Wheat-Free Rugelach Make the filling, omitting the currants. Sprinkle the dough with filling and sprinkle with salt as directed. Cut 25 to 30 pitted dates in half lengthwise. Lay 6 to 8 date halves end to end, with ends slightly overlapped, along one long edge of the dough. Roll the dough and continue as directed.

Cacao Nib Wheat-Free Rugelach Substitute ½ cup finely chopped cacao nibs for the walnuts. Use in place of filling as directed.

BROWNIE BOW TIES

What more can be said about a flaky pastry filled with an intensely bittersweet bite of chocolate brownie? Just that the flakiest cream cheese dough requires restraint in mixing; yes, you *do* want to see large streaks of unmixed cream cheese in the dough. Making the dough in a stand mixer yields the best results, but if you use a food processor, follow the method on page 245.

Makes 48 cookies

INGREDIENTS

1 recipe Rugelach cream cheese dough (page 248)

6 tablespoons (¾ stick) unsalted butter

4 ounces unsweetened chocolate, coarsely chopped

1 cup (7 ounces) sugar

1 teaspoon pure vanilla extract

¼ teaspoon salt

2 large eggs, cold

2 tablespoons unbleached all-purpose flour

A little milk for brushing on the cookies

Cinnamon stick or nutmeg for grating (optional)

EQUIPMENT

Cookie sheets, lined with parchment paper or foil

Stand mixer with paddle attachment or food processor

Make the dough for Rugelach as directed in the recipe on page 248 and chill it.

Melt the butter and chocolate in a heatproof bowl set directly in a wide skillet of barely simmering water. Stir frequently until the mixture is melted and smooth. Remove the bowl from the water. Set aside 2 tablespoons of the sugar. Stir the remaining sugar, the vanilla, and salt into the chocolate mixture. Whisk in the eggs. Add the flour and whisk until the mixture is smooth and glossy and cohesive, about 1 minute. Cover and refrigerate until the filling is firm and fudgy, at least 1 hour.

Preheat the oven to 350°F. Position racks in the upper and lower thirds of the oven.

Remove 1 piece of dough from the refrigerator. If the dough is rock-hard, let it sit until it is pliable enough to roll, but not too soft. On a floured surface with a floured rolling pin, roll the dough into a 9-by-11-inch rectangle a scant ⅛ inch thick. With a pastry wheel (for nice zigzag edges) or a knife, trim the dough to even the edges. Cut the dough crosswise into quarters and then lengthwise into thirds to make 12 squares. Place a rounded teaspoon (equal to 2 level teaspoons) of chocolate filling in the center of each square. Have a small dish of water at hand. Pick up 2 opposite corners of a square, moisten the edge of one with a wet fingertip, overlap the corners by about ½ inch, and gently press them together over the filling to seal the dough and slightly flatten the filling. Transfer to the lined cookie sheets. Repeat with the remaining squares of dough, arranging the cookies 1½ inches apart. If the dough becomes too soft to handle at any point, refrigerate it briefly to firm it. Roll and fill the remaining pieces of dough. Brush the cookies with just enough milk to moisten them and sprinkle liberally with the reserved 2 tablespoons sugar.

Bake for 18 to 20 minutes, until golden brown. Rotate the pans from top to bottom and from front to back halfway through the baking time to ensure even baking. Set the pans or just the liners on racks to cool. Let the cookies cool completely before stacking or storing. Grate a little cinnamon stick or nutmeg over each cookie before serving, if desired. May be kept in an airtight container for up to 3 days.

PECAN TASSIES

Tiny tartlets with the same flaky cream cheese dough used to make Rugelach (page 248). This is my adaptation of a recipe by one of my culinary heroes, Margaret S. Fox, from her book *Café Beaujolais*. The filling will remind you of pecan pie. Making the dough in a stand mixer yields the best results, but if you use a food processor, follow the method on page 245.

Makes 24 small pastries

INGREDIENTS

FOR THE PASTRY

1¼ cups (5.625 ounces) unbleached all-purpose flour

1 tablespoon sugar

⅛ teaspoon salt

8 tablespoons (1 stick) unsalted butter, cold

4 ounces cream cheese, cold

FOR THE FILLING

1 large egg white

¾ cup (5.25 ounces) lightly packed light brown or light muscovado sugar

1 tablespoon unsalted butter, melted

¾ cup (2.625 ounces) pecans, coarsely chopped

1 teaspoon pure vanilla extract

Pinch of salt

EQUIPMENT

2 miniature muffin pans with 12 cups each

Stand mixer with paddle attachment or food processor

To Make the Dough Combine the flour, sugar, and salt in the bowl of a stand mixer. Using the paddle attachment, mix briefly to distribute the ingredients. Cut the butter into 8 pieces and add them to the bowl. Mix on low speed until most of the mixture resembles very coarse bread crumbs with a few larger pieces of butter the size of hazelnuts. Cut the cream cheese into 1-inch cubes and add them to the bowl. Mix on medium-low speed until the mixture is damp and shaggy looking and holds together when pressed with your fingers, 30 to 60 seconds. Dump the dough onto the work surface, scraping the bowl. Knead two or three times to incorporate any loose pieces. There should be large streaks of cream cheese.

Divide the dough in half, pressing each into a square patty about 4 inches. Wrap and chill until firm, at least 2 hours and up to 3 days.

Preheat the oven to 350°F. Position a rack in the lower third of the oven. Grease the muffin cups.

Remove 1 piece of dough from the refrigerator. If the dough is rock-hard, let it sit until it is pliable enough to roll, but not too soft. On a floured surface with a floured rolling pin, roll the dough into a 9-by-11-inch rectangle a scant ⅛ inch thick. With a pastry wheel (for nice zigzag edges) or a knife, trim the dough to even the edges. Cut the dough crosswise into quarters and then lengthwise into thirds to make 12 squares. Gently fit a square of dough into each cup, allowing the sides to pleat naturally. Repeat with the other piece of dough. Set aside.

To Make the Filling In a medium bowl, whisk the egg white until foamy. Stir in the brown sugar, butter, pecans, vanilla, and salt. Divide the filling among the pastries, using a scant 1 teaspoon for each.

Bake for 15 to 20 minutes, or until the pastry is well-browned on the edges and underneath (lift one out with the point of a knife to check). Transfer in the pan to a rack to cool for 5 minutes. Remove the tassies from the pan and let them cool completely on the rack before storing. May be kept in an airtight container for about 3 days.

FLAKY WHOLE WHEAT WALNUT COOKIES

Sprinkle these with the sugar if you want "cookies." But if you salt the tops instead, you get flaky "crackers" to top with savory cheeses and serve with wine or cocktails. These are flakiest on the day they are made. After that they become a little sturdier—but much easier to spread with soft cheeses!

Makes sixteen 5-inch cookies

INGREDIENTS

2½ cups (11.25 ounces) whole wheat pastry flour

2 tablespoons packed brown sugar

½ teaspoon salt

½ pound (2 sticks) unsalted butter, cold

½ cup (1.75 ounces) walnuts or pecans

8 ounces cream cheese, cold

1 tablespoon plus 1 teaspoon coarse sugar or 2 teaspoons coarse salt

EQUIPMENT

Cookie sheets, lined with parchment paper or greased

Food processor

To Make the Dough Combine the flour, brown sugar, and salt (not the coarse salt) in a food processor and pulse a few times to mix. Cut the butter into ¾-inch cubes and add to the flour mixture along with the nuts. Pulse until the butter pieces range in size from very coarse bread crumbs to hazelnuts. Cut the cream cheese into 1-inch cubes and add to the mixture. Pulse until the dough looks damp and shaggy and holds together when pressed with your fingers. Dump the dough onto the work surface, scraping the bowl. Knead two or three times to incorporate any loose pieces. There should be large streaks of cream cheese.

Divide the dough into 4 pieces. Press each piece into a flat patty. Wrap and refrigerate until firm, at least 2 hours and up to 3 days.

Preheat the oven to 350°F. Position racks in the upper and lower thirds of the oven.

Remove the dough from the refrigerator. If necessary, let it stand at room temperature until it is pliable enough to roll, but not too soft. Cut each patty into 4 pieces. On a lightly floured surface, roll each into a 5-inch circle a scant ⅛ inch thick. Place on one of the lined or greased cookie sheets. Prick about 6 times with a fork and sprinkle with ¼ teaspoon coarse sugar or ⅛ teaspoon coarse salt. Repeat with the remaining dough, placing cookies almost touching each other on each sheet.

Bake for 15 to 17 minutes, until the cookies are golden brown at the edges. Rotate the sheets from top to bottom and from front to back halfway through the baking time to ensure even baking. For lined pans, set the pans or just the liners on racks to cool; for unlined pans, use a metal spatula to transfer the cookies to racks. Cool the cookies completely before storing or stacking. The cookies are flakiest on the day they are baked, but stored in an airtight container they remain delicious for about 5 days.

UPGRADES

You can substitute toasted and skinned hazelnuts (see page 17) for the walnuts or pecans: Put the nuts into the processor with the flour, sugar, and salt. Pulse until the nuts are chopped medium fine before adding the butter.

HOLIDAY SPICE BATONS

Flavorful and elegant. Fun to make. Kids can help scatter sugar and spices and roll up the dough. Each version is a little flavor story. Feel free to divide this large recipe in half to make only 40 pieces. Wrap and refreeze the remaining dough or use it to make a half recipe of one of the upgrades, or half of another recipe that calls for phyllo dough (pages 264–67).

Makes about 80 pieces

INGREDIENTS

2 teaspoons ground cinnamon

½ teaspoon ground cloves

1 cup (7 ounces) sugar

2 teaspoons grated orange zest

1 pound phyllo dough, at room temperature

½ pound (2 sticks) unsalted butter, melted

EQUIPMENT

Cookie sheets, lined with parchment paper or foil

Preheat the oven to 350°F. Position racks in the upper and lower thirds of the oven.

Combine the cinnamon, cloves, sugar, and orange zest in a small bowl and mix thoroughly. Place 1 sheet of phyllo dough on a smooth surface. Use a spoon to drizzle some melted butter all over the surface of the dough, using only the clear yellow portion of the butter and not the milky white part. Use a brush or your fingers to spread the butter over the entire sheet of dough, gently sliding and patting the butter. Add more butter if necessary. Cut the dough into rectangles about 6 by 8 inches.

Sprinkle each rectangle with about ½ teaspoon of the sugar and spice mixture. Starting from one of the long edges, turn over about ½ inch of dough and roll 2 turns. Fold each side to the center and continue rolling; the finished roll will be 4 inches long and ½ inch thick. Place seam side down on one of the lined pans. Repeat with the remaining dough and sugar, placing the cookies about ½ inch apart. For extra sparkle, you can brush the rolls with butter and sprinkle with any leftover sugar mixture or plain sugar.

Bake for 10 to 15 minutes, until both tops and bottoms are golden brown. Rotate the pans from top to bottom and from front to back halfway through the baking time to ensure even baking. Set the pans or just the liners on racks to cool. Let the cookies cool completely before stacking or storing. May be kept in an airtight container for up to 5 days.

UPGRADES

Chocolate Pecan Batons Substitute for the sugar and spice mixture: ½ cup (3.5 ounces) sugar, 1 teaspoon pure vanilla extract, 1 cup (3.75 ounces) finely chopped toasted pecans (see page 17), 1 cup finely chopped semisweet or bittersweet chocolate with 55 to 60% cacao. Use 1 teaspoon of filling per cookie.

Scandinavian Spice Batons Substitute for the sugar and spice mixture: 1 teaspoon ground cardamom, 1 teaspoon freshly grated nutmeg, 1 cup (7 ounces) sugar, 2 teaspoons finely grated lemon zest.

Coconut and Palm Sugar Batons Substitute for the sugar and spice mixture: 1 cup (3 ounces) unsweetened dried finely shredded coconut (see page 352) and 1 cup (7 ounces) sugar (granulated or grated palm sugar); use 1 teaspoon of filling per cookie.

Ginger Cardamom Batons Substitute for the sugar and spice mixture: 1 teaspoon ground cardamom, 1 teaspoon ground ginger, 1 cup (7 ounces) sugar, ½ teaspoon cayenne.

Sesame Batons Substitute for the sugar and spice mixture: 1 cup (7 ounces) sugar and 1 cup (5 ounces) sesame seeds; use 1 teaspoon of filling per cookie.

FLAKY CHOCOLATE TRIANGLES

Bittersweet chocolate filling, reminiscent of a gooey brownie, in a flaky pillow of phyllo pastry.

Makes about 80 pieces

INGREDIENTS

4 tablespoons unsalted butter

3½ ounces bittersweet chocolate (70% cacao)

¼ cup (1.75 ounces) sugar

½ teaspoon pure vanilla extract

Pinch of salt

1 large egg

1 tablespoon unbleached all-purpose flour

1 pound phyllo dough, at room temperature

½ pound (2 sticks) unsalted butter, melted

EQUIPMENT

Cookie sheets, lined with parchment paper or foil

Preheat the oven to 350°F. Position racks in the upper and lower thirds of the oven.

Melt the 4 tablespoons butter and the chocolate together in a heatproof bowl set directly in a wide pan of barely simmering water. Remove the bowl from the water and stir in the sugar, vanilla, and salt. Add the egg and the flour and stir briskly until smooth and blended. Set aside.

Place 1 sheet of phyllo dough on a smooth surface. Use a spoon to drizzle some melted butter all over the surface of the dough, using only the clear yellow portion of the butter and not the milky white part. Use a brush or your fingers to spread the butter over the entire sheet of dough, gently sliding and patting the butter. Add more butter if necessary. Cut the dough into rectangles about 6 by 8 inches.

Place a teaspoon of the chocolate filling ½ inch from one of the corners of the dough. Fold the phyllo over to make a tall rectangle 8 inches long and 3 inches wide, with the filling enclosed in the dough. Starting at the end with the filling, flag-fold the dough: Fold the lower right corner on the diagonal to the left, lining up the left edges to make a 3-inch right triangle. Fold the triangle upward, lining up the left edges. Fold the triangle on the diagonal toward the right, lining up the right edges. Fold excess phyllo over the triangle. Place seam side down on one of the lined cookie sheets. Repeat with the remaining dough and filling.

Bake for 12 to 15 minutes, or until both tops and bottoms are golden brown. Set the pans or just the liners on racks to cool. Let the cookies cool completely before stacking or storing. May be kept in an airtight container for up to 5 days.

UPGRADES

Milk Chocolate Almond Butter Triangles Substitute for the chocolate filling: 1 cup (9 ounces) well-stirred roasted almond butter (see footnote, page 267) mixed with 10½ ounces finely chopped milk chocolate. If the almond butter is unsalted, add pinches of salt to taste. Use 1 heaping teaspoon per cookie.

Goat Cheese and Honey Triangles Substitute for the chocolate filling: 11 ounces of fresh creamy-style (not aged) goat cheese or goat cream cheese mixed with 1½ cups (18 ounces) honey. Use 1 teaspoon per cookie, topped with a walnut half if desired.

CHOCOLATE PHYLLO LOGS

Fat and flaky little phyllo rolls filled with warm melty chocolate. These differ slightly in method from Chocolate Pecan Batons (page 263): all of the chocolate is in the very center of the log rather than scattered over the whole sheet. This concentrates all of the melty chocolate in one spot for maximum effect. Feel free to divide this large recipe in half to make only 40 pieces. Wrap and refreeze the remaining dough or use it to make a half recipe of one of the upgrades, or half of another recipe that calls for phyllo dough (pages 262–65). (Photograph on page 269)

Makes about 80 pieces

INGREDIENTS

1 pound phyllo dough, at room temperature

½ pound (2 sticks) unsalted butter, melted

10½ ounces semisweet or bittersweet chocolate (any cacao percentage), chopped into shards, or
   1⅔ cups purchased chocolate chips or chunks

½ cup (3.5 ounces) sugar.

EQUIPMENT

Cookie sheets, lined with parchment paper or foil

Preheat the oven to 350°F. Position racks in the upper and lower thirds of the oven.

Place 1 sheet of phyllo dough on a smooth surface. Use a spoon to drizzle some melted butter all over the surface of the dough, using only the clear yellow portion of the butter and not the milky white part. Use a brush or your fingers to spread the butter over the entire sheet of dough, gently sliding and patting the butter. Add more butter if necessary. Cut the dough into rectangles about 6 by 8 inches.

Place heaping teaspoons of chocolate pieces in a strip about 3 inches long, centered at one narrow end of a piece of buttered phyllo. Sprinkle ¼ teaspoon sugar over the whole piece of phyllo. Fold the end of the phyllo over the chocolate and roll 2 turns, then fold each side to the middle and finish rolling; the finished roll will be 3 inches long and about ¾ inch thick. Place seam side down on one of the lined cookie sheets. Repeat with remaining phyllo pieces, placing the cookies about ½ inch apart.

Bake for 12 to 15 minutes, or until both the tops and the bottoms are golden brown. Rotate the pans from top to bottom and from front to back halfway through the baking time to ensure even baking. Set the pans or just the liners on racks to cool. Let the cookies cool completely before stacking or storing. May be kept in an airtight container for up to 5 days.

UPGRADES

Cranberry Cocoa Logs Mix together ¾ cup (5.25 ounces) packed light brown sugar, 3½ ounces finely chopped bittersweet or semisweet chocolate (about 60% cacao), 2 tablespoons (0.4 ounce) unsweetened cocoa powder, 2 tablespoons instant coffee or espresso powder, 2 teaspoons ground cinnamon, and 1 cup (5 ounces) dried cranberries. Substitute a heaping teaspoon of this mixture for the chocolate.

Almond Logs Mix together 1 cup (7 ounces) sugar and 1 cup (3 ounces) sliced almonds and substitute this mixture for the chocolate.

Almond Butter Logs Omit the chocolate. Mix 1½ cups (13.5 ounces) well-stirred roasted almond butter* with 1½ cups (18 ounces) honey. If the almond butter is unsalted, stir in ½ to ¾ teaspoon salt, to taste. In place of the chocolate, shape a slightly rounded teaspoon of the almond mixture into a narrow 2-inch strip. Sprinkle the phyllo with sugar as directed, or mix the sugar first with the grated zest of a large orange, or substitute ½ cup Holiday Spice Sugar (page 336).

---

*Natural almond butter, which is unsweetened and must be stirred to blend in the separated almond oil, is better here than the "no-stir" variety. The latter is too sweet, and the emulsifiers that make it homogeneous produce a less luxurious filling.

HOW TO WORK WITH PHYLLO

Despite fears to the contrary, phyllo dough is easy and fun to work with. The dough comes in the form of flexible paper-thin sheets. The sheets are stacked, folded, and packed in a sealed bag inside a box (unless you buy them fresh from a bakery that makes them) and sold refrigerated or frozen. Thaw frozen phyllo in the unopened package in the refrigerator for several hours or overnight and then bring to room temperature on the counter before opening the package. Open the package when you are ready to use the dough, not before. Each sheet is delicate, but not so fragile that it requires a surgeon to handle it. (If sheets stick together because they are not yet thawed, rewrap and return them to the fridge to finish thawing rather than trying to force them apart. If thawed sheets are brittle or stuck together, they should be returned to the vendor—they are old or damaged in some way.)

Phyllo sheets dry out and lose their flexibility if you leave them exposed to air for too long, but there is no need to worry if you observe two rules: Don't open the package until your melted butter and fillings are at hand and you are ready to fill and shape your cookies. And, once you begin to work with the phyllo, continue until you are done with the recipe. Then put any leftover phyllo away immediately. If you leave phyllo sheets exposed to the air while you take a lengthy phone call or walk the dog, the sheets will dry out and crack when you try to fold or roll them. But if you work without dillydallying, the phyllo will remain supple long enough for you to finish your project. Cookbooks and phyllo packages often advise you to cover the stack of phyllo with a sheet of plastic wrap weighted with a wrung-out wet towel, to prevent the sheets from drying out as you work. The damp towel is *not* a good idea unless you can make certain that it never ever comes in direct contact with the phyllo—wet phyllo immediately dissolves into paste. The infamous wet towel (or a wet counter or wet hands) is probably the cause of most phyllo phobia. Keep the phyllo under a sheet of plastic wrap if you like, but it is not really necessary if you work at a reasonable pace from start to finish. Any leftover phyllo sheets should be wrapped airtight in plastic wrap or a plastic bag and returned to the fridge or freezer.

SESAME BUTTERFLIES

Crunchy, crispy, flaky all at once. Butterfly-shaped cookies modeled after the French classic, layered with caramelized toasted sesame seeds.

Makes eighty to ninety 2½-inch cookies

INGREDIENTS

½ cup (2.5 ounces) sesame seeds

½ cup (3.5 ounces) sugar

Generous ⅛ teaspoon salt

1 recipe Mock Puff Pastry (page 347) or 1 pound purchased puff pastry

EQUIPMENT

Cookie sheets, lined with parchment paper or foil

Preheat the oven to 400°F. Position racks in the upper and lower thirds of the oven.

Divide the sesame seeds, sugar, and salt equally between two bowls and mix thoroughly.

Cut the sheet of pastry in half and return half to the refrigerator. Sprinkle the work surface liberally with some sesame sugar from one bowl. Set the pastry on the sugared surface and sprinkle it evenly with more of the sugar mixture. Roll the pastry out to a 12½-inch square about ⅛ inch thick, turning and sprinkling the pastry and the surface frequently to use up the entire contents of the bowl. Use a pizza cutter or long knife to trim the edges evenly to make a 12-inch square. Cut the pastry into 3 equal strips, each 4 inches wide. Stack the strips on top of one another. With a pencil or a stick no wider than a pencil, press a deep indentation in the center along the length of the dough stack. Fold the dough in half, using the indentation as guide. Cut the dough into ¼-inch slices. Place them 2 inches apart on the lined cookie sheets. Repeat with the remaining sheet of pastry.

Bake for 10 to 15 minutes, or until deep golden brown and caramelized underneath. Rotate the pans from top to bottom and from front to back halfway through the baking time to ensure even baking. Set the pans or just the liners on a rack to cool. Let the cookies cool completely before storing. May be kept in an airtight container for up to 5 days.

UPGRADES

Ginger Cardamom Butterflies Substitute for the sesame seeds: ½ teaspoon ground cardamom, ½ teaspoon ground ginger, and ¼ teaspoon ground cayenne pepper.

Nutmeg Cardamom Butterflies Substitute for the sesame seeds: ½ teaspoon ground cardamom, ½ teaspoon ground nutmeg, and 1 teaspoon grated lemon zest.

Almond Butterflies Substitute for the sesame seeds: ½ cup (1.5 ounces) sliced almonds.

Coconut Butterflies Substitute for the sesame seeds: ½ cup (1.5 ounces) unsweetened dried finely shredded coconut (see page 352).

FLAKY CHEESE TASSIES

Lovely bits of creamy filling surrounded by flaky, buttery pastry. Fancy and delightful. And easy if you keep the pastry on hand in the freezer.

Makes seventy-two 1½-inch cookies

INGREDIENTS

4 ounces cream cheese, softened

1 teaspoon grated lemon zest

¼ cup (1.75 ounces) sugar

2 tablespoons fresh lemon juice

1 recipe Mock Puff Pastry (page 347) or 1 pound purchased puff pastry

EQUIPMENT

2 miniature muffin pans with 12 cups each

Preheat the oven to 400°F. Position racks in the upper and lower thirds of the oven. Butter the muffin cups unless they are nonstick pans.

Beat together the cream cheese, zest, and sugar until smooth. Gradually beat in the lemon juice until smooth.

Cut the sheet of pastry in half and return half to the refrigerator. On a lightly floured surface, roll the pastry out to a 12½-inch square about ⅛ inch thick. Use a pizza cutter or long knife to trim the edges to make the dough exactly 12 inches square. Cut the dough into 2-inch squares. Transfer 12 squares to the refrigerator. Place the remaining 24 squares in the muffin cups, pressing each down in the center to make a shallow cup. Place ½ teaspoon of filling into each cookie.

Bake for 15 to 20 minutes, or until well browned at the edges. Rotate the pans from top to bottom and from front to back halfway through the baking time to ensure even baking. Let cool for 5 minutes, then gently remove the cookies from the pans with a table knife. Repeat with the remaining dough and filling. (If more pans are available, bake up to 4 pans at once, rotating the pans halfway through the baking time.) Serve the day you bake them.

UPGRADES

Blackberry Tassies Substitute ¾ cup (8.25 ounces) seedless blackberry or other jam for the cream cheese mixture.

Hazelnut and Honey Tassies Substitute ½ cup (4 ounces) finely chopped toasted and skinned hazelnuts (see page 17) mixed with ½ cup (6 ounces) honey and a pinch of salt for the cream cheese mixture.

MELT-IN-YOUR-MOUTH

FROM FRENCH MACARONS (left) TO PEANUT BUTTER CLOUDS

Oooh … these are the cookies that start deceptively—with a little crunch, a nuance of chewiness, or an infinitesimal crackle—before dissolving quickly, tenderly, meltingly on the tongue. Sweet or rich, there is surprising, tantalizing variety. Airy sweet meringues—often flourless and fat-free—are the *über*-sweet nothings of the cookie world. My newest meringues are sensational, fragrant, even exotic—flavored with creamy peanut butter or sesame paste and rose water, or laced with chestnut flour or freeze-dried bananas! By contrast, rich shortbreads, Butter Cookies, and Mexican Wedding Cakes, otherwise described as sablé, or sandy, are divinely and luxuriously tender precisely because their abundance of flour and butter and generous lashing of nuts makes them so. Go figure. Intensely flavored but ethereal French Macarons reside here too, dreamy and in a class by themselves.

FRENCH MACARONS

Indescribable. Cookie royalty. Unlike American macaroons dense with coconut, French macarons (pronounced mah-kah-ROHN) are pillowy soft, sweet, ethereal, ever-so-slightly chewy yet melt-in-your mouth almond sandwich cookies. They are often tinted in colors (from delicate to neon) that signal the flavor of their fillings. Part of the magic involves an overnight rest that allows the cookies to merge with their moist fillings. Jam is a classic macaron filling (and really quite good), but chocolate ganache, citrus curd, and flavored buttercreams are even more exciting. You can fill macarons with sweetened chestnut spread right out of the jar, peanut butter, Nutella, or what have you. Macarons look sophisticated and hard to make, but they are easier than you think. (Photograph on page 274)

Makes thirty to thirty-six 1¾-inch sandwich cookies

INGREDIENTS

2 cups (8 ounces) powdered sugar

1⅓ cups (4.5 ounces) finely ground blanched almond meal (see Tech Support, page 278)

3 to 4 large egg whites, at room temperature

¼ teaspoon almond extract

3 to 6 drops of food coloring to match your flavor (optional)

¾ cup filling, such as Lemon Curd (page 337), Chocolate Ganache (page 343), Coffee or other Buttercream (pages 338–39), chestnut spread, Nutella, peanut butter, or jam

EQUIPMENT

Cookie sheets, lined with parchment paper

Medium-coarse sieve

Large pastry bag fitted with a ½-inch plain tip (optional)

Combine the powdered sugar and almond meal in a bowl and mix together thoroughly with a whisk or fork. Pass through a medium-coarse sieve to lighten and aerate the mixture (which makes it easier to fold).

In a glass measure, add enough egg whites to reach halfway between the ⅓ cup and ½ cup mark; or use a scale to weigh out 3.75 ounces of egg whites. Transfer these to a large bowl, and save the rest for another purpose or discard. With an electric mixer, beat the egg whites at medium speed until they form soft peaks when the beaters are lifted; add the almond extract and the coloring, if using. Beat at high speed until the mixture forms stiff but not dry peaks when the beaters are lifted. Pour all of the almond flour mixture over the egg whites. With a large rubber spatula, fold the almond mixture into the egg whites (see page 287 for the best technique) just until it is fully incorporated. The egg whites will deflate somewhat, but the batter will be thick and moist and almost pourable.

Drop heaping teaspoons of batter 1 inch apart on the lined cookie sheets. Or transfer the batter to the pastry bag and pipe out disks in the following manner: Hold the bag vertical with the tip about ⅜ inch from the pan liner. Squeeze the bag without moving it until a disk of batter 1½ inches in diameter is formed. Stop squeezing a second or two before moving the bag to pipe the next disk (see page 290 for piping smooth domes). Repeat, piping disks 1 inch apart. Let the macarons rest for 20 to 30 minutes, or until the surface of the disks is ever so slightly dry—this slightly dry crust will help form characteristic little "platforms" at the base of each macaron as they bake.

Meanwhile, preheat the oven to 400°F. Position racks in the upper and lower thirds of the oven.

Slide two sheets of macarons into the oven and immediately turn the temperature down to 300°F. Bake for 12 to 15 minutes, until the macarons are barely starting to turn golden (they will be golden on the bottom, though you will have to destroy one macaron to find out). Rotate the pans from top to bottom and from front to back halfway through the baking time to ensure even baking. Set the pans or just the liners on racks to cool.

When the cookies are cool, lift a corner of the parchment pan liner. Holding a cookie with the other hand, carefully peel the liner away from the cookie (don't try to pull the cookie off the liner or you will lose the bottom of the cookie). Repeat with the remaining cookies.

Spread ½ to 1 teaspoon filling on the flat side of a cookie and top with a cookie of matching size. Put the cookies on a tray and cover them with plastic wrap. Put the trays in the refrigerator to let the cookies mellow at least overnight and for up to 2 days before serving. Bring to room temperature for serving.

TECH SUPPORT

It's possible to grind almonds in a food processor with some of the powdered sugar, but for this recipe you want the almonds uniformly fine. I recommend using finely ground blanched almond meal from Bob's Red Mill (see Resources, page 362), often found at better supermarkets and specialty stores. It works beautifully, even though it is pricier than grinding your own.

UPGRADES

Lemon Macarons   Add 1 teaspoon of finely grated lemon zest and (if you insist) 4 to 6 drops of yellow food coloring just before the egg whites are fully beaten. Fill the cookies with Lemon Curd (page 337).

Raspberry or Strawberry Macarons   If you like, add 4 to 6 drops of red food coloring to the egg whites just before they are fully beaten. Fill cookies with raspberry or strawberry preserves, or any berry preserves.

Coffee Macarons   Add 1½ teaspoons instant espresso or coffee powder to the powdered sugar and almond meal. Fill cookies with Coffee Buttercream (page 339).

Chestnut Macarons   Fill cookies with sweetened chestnut spread.

Chocolate or Mocha Macarons   Mix 3 tablespoons of unsweetened cocoa powder (natural or Dutch-process) with the powdered sugar and almond meal. Fill cookies with Chocolate Ganache (page 343), Chocolate Butter Filling (page 344), or Coffee Buttercream (page 339).

MACARON CHAT

The key to successful macarons is counterintuitive, and the best recipe turns out to be the simplest recipe: beat egg whites, then fold in finely ground almonds and powdered sugar. To read this recipe is to fear that the egg whites will deflate while you fold in such a quantity of almonds and sugar. I tried to prevent this "problem" by beating a little cream of tartar and granulated sugar into the whites to stabilize them before folding in the almonds and powdered sugar; however, my macarons came out with thick meringue crusts instead of the glossy paper-thin crust with soft melt-in-your-mouth interiors I had hoped for. I reread my old French edition of Pierre Hermé's first cookbook and learned that, indeed, sweetened meringue produces meringues, while unsweetened meringue produces macarons! When I stopped trying to fix what was not broken, my macarons turned out perfectly. A little deflating is both inevitable and desirable when you fold this batter, but you still need a skillful folding stroke to prevent the batter from deflating too much!

Bragging rights go to macaron makers who consistently produce foamy-looking little "platforms" around the base of each cookie showing (like the cloud beneath a rocket at liftoff) how the batter inflated in the oven and lifted the cookie without cracking the top surface. The coveted platform is a sign of skillfully mixed batter, a brief rest to dry the surface of each cookie before baking, and a hot start in the oven. If you are not getting much sign of liftoff, try baking one sheet at a time in the center of the oven, and be sure to reheat the oven to 400°F again before baking subsequent sheets.

MELTING CHOCOLATE MERINGUES

Deceptively light and delicately crusted, these cookies are moist and meltingly bittersweet within. Without butter or egg yolks, they are the soul of simplicity and a nice way to use a distinctive chocolate.

Makes thirty 2-inch meringues

INGREDIENTS

6 ounces bittersweet or semisweet chocolate (not to exceed 62% cacao), coarsely chopped

2 large egg whites, at room temperature

⅛ teaspoon cream of tartar

½ teaspoon pure vanilla extract

¼ cup (1.75 ounces) sugar

¾ cup (2.625 ounces) chopped walnuts

EQUIPMENT

Cookie sheets, lined with parchment paper

Preheat the oven to 350°F. Position racks in the upper and lower thirds of the oven.

Melt the chocolate in a medium heatproof bowl set directly in a wide skillet of barely simmering water. Stir frequently until the chocolate is almost completely melted, then remove from the heat and stir to complete the melting. Set aside.

In a large bowl, beat the egg whites with the cream of tartar and vanilla until soft peaks form when you lift the beaters. Gradually add the sugar, continuing to beat until the egg whites are stiff but not dry. Pour the nuts, then all of the warm chocolate, over the egg whites and fold with a rubber spatula until the color of the batter is uniform (see page 287). Do not let the batter wait.

Drop tablespoonfuls of batter at least 1 inch apart onto the lined cookie sheets. Bake for 8 to 10 minutes, until the cookies look dry and feel slightly firm on the surface but are still gooey inside when you press them. Rotate the pans from top to bottom and from front to back halfway through the baking time to ensure even baking. Set the pans or just the liners on racks to cool. Let cool completely before storing. The cookies are best on the day they are baked, but may be kept (and are still delectable) in an airtight container for another 2 to 3 days.

CHESTNUT WALNUT MERINGUES

Chestnut flour (see page 354) and walnuts transform meringues into a richer, more complex sweet to enjoy as a simple cookie or to accompany a dish of ripe strawberries topped with unsweetened whipped cream . . .

Makes 30 to 40 meringues

INGREDIENTS

¼ cup (1 ounce) chestnut flour

⅔ cup (2.625 ounces) coarsely chopped walnuts (finely chopped if using a pastry bag)

1 cup (7 ounces) sugar

4 large egg whites, at room temperature

⅛ teaspoon cream of tartar

EQUIPMENT

Cookie sheets, lined with parchment paper

Large pastry bag fitted with a ½-inch or larger plain or star tip (optional)

Preheat the oven to 200°F. Position the racks in the upper and lower thirds of the oven.

In a small bowl, mix the chestnut flour and walnuts with ⅓ cup of the sugar. Set aside.

Combine the egg whites and cream of tartar in a clean dry bowl and beat at medium-high speed in a stand mixer (or at high speed with a handheld mixer) until the egg whites are creamy white, instead of translucent, and hold a soft shape when the beaters are lifted. Continue to beat, adding the remaining sugar a little at a time over 1½ to 2 minutes, until the whites are very stiff. Pour the chestnut flour mixture over the egg whites and fold in with a rubber spatula just until combined.

Drop heaping tablespoons of meringue, or any size and shape you like, 1½ inches apart onto the lined cookie sheets. Or scrape the batter into the pastry bag and pipe "kisses" or any size or shape you like.

Bake for 2 hours. Rotate the pans from top to bottom and from front to back halfway through the baking time to ensure even baking. Remove a test meringue and let it cool completely before taking a bite. (Meringues are never crisp when hot.) If the meringue is completely dry and crisp, turn off the heat and let the remaining meringues cool completely in the oven. If the test meringue is soft or chewy or sticks to your teeth, bake for another 15 to 20 minutes before testing another meringue.

To prevent the meringues from becoming moist and sticky, put them in an airtight container as soon as they are cool. May be stored airtight for weeks.

NOT-SO-PLAIN CHOCOLATE MERINGUES

White meringue with a huge amount of pulverized chocolate folded into it is the best chocolate meringue of all. Offset the sweetness of the meringue by choosing chocolate with at least 70% cacao. Or not.

Makes 30 to 35 meringues

INGREDIENTS

5 ounces bittersweet or semisweet chocolate (any cacao percentage), coarsely chopped, or
    finely chopped if using a pastry bag

⅔ cup (4.625 ounces) sugar

⅛ teaspoon salt

3 large egg whites, at room temperature

⅛ teaspoon cream of tartar

1 to 2 tablespoons unsweetened cocoa powder (optional)

EQUIPMENT

Cookie sheets, lined with parchment paper

Food processor

Large pastry bag fitted with a ⅝-inch plain round tip (optional)

Preheat the oven to 200°F. Position racks in the upper and lower thirds of the oven.

Pulse the chocolate with about a third of the sugar and the salt in a food processor until the mixture looks like fine crumbs. In a clean dry bowl of a stand mixer or another large bowl, combine the egg whites and cream of tartar. Beat at medium-high speed (or at high speed with a hand mixer) until the egg whites are creamy white, instead of translucent, and hold a soft shape when the beaters are lifted. Continue to beat, adding the remaining sugar a little at a time, taking 1½ to 2 minutes to add it all, until the egg whites are very stiff.

Pour the chocolate mixture over the egg whites and fold in with a rubber spatula just until combined.

Drop heaping teaspoons of batter 1½ inches apart on the lined cookie sheets. Or scrape the batter into the pastry bag and pipe "kisses" or any size or shape you like. If desired, use a fine strainer to dust a little cocoa powder over the meringues.

Bake for about 2 hours, rotating the pans from top to bottom and from front to back halfway through the baking time to ensure even baking. Remove a test cookie and let it cool completely before taking a bite. (Meringues are never crisp when hot.) If the cookie is completely dry and crisp, turn off the oven and let the cookies cool in the oven. If the test cookie is soft or chewy or sticks between your teeth, leave the oven on for another 15 or 20 minutes. Turn the oven off and let the cookies cool in the oven. Remove the cookies from the oven and let cool completely. To prevent them from becoming moist and sticky, put them in an airtight container as soon as they are cool. May be stored airtight for several weeks.

UPGRADES

Mocha Meringues   Combine 1½ teaspoons instant espresso powder with the sugar beaten into the egg whites.

Chocolate Banana Meringues   Pulverize a rounded ½ cup (1 ounce) freeze-dried banana slices with the chocolate and sugar.

EGG WHITE BASICS

Beating egg whites skillfully is the key to tender meringues and amaretti, shapely meringue mushrooms, and superb macarons.

Beat egg whites at room temperature in a nonplastic bowl—stainless steel, glass, or crockery. Grease prevents egg whites from beating up to their potential stiffness and volume. Make sure there are no bits of egg yolk in the egg whites. The bowl and beaters should be clean and dry.

Egg whites also beat up fluffier at room temperature, so take them out in advance or put the bowl of egg whites in a larger container of warm water for a few minutes. It's OK if they get warm.

Older egg whites work better as well: separate the eggs a day or more in advance and store the egg whites, covered, in the fridge until needed. This is especially useful when making French macarons, where no sugar is used in the beating step to help stabilize the whites.

For the fluffiest, stiffest, and most voluminous meringue, sugar should not be added too soon, and it should be added gradually. Before adding sugar, beat the egg whites until they are no longer yellow or translucent but white and creamy like shaving cream and they hold a soft shape when the beaters are lifted. Some recipes tell you how long to take to add the sugar . . . to help you get it right. Then begin to spoon or sprinkle in the sugar a little at a time. If your meringue seems lazy and heavy in the bowl, rather than stiff and perky, you have probably rushed by adding sugar too soon or too fast.

For tender rather than tough or hard meringues, it is important that some, but not all, of the sugar be dissolved in the egg whites. To that end, a portion of the sugar (with or without other dry ingredients) may be held to the end, to be folded or briefly beaten in. This ensures that some sugar remains undissolved and your meringues will be tender rather than hard like a china plate.

FOLDING DRY INGREDIENTS INTO STIFF MERINGUE

Recipes such as French macarons, amaretti, and chocolate meringues require folding large quantities of ground nuts or chocolate and sugar into whipped egg whites or meringue. Here's how to accomplish this without deflating the egg whites or meringue more than is necessary:

Have the lined pans and a pastry bag and tip (if using) ready. Use a large flat (not spoon-shaped) rubber spatula and a flexible wrist. If you are inexperienced, or if the meringue has filled your mixer bowl, transfer the meringue to a large wide bowl (much bigger than you think you need!) for easier folding. Fold dry into wet, rather than the other way around, as follows: Pour some or all (according to the individual recipe) of the dry mixture on top of the meringue. Cut through the center of the nuts and meringue with the spatula blade. Rotate your wrist away from you to scrape the spatula blade up the side of the bowl toward you, bringing a big scoop of meringue and nuts along with it. Lift the spatula out of the bowl and rotate your wrist even farther backward (away from you) to dump the meringue and nuts back over the center of the bowl. Don't smooth or smear or mash or stir the ingredients (even if you have seen some cooks do this!). Repeat the stroke, each time cutting through the batter where it looks most in need of blending.

At first it will seem impossible to blend so much dry mix into such fluffy meringue without smearing or stirring, but after a few strokes you will see progress. Rotate the bowl as you work, and as necessary, scrape the bottom of the bowl to capture loose dry ingredients and scrape the spatula against the rim of the bowl. If you are folding dry ingredients in more than one addition, fold each addition until just two-thirds blended before adding the next. Fold the last addition (or one single addition) just until the ingredients are blended. If you keep faith with the folding stroke, you will finish with firm meringue batters that remain fairly stiff and French macaron batters—which should be somewhat deflated—that are deflated just enough.

MERINGUE MUSHROOMS

Crisp, sweet, festive, and fun. Meringue mushrooms are a classic trompe l'oeil sweet. Use them to garnish a traditional Yule log cake, add them to a cookie tray, or package them in little produce baskets wrapped in cellophane like real mushrooms and give them as gifts. They keep well for many weeks, even months if stored airtight. They never fail to amaze and delight. (Photograph on page 291)

Makes about 40 mushrooms with 1¼-inch caps

INGREDIENTS

3 large egg whites, at room temperature

⅛ teaspoon cream of tartar

¾ cup (5.25 ounces) sugar

About 2 teaspoons unsweetened cocoa powder

2 ounces bittersweet or semisweet chocolate, cut into small pieces

EQUIPMENT

Cookie sheets, lined with parchment paper

Large pastry bag fitted with a ½-inch plain tip

Preheat the oven to 200°F. Position racks in the upper and lower thirds of the oven.

In a clean dry bowl with an electric mixer, beat the egg whites and cream of tartar on medium speed until soft peaks form when the beaters are lifted. On high speed, gradually add ½ cup of the sugar about a tablespoon at a time. The mixture should stand in stiff peaks when the beaters are lifted. Use a rubber spatula to fold in the remaining ¼ cup sugar. Scrape the meringue into the pastry bag. Pipe pointed "kisses" about 1 inch high to make "stems" on the lined cookie sheets. Do not worry if the tips bend over or sag. Pipe domes to make mushroom "caps." Sieve a light dusting of cocoa over the caps and stems and fan them or blow on them vigorously to blur the cocoa and give the mushrooms an authentic look. Bake 2 hours until crisp and completely dry. Rotate the pans from top to bottom and from front to back halfway through the baking time to ensure even baking. If not assembling immediately, store caps and stems airtight as soon as they are cool to prevent them from becoming moist and sticky.

To Assemble the Mushrooms   Place the chocolate in a small bowl set directly in a wide skillet of barely simmering water. Immediately turn off the heat and stir the chocolate until melted and smooth. Use a sharp knife to cut ¼ inch to ½ inch off of the tip of each stem to create a flat surface. Spread a generous coat of melted chocolate over the flat side of several mushroom caps. Allow the chocolate to set partially before attaching the cut surface of the stems. Repeat until all of the mushrooms are assembled. Set aside the assembled mushrooms until the chocolate has hardened and the caps and stems are "glued" together. To prevent them from becoming sticky, put them in an airtight container as soon as they are cool. May be stored airtight for 3 to 4 weeks.

UPGRADES

Coffee Meringue Mushrooms   Stir 1½ teaspoons instant coffee or espresso powder into the portion of sugar that is gradually beaten into the egg whites.

Chestnut Meringue Mushrooms   Mix 3 tablespoons chestnut flour (see page 354) with the ¼ cup of the sugar that is folded in at the end.

PIPING MERINGUE MUSHROOMS

How to Pipe Stems Always pipe the mushroom stems first, while the meringue is still stiff enough to stand high. Hold the bag perpendicular to the cookie sheet, with the tip opening a fraction of an inch away from the sheet. Start squeezing gently, without moving the bag at first (to form a wide base for the stem), then raise the bag as you squeeze. Continue to raise the bag after you've stopped squeezing, to form a tall point. It's OK if the tip bends over.

How to Pipe Smooth Domes Piped mushroom caps, as well as amaretti and French macarons, often have pointy tops, which you then have to smooth out with a wet finger before baking. But you can learn to pipe smooth domes to begin with.

To pipe smooth domes, hold your pastry bag completely perpendicular to the cookie sheet and as far from the sheet as the height of your intended dome—½ inch from the sheet for a dome that will be ½ inch tall, ¾ inch above the sheet for a dome ¾ inch tall—regardless of diameter. Hold the bag perfectly still while you are squeezing the bag: do not move it up and down or around. Squeeze until the batter fills the space between the baking sheet and the pastry tip—and keep squeezing if you want a wider diameter. When you stop squeezing, don't move the bag. Points form when we move or lift the bag while meringue is still coming out of it. Since there is always a time lag between the brain saying "stop" and the hands actually stopping, try to think "stop" a few nanoseconds before you are done and hold the bag still for several nanoseconds after you stop squeezing. When no more batter is coming out, don't lift the bag up. Instead, move it in a tiny circle and then sideways away from the dome—still without squeezing. The pastry tip will skim across the surface of the dome, cutting off the beginning of any point—as long as you are not squeezing.

Smooth domes are easier to pipe than to read about. Once you get the hang of it, you'll never again have to spend time smoothing out pointy domes.

COCONUT MERINGUES

These sweet, flavorful cookies are wildly versatile. Just enjoy them or make a dreamy dessert by nestling them with whipped cream and berries, sliced bananas or mangoes, or even grilled pineapple slices. Or sandwich meringue with softened ice cream and then freeze until serving time. Serve with fruit and whipped cream or just pass a bowl of chocolate sauce . . . You can even streamline the recipe by skipping the coconut-toasting step.

Makes 25 to 30 meringues

INGREDIENTS

½ cup (1.5 ounces) unsweetened dried shredded coconut (see page 352)

⅔ cup (4.625 ounces) sugar

3 egg large whites, at room temperature

⅛ teaspoon cream of tartar

⅓ cup (0.5 ounce) dried flaked coconut, also called coconut chips, for decoration (optional)

EQUIPMENT

Cookie sheets, lined with parchment paper

Large pastry bag fitted with a ½-inch or ⅝-inch plain tip (optional)

Preheat the oven to 300°F. Position racks in the upper and lower thirds of the oven.

To Toast the Shredded Coconut Have a medium bowl ready near the stove. Spread the coconut in a wide heavy skillet over medium heat. Stir constantly until the coconut begins to color slightly. Turn the heat down and continue to stir until the coconut approaches golden brown. Remove the pan from the heat and continue to stir, letting the residual heat of the pan finish toasting the coconut slowly and evenly. The whole process takes less than 5 minutes. Immediately scrape the coconut into the bowl.

Stir 3 tablespoons of the sugar into the coconut. Set aside.

In a clean dry bowl with an electric mixer, beat the egg whites and cream of tartar on medium speed until soft peaks form when the beaters are lifted. On high speed, gradually add the remaining sugar about a tablespoon at a time, taking 1 to 1½ minutes. The mixture should stand in stiff peaks when the beaters are lifted. Use a rubber spatula to fold in the toasted coconut mixture just until incorporated. Drop heaping teaspoons of batter 2 inches apart on the lined cookie sheets. Or scrape the batter into the pastry bag and pipe "kisses" or any size or shape you like. Sprinkle each with coconut chips if using.

Bake for 10 to 15 minutes, or until the meringue or the shaved coconut begins to turn golden, whichever happens first. Turn the oven down to 200°F and continue to bake for the remainder of 2 hours. Rotate the pans from top to bottom and from front to back halfway through the baking time to ensure even baking. Remove a test cookie and let it cool completely before taking a bite. (Meringues are never crisp when hot.) If the cookie is completely dry and crisp, turn off the oven and let the cookies cool in the oven. If the test cookie is soft or chewy or sticks between your teeth, leave the oven on for another 15 or 20 minutes. Cool the meringue in the turned-off oven. Cool completely before using or storing. May be kept in an airtight container for at least 2 months.

BANANA OR RASPBERRY MERINGUES

What to do with those intriguing containers of freeze-dried fruit? Banana meringues are easy, airy, crunchy, flavorful, and unusual. Make them into dessert with juicy strawberries and whipped cream or crème fraîche and/or vanilla ice cream. Stop there or spoon on some dulce de leche (page 337) and add a handful of toasted pecans (see page 17). If it's a diet day, cut the dulce, stick with the strawberries, and trade in the cream or ice cream for yogurt. Still seriously good. Raspberry meringues are pink and especially tasty with nuts and chocolate.

Makes 25 to 30 meringues

INGREDIENTS

½ cup (0.75 ounce) freeze-dried banana slices or ⅓ cup (0.45 ounce) freeze-dried raspberries

½ cup plus 2 tablespoons (4.375 ounces) sugar

3 large egg whites, at room temperature

⅛ teaspoon cream of tartar

EQUIPMENT

Cookie sheets, lined with parchment paper

Mortar and pestle or food processor

Large pastry bag fitted with a ½-inch or larger plain or star tip (optional)

Preheat the oven to 200°F. Position racks in the upper and lower thirds of the oven.

Pulverize the fruit with 2 tablespoons of the sugar with a mortar and pestle or in a food processor. Set aside.

In a clean dry bowl with an electric mixer, beat the egg whites and cream of tartar on medium speed until soft peaks form when the beaters are lifted. On high speed, gradually add the remaining sugar about a tablespoon at a time, taking 1 to 1½ minutes. The mixture should stand in stiff peaks when the beaters are lifted. Use a rubber spatula to fold in the reserved sugar-fruit powder just until incorporated. Scoop heaping teaspoons of batter and place 2 inches apart onto the lined cookie sheets. Or scrape the batter into the pastry bag and pipe "kisses" or any size or shape you like.

Bake for 2 hours. Rotate the pans from top to bottom and from front to back halfway through the baking time to ensure even baking. Remove a test cookie and let it cool completely before taking a bite. (Meringues are never crisp when hot.) If the cookie is completely dry and crisp, turn off the oven and let the cookies cool in the oven. If the test cookie is soft or chewy or sticks between your teeth, leave the oven on for another 15 or 20 minutes. Cool the meringues in the turned-off oven. To prevent the meringues from becoming moist and sticky, put them in an airtight container as soon as they are cool. May be stored airtight for at least 2 months.

UPGRADES

Banana Pecan Meringues Fold ⅔ cup (2.33 ounces) coarsely chopped, lightly toasted pecans (see page 17) into the batter with the banana powder and sugar. Shape with a spoon.

Coconut Banana Meringues Fold ⅓ cup (1 ounce) toasted unsweetened dried shredded coconut (see pages 16 and 352) into the batter with the banana powder and sugar. If desired, sprinkle the meringue (before baking) with dried shaved coconut (coconut chips). Shape with a spoon.

Raspberry Meringues with Nuts and Chocolate Fold ⅔ cup (2.33 ounces) coarsely chopped walnuts, pecans, or toasted almonds and ⅔ cup (4 ounces) chopped semisweet or bittersweet chocolate or chocolate chips into the batter with the raspberry powder and sugar. Shape with a spoon.

PEANUT BUTTER CLOUDS

Peanut butter folded into meringue makes wonderfully light, crunchy cookies that melt on the tongue with peanut flavor. Make a sundae by piling them into glasses or bowls with vanilla ice cream, sliced strawberries, and unsweetened whipped cream and consider passing a bowl of warm chocolate or caramel sauce . . . and perhaps a pinch of flaky sea salt, such as Maldon or fleur de sel, or other imported or domestic salts available from specialty shops or better supermarkets. Sesame Kisses (page 298) will charm any halvah lover (I'm one). They are marvelous with strawberries and ice cream too, and with a drizzle of honey.

Makes 30 to 36 meringues

INGREDIENTS

3 egg whites, at room temperature

⅛ teaspoon cream of tartar

⅔ cup (4.625 ounces) sugar

⅓ cup (3 ounces) chunky or smooth natural peanut butter, well stirred before measuring

3 tablespoons finely chopped salted peanuts

EQUIPMENT

Cookie sheets, lined with parchment paper

Pastry bag fitted with a ½-inch or larger plain or star tip (optional)

OPPOSITE: Sesame Kisses (page 298)

Preheat the oven to 200°F. Position racks in the upper and lower thirds of the oven.

Combine the egg whites and cream of tartar in a clean dry bowl. Beat at medium-high speed with a heavy-duty stand mixer (or at high speed with a handheld mixer) until the egg whites are creamy white (instead of translucent) and hold a soft shape when the beaters are lifted. Continue to beat on medium-high speed, adding the sugar a little at a time, taking 1½ to 2 minutes in all, until the whites are very stiff. Scatter small spoonfuls of peanut butter over the meringue. With a large rubber spatula, fold the peanut butter into the meringue; it's OK if it's not perfectly blended.

Drop rounded tablespoons of meringue—or use the pastry bag to pipe any size and shape you like—1½ inches apart onto the lined cookie sheets. Sprinkle each meringue with a pinch of the chopped peanuts. Bake for 1½ hours. Rotate the pans from top to bottom and from front to back halfway through the baking time to ensure even baking. Remove a test meringue and let it cool completely before taking a bite. (Meringues are never crisp when hot.) If the meringue is completely dry and crisp, turn off the heat and let the remaining meringues cool completely in the oven. If the test meringue is soft or chewy or sticks to your teeth, bake for another 15 to 20 minutes before testing another meringue.

To prevent the cookies from becoming moist and sticky, put them in an airtight container as soon as they are cool. May be stored in an airtight container for at least 2 weeks.

UPGRADES

Sesame Kisses (Photograph on page 297) | Add ½ teaspoon pure vanilla extract or ¾ teaspoon rose water or orange flower water to the egg whites with the cream of tartar. Substitute ⅓ cup (3 ounces) well-stirred tahini (preferably roasted, not raw) mixed with ⅛ teaspoon salt for the peanut butter. Substitute 2 teaspoons sesame seeds for the chopped peanuts.

LUCY'S CHOCOLATE MINIS

Richer than a cupcake but lighter than a brownie. These two-bite chocolate cakes are perfect just as they are, but you can also doll them up with frosting. Don't substitute standard-size muffin pans, because they don't bake properly as full-size cupcakes.

Makes 36 cakes

INGREDIENTS

¾ cup plus 2 tablespoons (4 ounces) unbleached all-purpose flour

2 tablespoons natural (nonalkalized) cocoa powder

¼ teaspoon salt

14 tablespoons (1¾ sticks) unsalted butter, cut into chunks

4 ounces bittersweet chocolate (70% cacao), coarsely chopped

1⅓ cups (9.33 ounces) sugar

1 teaspoon pure vanilla extract

4 large eggs

EQUIPMENT

3 miniature cupcake pans with 12 cups each, lined

Preheat the oven to 350°F. Position a rack in the lower third of the oven.

Combine the flour, cocoa, and salt in a small bowl and mix thoroughly with a whisk or fork.

Place the butter and chocolate in a medium to large heatproof bowl set directly in a wide skillet of barely simmering water. Stir frequently until the chocolate and butter are melted and quite warm to the touch. Remove the bowl from the water bath. Whisk in the sugar and vanilla. Add the eggs one at a time, whisking well to blend each before adding the next. Add the flour mixture and whisk just until smooth and blended, not longer. Spoon about 1½ tablespoons of the batter into each muffin cup—the batter will come almost to the top of each liner. Bake for 14 to 18 minutes, until a toothpick inserted into the center of the cakes comes out with just a few moist crumbs clinging to it. Rotate the pans from front to back halfway through the baking time to ensure even baking. Cool the cakes on a rack. May be kept in an airtight container for 2 to 3 days.

UPGRADES

Mini Chocolate Cupcakes with Minty White Chocolate Ganache Frost Lucy's Minis with Minty White Chocolate Ganache Frosting (page 342). Garnish each cake with a small unblemished mint leaf.

Mini Chocolate Cupcakes with Fast Fudge Frosting Frost Lucy's Minis with Fast Fudge Frosting (page 343).

CAKEY BROWNIES

A little relief from dense, creamy brownies, these have a bit of extra height and a pleasing cakey texture from an additional egg, more flour, and a little baking powder. Plenty of chocolate flavor intensity and balanced sweetness comes from a blend of two kinds of chocolate.

Makes sixteen 2-inch brownies

INGREDIENTS

⅔ cup (3 ounces) unbleached all-purpose flour

½ teaspoon salt

½ teaspoon baking powder

3 ounces unsweetened chocolate

2 ounces bittersweet (70% cacao) chocolate

10 tablespoons (1¼ sticks) unsalted butter

1¼ cups (8.75 ounces) sugar

1 teaspoon pure vanilla extract

3 large eggs

1 cup (3.5 ounces) walnuts, pecans, or other nuts (optional)

EQUIPMENT

An 8-inch square pan, the bottom and all 4 sides lined with foil (see page 24)

Preheat the oven to 325°F. Position a rack in the lower third of the oven.

Combine the flour, salt, and baking powder in a medium bowl and mix together thoroughly with a whisk or fork.

Melt the chocolates and butter in a heatproof bowl set directly in a wide pan of barely simmering water. Stir frequently until the chocolate is melted and smooth. Remove from the heat and, using a rubber spatula or wooden spoon, stir in the sugar and vanilla. Add the eggs one at a time, stirring briskly until each is incorporated. Stir in the flour mixture until blended. Stir in the nuts, if using.

Scrape the batter into the pan and spread it evenly. Bake for 35 to 40 minutes, until a toothpick inserted in the center comes out with a few gooey crumbs. Cool on a rack.

Remove the brownies from the pan by lifting the edges of the foil. Transfer to a cutting board and cut into 16 or more squares. May be kept in an airtight container for up to 3 days.

LIGHT CAKEY BROWNIES

Consider these chocolate squares for people who don't want gooey, chewy, creamy, or dense but still love chocolate. I reorganized ingredients and changed the mixing method to produce these airy brownies with a delicate melt-in-your-mouth crumb. These aren't hard to make, but you must use a mixer. And finally, if you do want a little gooey, chewy, sticky pleasure, these make a great base for Rocky Road Brownies (page 224). Really.

Makes sixteen 2¼-inch or 25 smaller brownies

INGREDIENTS

4 ounces unsweetened chocolate

8 tablespoons (1 stick) unsalted butter

½ cup plus 2 tablespoons (2.75 ounces) unbleached all-purpose flour

¼ teaspoon baking powder

3 large eggs

1¼ cups (8.75 ounces) sugar

¼ teaspoon salt

EQUIPMENT

A 9-inch square metal baking pan, the bottom and all 4 sides lined with foil (see page 24)

Stand mixer with whisk attachment or handheld electric mixer

Large sieve or sifter

Preheat the oven to 350°F. Position a rack in the lower third of the oven.

Melt the chocolate and butter in a heatproof bowl set directly in a wide skillet of barely simmering water. Stir frequently until the chocolate is melted and smooth. Remove the bowl from the water and cool to lukewarm.

Combine the flour and baking powder in a bowl and mix together thoroughly with a whisk or fork.

In the bowl of a stand mixer or a regular mixing bowl (if using a handheld mixer), combine the eggs, sugar, and salt. Beat on high speed until the mixture is thick, pale yellow, and about double in volume (about 2 minutes in a heavy-duty stand mixer or a bit longer with a handheld mixer). Scrape the warm chocolate over the eggs. Fold with a large rubber spatula until the chocolate is partially incorporated. Sift the flour mixture over the top and fold just until the chocolate and flour are blended into the batter. Scrape the batter into the lined pan and tilt the pan to level the batter. Bake for 20 to 25 minutes, until a toothpick comes out with a few moist crumbs clinging to it. Set the pan on a rack to cool completely. Lift the brownies from the pan by grasping the edges of the foil. Peel the foil from the sides of the brownie. Slide a long metal spatula under the brownies to detach them from the foil. Cut the brownies into squares. May be kept in an airtight container for up to 3 days.

MEXICAN WEDDING CAKES

Tender nut-studded round or crescent-shaped cookies rolled in powdered sugar turn up around the globe; only the nuts and the names are different. Use pecans to make Mexican Wedding Cakes (aka polvorones), almonds for Viennese crescents or Greek kourabiedes, and walnuts for Russian tea cakes. Try toasted and skinned hazelnuts, macadamias, Brazil nuts, hickory nuts, pistachios, or peanuts . . .

There are both ground nuts and crunchy chopped nuts in this recipe. If you prefer all the nuts to be ground—for an even more tender, melt-in-your-mouth cookie—skip the first paragraph of the instructions. After pulverizing the sugar, put all the nuts into the processor with the flour and salt and pulse until the nuts are all finely ground.

Makes about forty-eight 1½-inch cookies

INGREDIENTS

1½ cups nuts

¼ cup (1.75 ounces) granulated sugar

2 cups (9 ounces) unbleached all-purpose flour

½ teaspoon salt

½ pound (2 sticks) unsalted butter, softened and cut into small chunks

2 teaspoons pure vanilla extract

1 large egg yolk (optional)

½ cup (1.5 ounces) powdered sugar

EQUIPMENT

Cookie sheets, lined with parchment paper or ungreased

Food processor

Pulse the nuts in a food processor until half of them look pulverized and the rest look chopped. Transfer the nuts to a bowl and set aside. Wipe the bowl of the food processor with a paper towel to remove excess oil from the nuts.

Put the granulated sugar in the processor and process until it is fine and powdery. Add the flour and salt and pulse just to mix. Add the butter, vanilla, and the egg yolk, if using. Process until the mixture looks damp and begins to clump together. Add the nuts and pulse just until combined. Transfer the dough to a bowl. Cover and refrigerate the dough for at least 2 hours, and preferably overnight.

Preheat the oven to 325°F. Position racks in the upper and lower thirds of the oven.

Shape slightly more than level tablespoons of dough into 1¼-inch balls or crescent shapes. Place the cookies 2 inches apart on the lined or ungreased pans. Bake for 22 to 24 minutes, or until lightly colored on top and golden brown on the bottom. Rotate the cookie sheets from top to bottom and from front to back halfway through the baking time to ensure even baking.

Let the cookies cool on the pan for 5 minutes and then sieve powdered sugar over them. For lined pans, set the pans or just the liners on racks to finish cooling; for unlined pans, use a metal spatula to transfer the cookies to a rack. Cool the cookies completely before storing. May be stored in an airtight container for at least 2 weeks. Sieve additional powdered sugar over the cookies before serving if necessary.

UPGRADES

Nutty Thumbprint Cookies Mexican Wedding Cake dough is perfect—and far more interesting than the usual—for thumbprint cookies. The dough holds its round shape and thumbprint depression in the oven; with so little sugar, it is a perfect container for the sweet preserves traditional in this American classic and for myriad other fillings. | Shape the dough into balls. Dip the handle of a wooden spoon (or your finger) in flour and press it into each ball to form a depression. Bake and cool as directed. Fill with Chocolate Ganache (page 343), Chocolate Butter Filling (page 344), or Nutella; alternatively, shortly before serving, fill with jam, preserves, Lemon Curd (page 337), or any dulce de leche (page 337). You will need at least ½ cup of filling for 48 cookies.

WHEAT-FREE MEXICAN WEDDING OR RUSSIAN TEA CAKES

Meltingly tender, rich, nutty . . . everything they should be. This versatile dough can also be used to make thumbprint cookies and simple and superb sablés (see the upgrades).

Makes thirty-six to forty 1½-inch round or crescent-shaped cookies

INGREDIENTS

1½ cups (5.25 ounces) walnuts or pecans

⅓ cup plus 1 tablespoon (2 ounces) white rice flour, preferably extra-fine (see Note, page 153)

1¼ cups plus 2 tablespoons (5 ounces) oat flour (see Note, page 153)

¼ teaspoon salt

⅛ teaspoon baking soda

⅓ cup (2.33 ounces) granulated sugar

2 ounces cream cheese, cold, cut into chunks

12 tablespoons (1½ sticks) unsalted butter, slightly softened, cut into chunks

1 teaspoon pure vanilla extract

½ cup (1.5 ounces) powdered sugar

EQUIPMENT

Cookie sheets, lined with parchment paper or greased

Food processor

Combine the nuts, flours, salt, baking soda, and sugar in a food processor. Pulse until the nuts are coarsely chopped. Add the cream cheese, butter, and vanilla. Process just until the dough forms a ball around the blade.

Preheat the oven to 325°F. Position racks in the upper and lower thirds of the oven.

Shape slightly more than level tablespoons of dough into 1-inch balls or crescent shapes. Place the cookies at least 1½ inches apart on the lined or greased pans. Bake for 15 to 20 minutes, until the cookies are golden brown on the bottom. Rotate the pans from top to bottom and from front to back halfway through the baking time to ensure even baking.

Let the cookies cool on the pan for 5 minutes, then sieve powdered sugar over them. For lined pans, set the pans or just the liners on racks to finish cooling; for unlined pans, use a metal spatula to transfer the cookies to racks. Let the cookies cool completely before storing. May be kept in an airtight container for at least 2 weeks. Before serving, sieve additional powdered sugar over the cookies if necessary.

UPGRADES

Wheat-Free Nutty Thumbprint Cookies Shape the dough into balls. Dip the handle of a wooden spoon (or your finger) in flour and press it into each ball to form a depression. Bake and cool as directed. Fill with Chocolate Ganache (page 343), Chocolate Butter Filling (page 344), or Nutella; alternatively, shortly before serving, fill with jam, preserves, Lemon Curd (page 337), or any dulce de leche (page 337).

Wheat-Free Sablés Substitute an equal volume of any nut that you like for the walnuts if desired. For divine Alfajores, fill these with any dulce de leche (page 337). | Make the dough as directed but, if you like, process the nuts until fine, rather than coarsely chopped. Either way, form the dough into a 10- to 12-inch log 2 inches in diameter. Wrap well and chill for at least 2 hours or overnight. Slice into scant ¼-inch-thick slices and place them 1½ inches apart on the pan. Bake for 8 to 10 minutes, until golden brown at the edges and deep brown underneath.

BASIC BUTTER COOKIES

Magnificently plain, tender, crunchy cookies celebrate the taste of butter without being too rich or greasy. No embellishments needed, but let them tempt you to try my variations and invent your own.

Makes about forty-eight 2-inch cookies

INGREDIENTS

14 tablespoons (1¾ sticks) unsalted butter, softened

¾ cup (5.25 ounces) sugar

¼ teaspoon salt

1½ teaspoons pure vanilla extract

1 large egg yolk (optional)

2 cups (9 ounces) unbleached all-purpose flour

EQUIPMENT

Cookie sheets, ungreased or lined with foil, dull side up

A 2-inch cookie cutter, round or other shape (optional)

With the back of a large spoon in a medium mixing bowl or with a mixer, beat the butter with the sugar, salt, and vanilla until smooth and creamy but not fluffy, about 1 minute with the mixer. Beat in the egg yolk, if using. Add the flour and mix just until incorporated. Scrape the dough into a mass and knead it with your hands a few times just to be sure the flour is completely incorporated.

For slice-and-bake cookies, form a 12-by-2-inch log. For rolled-and-cut cookies, form 2 flat patties. Wrap and refrigerate the dough for at least 2 hours, and preferably overnight. The dough may be frozen for up to 3 months.

Preheat the oven to 350°F (or 325°F, if using the egg yolk). Position racks in the upper and lower thirds of the oven.

To Slice and Bake Cookies Use a sharp knife to cut the cold dough log into slices ¼ inch thick. Place cookies at least 1½ inches apart on the ungreased or lined cookie sheets.

To Roll and Cut Cookies Remove 1 patty from the refrigerator and let it sit at room temperature until supple enough to roll but still quite firm, about 20 minutes. It will continue to soften as you work. Roll the dough between 2 sheets of wax paper or between heavy plastic sheets cut from a resealable plastic bag to a thickness of ¼ inch. Turn the dough over once or twice while you are rolling it out to check for deep wrinkles; if necessary, peel off and smooth the paper or plastic over the dough before continuing to roll it. When the dough is thin enough, peel off the top sheet of paper or plastic and keep it in front of you. Invert the dough onto that sheet and peel off the second sheet. Cut cookie shapes as close together as possible to minimize scraps, dipping the edges of the cookie cutters in flour as necessary to prevent sticking. Use the point of a paring knife to lift and remove scraps as you transfer cookies to cookie sheets. Place the cookies at least 1½ inches apart on the ungreased or lined cookie sheets. If the dough gets too soft at any time—while rolling, cutting, removing scraps between cookies, or transferring cookies—slide a cookie sheet underneath the paper or plastic and refrigerate the dough for a few minutes until firm. Repeat with the second piece of dough. Gently press all of the dough scraps together (don't overwork them with too much kneading) and reroll.

Bake for 12 to 14 minutes (a bit longer, if using the egg yolk dough), or until light golden brown at the edges. Rotate the cookie sheets from top to bottom and from front to back halfway through the baking time to ensure even baking. Repeat until all the cookies are baked.

For lined pans, set the pans or just the liners on racks to cool. For unlined pans, let the cookies firm up on the pans for about 1 minute, then transfer them to a rack with a metal spatula. Cool completely before stacking or storing. The cookies are delicious fresh but even better the next day. May be kept in an airtight container for at least 1 month.

UPGRADES

Butter Cookies Dipped in or Drizzled with Chocolate Half-dip cooled cookies in Tempered Chocolate Cookie Dip (page 345) or Easy Chocolate Cookie Dip (page 344) or drizzle (instead of dipping the cookies) with melted chocolate.

Brown Sugar Butter Cookies Substitute ¾ cup packed light or dark brown sugar for the sugar. These cookies may soften a little if stored for longer than a week.

Whole Wheat or Buckwheat Butter Cookies Substitute 1 scant cup (4 ounces) whole wheat, spelt, or kamut flour for 1 cup of the all-purpose flour. Or substitute ¾ cup (3 ounces) of buckwheat flour for ¾ cup of the all-purpose flour.

Butter Cookies with Ground Nuts In a food processor, pulse the flour with 1 cup of any nuts (weights vary) until the nuts are finely ground. Proceed with the recipe.

Bourbon Pecan Butter Cookies Add 1 tablespoon plus 1 teaspoon bourbon with the vanilla extract. Mix in 1 cup (4 ounces) chopped toasted pecans (see page 17) before adding the flour.

Eggnog Cookies Use the egg yolk dough and add 1 tablespoon plus 1 teaspoon rum or brandy and ¼ teaspoon freshly grated nutmeg with the vanilla.

THE BASIC BUTTER COOKIE

A perfect, poetically plain butter cookie has a fine sandy texture (*sablé* in French) and the pure flavor of butter, flour, and sugar. The tender buttery crunch might be described as friable or frangible—quite different from the coarser, noisier crunch of biscotti, for example. A star in its own right, a good butter cookie is a launching pad for dozens of new cookies. Add nuts, seeds, dried fruits, flavors, spices, flaky sea salt, or pulverized vanilla beans. You can build even more variety into the repertoire by varying the size of inclusions, from large nut pieces to finely ground nuts; everything you add—its particle size, its softness or coarseness—changes the eating quality of these perfect plain cookies.

Good butter cookies are all in the details. For tender flavorful cookies rather than tough heavy doorstops, measure the flour carefully (see page 14) and mix only as much as the recipe advises. Beating or mixing the butter and sugar only until smooth and creamy (not fluffy) produces cookies with more concentrated flavor and a perfect crisp-tender texture. Butter and sugar beaten until fluffy may produce butter cookies with a dry, coarse, airy texture and diminished flavor.

Resting and chilling the dough improves flavor and texture by allowing the flour to absorb moisture and the butter to infuse with any added flavors. Except when the dough contains bits of chocolate or cacao nibs, which tend to scorch, bake butter cookies on ungreased cookie sheets (or foil-lined rather than parchment-lined sheets) for the added flavor from browning and caramelizing the bottoms and edges of the cookies. Adding an optional egg yolk to enrich flavor will make butter cookies even more tender.

COFFEE WALNUT COOKIES

Walnuts and freshly ground coffee beans make delicately flavored cookies. Coffee lovers might enjoy them with a dish of coffee ice cream and a cup of espresso, but they are very good with grilled fresh pineapple slices and vanilla ice cream.

Makes about forty-five 2-inch cookies

INGREDIENTS

2 cups (9 ounces) unbleached all-purpose flour

1 cup (3.5 ounces) walnut halves or pieces

¾ cup (5.25 ounces) sugar

¼ teaspoon salt

2 teaspoons freshly and finely ground medium-roast (not espresso-roast) coffee beans,
    plus about 45 whole beans

12 tablespoons (1½ sticks) unsalted butter

1 tablespoon plus 1 teaspoon brandy

1½ teaspoons pure vanilla extract

EQUIPMENT

Cookie sheets, ungreased or lined with foil, dull side up

Food processor

A 2-inch cookie cutter, round or other shape (optional)

Combine the flour, walnuts, sugar, and salt in a food processor and pulse until the walnuts are finely ground. Add the ground coffee and pulse to mix.

Add the butter (cut into several pieces if firm) and pulse until the mixture looks damp and crumbly. Drizzle in the brandy and vanilla and pulse until the dough begins to clump up around the blade. Remove the dough, press it into a ball, and knead it by hand a few times to complete the mixing.

For slice-and-bake cookies, form the dough into a 12-by-2-inch log. (For more petite cookies, or for oval cookies, make a longer, thinner log.) For rolled-and-cut cookies, divide the dough in half and form 2 flat patties. Wrap the dough and refrigerate for at least 2 hours, and preferably overnight or up to 3 days.

The dough can also be frozen for up to 3 months.

Preheat the oven to 350°F. Position racks in the upper and lower thirds of the oven.

For Slice-and-Bake Cookies Use a sharp knife to cut the cold dough log into ¼-inch-thick slices. For oval cookies, slice on the diagonal. (If the dough crumbles when you cut into it, let it soften for several minutes.) Place the cookies at least 1 inch apart on the ungreased or lined pans. Press a coffee bean into the center of each cookie.

For Rolled-and-Cut Cookies Remove 1 dough patty from the refrigerator and let it stand at room temperature until supple enough to roll but still quite firm; it will continue to soften as you work. Roll the dough to a thickness of ¼ inch between 2 sheets of wax paper or between heavy plastic sheets cut from a resealable plastic bag. Flip the dough over once or twice while you are rolling it out to check for deep wrinkles; if necessary, peel off and smooth the paper or plastic over the dough before continuing to roll it out. When the dough is thin enough, peel off the top sheet of paper or plastic and place it next to the dough. Invert the dough onto the sheet and peel off the second sheet. Using a cookie cutter, cut out cookies, as close together as possible to minimize scraps, dipping the edges of the cutter in flour as necessary to prevent sticking. Use the point of a paring knife to lift and remove the scraps as you transfer cookies to the lined or ungreased pans, placing them at least 1 inch apart. Press a coffee bean into the center of each. If the dough gets too soft at any time while rolling, cutting, removing scraps between cookies, or transferring the cookies, slide a cookie sheet underneath the paper or plastic and refrigerate the dough for a few minutes, until firm. Repeat with the second piece of dough. Then gently press all of the dough scraps together (without working or kneading them more than necessary), reroll, and cut out more cookies.

Bake the cookies for 12 to 14 minutes, until light golden brown at the edges. Rotate the sheets from top to bottom and from front to back halfway through the baking to ensure even baking.

For lined pans, set the pans or just the liners on racks to cool. For unlined pans, let the cookies firm up on the pans for about 1 minute, then transfer them to a rack with a metal spatula. Cool the cookies completely before stacking or storing. These cookies are delicious fresh but are even better the next day. May be kept in an airtight container for at least 1 month.

ALMOND SABLÉS

Richer and little less sweet than plain butter cookies, ground almonds make them even more tender and sablé. Sliced and baked a little thinner, these make luscious Alfajores sandwiched with dulce de leche (page 337). If you prefer to roll and cut these in shapes, follow instructions for rolling and cutting Basic Butter Cookies (page 310).

Makes forty-eight 2-inch cookies

INGREDIENTS

½ cup (3.5 ounces) granulated sugar

Rounded ¼ teaspoon salt

⅔ cup (3.33 ounces) whole almonds (see Note)

½ pound (2 sticks) unsalted butter, slightly softened

2 teaspoons pure vanilla extract

⅛ teaspoon almond extract

2 cups (9 ounces) unbleached all-purpose flour

⅓ cup (2.33 ounces) turbinado, evaporated cane (Sugar in the Raw), or coarse granulated sugar (optional)

EQUIPMENT

Cookie sheets, ungreased or lined with foil, dull side up

Food processor

Pulse the sugar and salt in a food processor until the sugar is fine and powdery. Add the almonds and pulse until they are finely ground. Add the butter in large chunks, along with the vanilla and almond extracts. Pulse until the butter is smooth. Add the flour and pulse until a soft dough begins to form around the blade. Transfer the dough to a large bowl and knead it briefly to make sure it is mixed evenly.

Form a log about 12 inches long and 1¾ inches in diameter. Wrap the log in wax paper or foil. Refrigerate for at least 2 hours and preferably overnight.

Preheat the oven to 350°F. Position a rack in the center of the oven.

Spread the coarse sugar on a sheet of wax paper or a flat dish. Roll the dough log in the sugar, pressing so that the sugar adheres. Cut the log into slices ¼ inch thick and place them at least 1 inch apart on the ungreased or lined cookie sheets. Bake for 12 to 15 minutes, until the edges are golden brown, rotating the pan from front to back halfway through the baking time to ensure even baking. For lined pans, set the pans or just the liners on racks to cool. For unlined pans, let the cookies set on the pan for a minute or two before transferring them to a rack with a metal spatula. Cool the cookies completely before storing. May be kept in an airtight container for up to 1 month.

NOTE

Whole almonds with skins work perfectly. They taste as good or better than store-bought blanched almond meal, and it's simple to pulverize them as the cookies are made in the processor anyway.

UPGRADES

You may substitute any nut for the almonds . . .

Hazelnut Sablés/Nutella Sandwiches For half or all of the almonds, substitute an equal measure of hazelnuts. If desired, slice and bake thinner (⅛ inch) and sandwich the cooled cookies with Nutella.

WHOLE WHEAT SABLÉS

There is nothing chewy, dense, or heavy here—just meltingly tender, buttery cookies with the nutty flavor of whole wheat. The flavor of wheat is perfection with almost any nut or dried fruit combination, or with cacao nibs. Hemp seeds are fabulous in the upgrade that follows. Spelt or kamut flours—both older forms of wheat—may be substituted for the scant cup of whole wheat flour.

Makes about forty-eight 2-inch cookies

INGREDIENTS

2 cups (9 ounces) whole wheat pastry flour, or 1 cup (4.5 ounces) unbleached all-purpose flour plus
    1 scant cup (4 ounces) whole wheat flour

14 tablespoons (1¾ sticks) unsalted butter, softened

½ cup (3.5 ounces) sugar

¼ teaspoon salt

1 teaspoon pure vanilla extract

EQUIPMENT

Cookie sheets, ungreased or lined with foil, dull side up

Combine the flours in a bowl and mix together thoroughly with a whisk or fork.

In a medium bowl, with the back of a large spoon or with an electric mixer, beat the butter with the sugar, salt, and vanilla until smooth and creamy but not fluffy, about 1 minute with the mixer. Add the flour and mix just until incorporated. Scrape the dough into a mass and, if necessary, knead it with your hands to be sure the flour is completely incorporated.

Form the dough into a 12-by-2-inch log. Wrap and refrigerate for at least 2 hours, and preferably overnight.

Preheat the oven to 350°F. Position racks in the upper and lower thirds of the oven.

Use a sharp knife to cut the cold dough log into ¼-inch-thick slices. Place the cookies at least 1½ inches apart on the ungreased or lined cookie sheets.

Bake for 12 to 14 minutes, until the cookies are light golden brown at the edges. Rotate the pans from top to bottom and from front to back halfway through the baking time to ensure even baking. For lined pans, set the pans or just the liners on racks to cool. For unlined pans, let the cookies firm up on the pans for about 1 minute, then transfer them to a rack with a metal spatula. Let the cookies cool completely before storing.

The cookies are delicious fresh but are even better the next day. May be kept in an airtight container for at least 1 month.

UPGRADES

You can add ⅓ cup (1.33 ounces) roasted cacao nibs with or without 1 cup chopped nuts (raw or toasted) of any kind to the creamed butter and sugar mixture before adding the flour. Also see Whole Wheat Hazelnut Cookies with Currants and Cacao Nibs (page 115).

Hemp Seed Whole Wheat Sablés These have a subtle nutty flavor reminiscent of sunflower seeds. (Photograph on page 323) | Add ½ to ⅔ cup (2.25 to 3 ounces) hemp seeds to the creamed butter before adding the flour. You can vary the recipe further by adding ½ cup (1.75 ounces) finely chopped pecans and 2 tablespoons toasted sesame seeds.

WHOLE-GRAIN COOKIES

Divine cookies made with whole grains require a suspension of preconceived notions: whole grains need not be restricted to recipes that are "healthy" any more than almonds are! But if you equate whole grains with old-fashioned "health food," leaden pastries, or granola cuisine, you may find it hard to imagine that these grains are equally capable of making elegant, tender buttery flavorful cookies.

You will find stunningly good and healthy graham crackers in the collection, as well as decadently buttery whole wheat sablés and shortbread. Oh, and the grains are so tasty, there is no need to camouflage or hide them . . .

Successful whole-grain cookies also require the right kinds of recipes. Protein and gluten—abundant in many whole grains—are prime suspects in tough and heavy cookies. To capture the greatness of the grain in a good cookie, I steer clear of recipes with lots of liquid or mixing. Liquid activates gluten development, and mixing makes it stronger. Shortbread and butter cookies are made without milk or eggs (which are about 20 percent water) or any other liquid other than the small amount of water in the butter. With no liquid to absorb, whole-grain flours behave just like finely ground nuts—they make shortbread and butter cookies tender. In fact, one batch of whole wheat shortbread had to be cut into dainty squares rather than long fingers or wedges because the crumb was so darn tender that long pieces broke in half from their own weight when picked up! Of course, the butter and sugar in these recipes also tenderize the cookies. Graham crackers work differently. In these, the flours are coated with fat before the liquid is added—the fat waterproofs the flour and protects it from the liquid. The way I see it, the gluten is essentially outsmarted. Meanwhile, a little leavening and the steam from the liquid opens up the texture and makes it tender. The result is flavorful, crunchy, and moderate in both fat and sugar—and still not tough.

OPPOSITE: Hemp Seed Whole Wheat Sablés (page 321)

PEANUT BUTTER COOKIES

Lots of extra peanut flavor here, from lots of pure natural peanut butter. Chilling the dough improves the flavor, but if you must mix and bake the cookies immediately, use melted instead of softened butter to boost the flavor and expect a slightly chewier cookie.

Makes thirty-six 2¼-inch cookies

INGREDIENTS

1½ cups (6.75 ounces) unbleached all-purpose flour

½ teaspoon baking soda

1 teaspoon flaky sea salt or ¾ teaspoon fine sea salt

8 tablespoons (1 stick) unsalted butter, softened

¼ cup (1.75 ounces) packed dark brown sugar, lump free

¾ cup (5.25 ounces) granulated sugar

1 large egg

1 teaspoon pure vanilla extract

1¼ cups (11.25 ounces) natural (but *not* unsalted) chunky peanut butter—stir well to blend in the oil
   before measuring

EQUIPMENT

Cookie sheets, lined with parchment paper or greased

Combine the flour, baking soda, and salt in a medium bowl and mix together thoroughly with a whisk or fork.

In a large bowl, with the back of a large spoon or an electric mixer, mix the butter with the sugars until smooth and creamy, but not fluffy, about 1 minute with the mixer. Add the egg, vanilla, and peanut butter and mix until blended. Add the flour mixture and stir just until it is evenly incorporated. Wrap and refrigerate the dough for at least 2 hours, and preferably overnight or up to 3 days.

Preheat the oven to 325°F. Position racks in the upper and lower thirds of the oven.

Scoop slightly more than 1 level tablespoon and form the dough into 1¼-inch balls. Place the balls 2 inches apart on the lined or greased cookie sheets. Flatten each ball to a thickness of ⅜ inch with a fork, pressing the back of the tines into the dough in two directions to make a crosshatch pattern. Or partially flatten the balls with the bottom of a glass (dipped in flour if it sticks), then press each cookie with a cookie stamp or other textured object.

Bake for 14 to 16 minutes, until the cookies are lightly colored on top and golden brown underneath. Rotate the sheets from top to bottom and from front to back halfway through the baking time to ensure even baking. For lined pans, set the pans or just the liners on racks to cool; for unlined pans, use a metal spatula to transfer the cookies to racks. Cool the cookies completely before stacking or storing. May be kept in an airtight container for at least 2 weeks.

SALTED PEANUT TOFFEE COOKIES

Encrusted with toffee-coated peanuts and accented with flaky sea salt, these updated peanut butter cookies have a tender melt-in-your-mouth shortbread texture. They are festive enough for a party but easy enough for every day.

Makes about fifty-six 1½-inch cookies

INGREDIENTS

1⅓ cups (6 ounces) unbleached all-purpose flour

½ teaspoon baking soda

1 teaspoon flaky sea salt or ¾ teaspoon fine sea salt

8 tablespoons (1 stick) unsalted butter, melted

½ cup (3.5 ounces) packed light or dark brown sugar

½ cup (3.5 ounces) granulated sugar

1 large egg

1 teaspoon pure vanilla extract

1 cup (9 ounces) natural (but *not* unsalted) chunky peanut butter—stir well to blend in the oil before measuring.

5 ounces store-bought Coconut Toffee Peanuts or Toffee Peanuts, coarsely chopped

EQUIPMENT

Cookie sheets, lined with parchment paper or greased

Combine the flour, baking soda, and salt in a medium bowl and mix together thoroughly with a whisk or fork.

In a large bowl, mix the melted butter with the sugars. Whisk in the egg, vanilla, and peanut butter, add the flour mixture, and mix with a rubber spatula or wooden spoon just until evenly incorporated.

Cover the dough and refrigerate for an hour or two and up to 2 days.

Preheat the oven to 325°F. Position racks in the upper and lower thirds of the oven.

Pour the chopped nuts into a shallow bowl. Scoop about 2 level teaspoons of dough for each cookie, shape into a 1-inch ball or a fat little log, and coat the top and sides heavily with the chopped nuts, pressing in any pieces that fall off so that there are no bald spots. Place 2 inches apart on the lined or greased pans.

Bake the cookies for 15 to 18 minutes, until they are lightly colored on top (and underneath). Rotate the sheets from top to bottom and from front to back halfway through the baking time to ensure even baking. The cookies will seem very soft to the touch (and the one you turn over to assess color may even fall apart), but they will firm up as they cool. For lined pans, set the pans or just the liners on racks to cool; for unlined pans, use a metal spatula to transfer the cookies to racks. Cool the cookies completely before storing. May be kept in an airtight container for at least 2 weeks.

UPGRADES

Salted Peanut Toffee Thumbprints with White Chocolate Surprisingly, white chocolate tastes better than dark or milk chocolate in these cookies (and this from a huge fan of bittersweet chocolate!). And chopped pieces from a bar of "real" white chocolate taste better than white chocolate chips. | Have ready 4 ounces white chocolate cut into little pieces or ⅔ cup (4 ounces) white chocolate chips. Bake the cookies in the shape of balls as described. As soon as the pans come out of the oven, press the back of a chopstick or dowel into the center of each hot cookie and move it around gently to widen the hole. Tuck pieces of chocolate (or chips) into each depression while the cookies are still hot.

Salted Peanut Toffee Thumbprints with Jam Have ready about ½ cup (5.5 ounces) strawberry or other jam or preserves. Bake the cookies in the shape of balls as described. As soon as the pans come out of the oven, press the back of a chopstick or dowel into the center of each hot cookie and move it around gently to widen the hole. Cool the cookies. Just before serving, fill the depressions with jam.

Salted Peanut Cookies with Thai Curry Cashews Made by Sunridge Farms, Thai Curry Cashews can be found in bulk bins in some supermarkets. | Substitute Thai Curry Cashews for the toffee peanuts.

Spicy Salted Peanut Toffee Cookies Add ½ to 1 teaspoon Thai curry paste or other hot sauce to the dough with the peanut butter.

TWICE-BAKED SHORTBREAD

There are a couple of secrets to this tender, buttery, crunchy shortbread. For the best flavor and texture, let the dough rest in the pan for at least 2 hours or overnight before baking. A second short bake toasts each piece ever so slightly, adding extra flavor and resulting in a light, crunchier texture through and through. Shortbread keeps for many weeks in a sealed container, and it makes a wonderful gift.

Makes fourteen to sixteen 2-inch squares, or 16 wedges

INGREDIENTS

11 tablespoons unsalted butter, melted and still warm

¼ cup plus 1 tablespoon (2.125 ounces) granulated sugar

1 teaspoon pure vanilla extract

¼ teaspoon salt

1½ cups (6.75 ounces) unbleached all-purpose flour

Turbinado, Demerara, or granulated sugar for sprinkling

EQUIPMENT

An 8-inch square baking pan or a 9½-inch round fluted tart pan with a removable bottom

Cookie sheet, lined with parchment paper

Line the bottom and sides of the baking pan with foil (see page 24) or grease the tart pan.

In a medium bowl, combine the melted butter with the sugar, vanilla, and salt. Add the flour and mix just until incorporated. Pat and spread the dough evenly in the pan. Let rest for at least 2 hours or overnight (no need to refrigerate).

Preheat the oven to 300°F. Position a rack in the lower third of the oven.

Bake the shortbread for 45 minutes. Remove the pan from the oven, leaving the oven on. Lightly sprinkle the surface of the shortbread with sugar. Let the shortbread cool for 10 minutes.

Remove the shortbread from the pan, taking care to avoid breaking it. Use a thin sharp knife to cut it into oblong "fingers," wedges, or squares. Place the pieces slightly apart on the parchment-lined pan and bake for 15 minutes. Cool the shortbread on a rack. May be kept in an airtight container for several weeks.

UPGRADES

Nutty Shortbread Shortbread with ground nuts is extra flavorful and tender. Try walnuts, pecans, untoasted or toasted and skinned hazelnuts or almonds, peanuts, or any nuts you fancy. | Decrease the flour to 1¼ cups. Add ½ cup (1.75 ounces) walnut or pecan pieces to the flour and pulse in a food processor until the nuts are finely ground. Proceed with the recipe.

Bourbon Pecan or Peanut Shortbread Decrease the flour to 1¼ cups. Add ½ cup (1.75 ounces) pecans or roasted peanuts (salted or not). Substitute packed brown sugar for the granulated sugar, and add 1 tablespoon bourbon with the vanilla. If using salted peanuts, omit the salt from the recipe.

Nutmeg or Cardamom Shortbread Add ¾ teaspoon freshly grated nutmeg or ½ teaspoon ground cardamom to the flour.

Pecan Penuche Shortbread Sweet, slightly addictive shortbread with the flavor of brown sugar fudge. | Measure and set aside ⅔ cup (3.33 ounces) coarsely chopped pecans. Make the dough substituting ½ cup (3.5 ounces) packed brown sugar or light muscovado sugar for the granulated sugar and adding 1 tablespoon dark rum with the vanilla. Add half of the pecans with the flour. Before baking, sprinkle the dough with the remaining nuts and press gently to make them adhere. Sprinkle with turbinado sugar.

GOLDEN KAMUT SHORTBREAD

Kamut is an ancient form of wheat. It makes exceptional shortbread, as the flour itself has a buttery flavor. The texture is tender, dry, and sandy; the color is golden; and the flavor is delicately sweet from the grain. Try this shortbread sprinkled with flaky sea salt and freshly ground pepper in addition to sugar. Kamut flour is found in the baking aisle of better supermarkets and by mail order (see Resources, page 362).

Makes fourteen to sixteen 2-inch squares, or sixteen wedges

INGREDIENTS

11 tablespoons unsalted butter, melted and still warm

¼ cup plus 1 tablespoon (2.125 ounces) sugar

1 teaspoon pure vanilla extract

¼ teaspoon salt

¾ cup (3.375 ounces) unbleached all-purpose flour

¾ cup (3.375 ounces) kamut flour

Turbinado, Demerara, or granulated sugar for sprinkling

Flaky sea salt and freshly ground black pepper (optional)

EQUIPMENT

An 8-inch square baking pan or a 9½-inch round fluted tart pan with a removable bottom

Cookie sheet, lined with parchment paper

Line the bottom and 4 sides of the baking pan with foil (see page 24) or grease the tart pan.

In a medium bowl, combine the melted butter with the sugar, vanilla, and salt. Add the flours and mix just until incorporated. Pat and spread the dough evenly in the pan. Let rest for at least 2 hours or overnight (no need to refrigerate).

Preheat the oven to 300°F. Position a rack in the lower third of the oven.

Bake the shortbread for 45 minutes.

Remove the pan from the oven, leaving the oven on. Lightly sprinkle the surface of the shortbread with sugar. If desired, sprinkle a little flaky sea salt and grind a little black pepper over the shortbread: do this by eye, as though seasoning a salad. Let the shortbread cool for 10 minutes.

Remove the shortbread from the pan, taking care to avoid breaking it. Use a thin sharp knife to cut wedges or squares. Place the pieces slightly apart on the parchment-lined pan and put it into the oven for 15 minutes. Cool the shortbread on a rack. May be kept in an airtight container for several weeks.

UPGRADES

Aniseed and Almond Shortbread This shortbread is sweet enough to be cookies, but not too sweet to nibble with a good glass of red wine. Whole wheat flour adds an extra-toasted nutty flavor to the classic almond and anise combination. Serve with strawberries and lightly sweetened whipped cream (flavored with a few drops of rose water if you like) for a simple but sophisticated dessert. Or nibble with a glass of single-malt Scotch. | Use the square baking pan. Reduce the vanilla to ½ teaspoon and add 1 tablespoon plus 1 teaspoon slightly crushed aniseed with the sugar. Substitute an equal amount of whole wheat flour for the kamut flour. Before baking, sprinkle the shortbread with ½ cup (2.5 ounces) chopped or slivered almonds and press them gently into the dough. (Note that although slivered almonds look best, they are stubborn when it's time to cut the shortbread; plan to cut squares and expect some ragged edges . . . nice and rustic!) Omit the salt and pepper.

COMPONENTS

Here you will find a small collection of mixtures and components that you may use over and over again for the recipes in this book and beyond. Look for spicy sugars for dusting and dredging all kinds of cookies (not to mention sprinkling on fruit, cereal, or buttered toast). There are fillings and frosting for sandwich cookies, thumbprint cookies, polvorones, and miniature cakes, or just to slather on graham crackers, toast, or scones. Look for Lemon Curd, chocolate fillings and frostings, three kinds of dulce de leche, the easiest classic butter cream, and fruit fillings (pear, sour cherry, spicy fig . . .), for marvelous Egyptian cookies called meneinas. For dipping cookies in chocolate, you'll find instructions for tempering chocolate like a pro, plus a recipe that requires no tempering at all! My shortbread crust for cheesecake and pudding bars is here, along with a recipe for mock puff pastry that is better than any store bought "real" puff pastry you can find.

SPICED SUGARS

Coating cookies with spiced sugar adds a layer of fragrance and flavor that is more interesting than simply mixing the spice into the dough. Cinnamon is the usual—and always very good—but don't miss nutmeg, cardamom, or even star anise, Chinese five-spice powder, or garam masala. Looking through my cupboards (and my old recipes), I found a little jar of cinnamon sugar—½ teaspoon of cinnamon in ¼ cup of sugar—and a much more recent batch with four times as much cinnamon! Spicy sugars can be as gentle or as fierce as you like them. If you are uncertain about a flavor, start with a little and taste as you increase the dose. I like a little salt as well. If you love a particular spicy sugar, double or quadruple the recipe, omitting the salt, and keep it on hand. Each time you use some of the sugar, mix a tiny pinch of salt into the portion you are using, if desired. Spiced sugars last indefinitely.

VANILLA SUGAR

Keep this on hand for baking, to sprinkle on fruit or cereal, and to mix into anything that will taste good sweetened with vanilla.

Makes 2 cups

INGREDIENTS
1 whole vanilla bean or pieces of scraped bean left over from other
     cooking, or 1 teaspoon or more ground or powdered vanilla bean
2 cups (14 ounces) sugar

If using a whole vanilla bean, slice down the middle and scrape the seeds into the sugar. Stir well and put the sugar in a jar with the scraped bean pieces. Or stir the ground or powdered vanilla into the sugar. In a week or so, the sugar will be fragrant and flavorful. If you use a little vanilla sugar at a time, and not too frequently, you can replace the amount taken out with more plain sugar, stirring it in well.

CINNAMON SUGAR

Makes ¼ cup

INGREDIENTS
¼ cup (1.75 ounces) sugar
1 teaspoon to 1 tablespoon ground cinnamon
Pinch of salt to taste (optional)

Mix together thoroughly the sugar, cinnamon, and salt, if using, before using or storing in an airtight container.

UPGRADES
Nutmeg Sugar Substitute 2 to 4 teaspoons freshly grated nutmeg for the cinnamon.
Cardamom Sugar Substitute ¼ teaspoon to 2 teaspoons ground cardamom for the cinnamon.
Garam Masala Sugar Substitute ¾ teaspoon garam masala for the cinnamon.
Chile or Chili Sugar Substitute up to ½ teaspoon ground chile or chili powder for the cinnamon.
Chinese Five-Spice Sugar Substitute 1 teaspoon Chinese five-spice powder for the cinnamon.
Star Anise Sugar Substitute ½ teaspoon ground or finely grated star anise for the cinnamon.
Lavender Sugar Substitute ½ teaspoon dried lavender buds for the cinnamon. Pulverize the lavender buds with the sugar and salt in a mini food processor or with a mortar and pestle.
Holiday Spice Sugar Reduce the cinnamon to ½ teaspoon and add ⅛ teaspoon ground cloves and ½ teaspoon finely grated orange zest.

LEMON CURD

Fill crisp, crunchy, or sandy cookies—such as Basic Butter Cookies (page 310), Vanilla Sugar Cookies (page 38), Almond Sablés (page 318), or Pecan Polvorones with Muscovado Filling (page 200)—with this tangy filling shortly before serving to prevent cookies from softening. Lemon curd is also a divine filling for French Macarons (page 276), where it's meant to merge with and soften the cookies overnight. (And, if making macarons, you will have leftover egg yolks that can be used up in this recipe.) This recipe makes enough to fill up to 80 sandwich cookies or 250 thumbprints. Don't forget that leftover lemon curd is delicious on toast or scones.

Makes 1½ cups

INGREDIENTS
3 large eggs, or 1 whole egg plus 3 egg yolks
½ cup strained fresh lemon juice
Grated zest of 1 lemon
½ cup (3.5 ounces) sugar
6 tablespoons unsalted butter, cut into pieces

Whisk the eggs lightly in a medium heatproof bowl to combine the yolks and whites. Combine the lemon juice, zest, sugar, and butter in a small nonreactive saucepan and bring to a simmer over medium heat. Gradually pour the hot liquid over the eggs, whisking constantly until all the liquid has been combined with the eggs. Return the mixture to the saucepan and whisk over medium heat until thickened and just beginning to simmer around the edges. Remove from the heat and strain the mixture into a clean container, pressing gently on the solids.

Refrigerate before using. Lemon curd may be refrigerated, covered, for up to 1 week.

VANILLA DULCE DE LECHE

Dulce de leche from scratch is divine. And no big deal.

Makes 1 cup

INGREDIENTS
½ vanilla bean
1 quart whole milk
½ cup (3.5 ounces) sugar
½ teaspoon baking soda
Pinch of salt (optional)

With a sharp paring knife, cut the vanilla bean in half lengthwise. In a large saucepan, combine the vanilla bean pieces with the milk, sugar, baking soda, and salt, if desired. Bring the mixture to a simmer, stirring frequently. At first the milk will thicken a little; then it will curdle. It will eventually smooth out again as you cook it. Continue to cook, stirring and scraping the sides and corners and all over the bottom of the pot frequently, until the mixture thickens and becomes a little chewy when spooned over an ice cube or when a spoonful dropped onto a plate holds a shape like thick caramel sauce. This may take 40 to 60 minutes. The mixture becomes especially foamy in the last stages of cooking. Scrape the mixture into a heatproof bowl or jar. Cool slightly, then taste and adjust the salt, if desired. You can leave the spent pieces of vanilla bean in the mixture if you like. May be kept in the refrigerator for at least 1 month.

UPGRADES
Plain Dulce de Leche Omit the vanilla bean.
Honey Vanilla Dulce de Leche Add 2 tablespoons honey with the sugar.
Coconut Dulce de Leche Substitute one 13- to 15-ounce can of coconut milk for an equal amount of the cow's milk.

NEW CLASSIC BUTTERCREAM

This is real French buttercream without the trickiest steps. Classic buttercream requires pouring hot sugar syrup over eggs while beating steadily—without scrambling the eggs or splattering the syrup around the sides of the bowl. The mixture is then reheated (to be sure the eggs are safe from salmonella) and then beaten again to cool it before the butter is added. Home cooks are at an extra disadvantage because small batches are tricky. This recipe produces classic results with fewer, easier steps, and it makes enough for 6 dozen French Macarons (page 276).

Makes about 1½ cups

INGREDIENTS

2 large egg yolks or 1 whole large egg, at room temperature
Pinch of salt
2 tablespoons water
⅓ cup (2.33 ounces) sugar
12 tablespoons (1½ sticks) unsalted butter, softened but not too squishy

EQUIPMENT

Instant-read thermometer
Medium-fine strainer

Have a clean bowl (or mixer bowl if using a stand mixer) near the stove with a strainer set over it.

In a 1-quart stainless-steel bowl (because glass bowls are too slow to heat), whisk the egg yolks (or whole egg), salt, and water together thoroughly. Whisk in the sugar. Set the bowl in a wide skillet filled with enough hot water to reach above the depth of the egg mixture. Over medium heat, with a heatproof silicone spatula, stir the egg mixture,

sweeping the sides and bottom of the bowl constantly to prevent the eggs from scrambling. Adjust the burner so the water barely simmers and continue to stir until the mixture registers between 175° and 180°F on an instant-read thermometer. Swish the thermometer stem in the hot skillet water to rinse off the raw egg in between temperature readings.

Remove the bowl from the skillet and scrape the mixture into the strainer. Rap the strainer to coax the mixture through it, but do not press on any bits that are left in the strainer. Turn the strainer and scrape the mixture clinging to the underside into the bowl. Beat at high speed for 3 to 4 minutes, or until the mixture is a cool, thick, fluffy foam like soft whipped cream.

Cut the butter into several chunks and beat it into the foam until it is thick and smooth. The foam will deflate when you add the butter. If the butter is too cold, the mixture will curdle or separate at first, but it will smooth out as you continue to beat, and if it doesn't you can set it into the warm water in the skillet for a few seconds and then continue to beat. If either the foam or the butter is too warm when you combine them, the buttercream will seem soupy instead of creamy. If it doesn't thicken up with beating, you can fix it by setting the bowl in a bowl of ice and water or in the refrigerator for 5 to 10 minutes; then resume beating until the mixture is creamy and smooth.

Refrigerate or freeze buttercream to store. To soften, break chilled or frozen buttercream into chunks with a fork. Microwave on low for several seconds, then stir smooth with a rubber spatula. Or set the bowl in hot water until some buttercream melts around the sides of the bowl. Stir and replace the bowl in hot water, then stir again. Repeat until the buttercream is smooth and spreadable.

UPGRADES

Vanilla Buttercream Add ¼ teaspoon (or more to taste) pure vanilla extract after the butter.

Honey Buttercream Substitute ¼ cup plus 2 tablespoons of honey for the sugar. Omit the water. To the finished buttercream, add a tiny pinch or two of salt to your taste.

Honey Vanilla Buttercream Reduce the sugar to ¼ cup and add 2 tablespoons honey to it before heating. Add ½ teaspoon pure vanilla extract after the butter. To the finished buttercream, add a tiny pinch or two of salt to your taste.

Coffee Buttercream Flavor the finished buttercream with 1½ to 2 teaspoons instant espresso or coffee crystals dissolved in ¼ teaspoon water.

New Classic Chocolate Buttercream Stir 7 to 10 ounces (to taste) melted and barely lukewarm white chocolate, milk chocolate, or semisweet or bittersweet chocolate (with up to 62% cacao) plus 2 tablespoons warm water into a finished batch of New Classic Buttercream.

FILLINGS FOR MENEINAS

After tasting Meneinas (page 198) with their fragrant date and walnut filling, I couldn't help dreaming up equally marvelous fillings—with pears, apricots, cherries, or figs—to honor them.

DATE AND WALNUT FILLING

This is the original, authentic filling for Meneinas (page 198), which was given to me with that recipe. It's simple and spendid.

Makes 2 cups

INGREDIENTS

2 cups (about 12 ounces) chopped, moist pitted dates
2 tablespoons unsalted butter
Salt
2 small or medium bright-skinned tangerines, preferably unsprayed or organic
1 cup (3.5 ounces) chopped walnuts

EQUIPMENT

Potato masher

Combine the dates, butter, and a pinch of salt in a medium saucepan. Grate the zest from the tangerines directly into the pan to capture the oils released from the skin. If the dates are dry, add 2 to 3 tablespoons tangerine juice or water. Cook over low heat, mixing and mashing (a potato masher works!) to form a smooth stiff paste. Off the heat, stir in the walnuts. When cool, taste and adjust the salt (or other seasonings) to your liking. May be kept in the refrigerator for at least 1 month.

SPICED FIG FILLING

For fig fanciers or any cook with a global spice rack.
Makes 1½ cups

INGREDIENTS
2 cups (12 ounces) lightly packed chopped pitted figs
3 tablespoons sugar
1 tablespoon honey
2 teaspoons crushed fennel seeds
½ teaspoon ground cinnamon
⅛ teaspoon ground cloves
⅛ teaspoon freshly ground white pepper
¼ teaspoon ground ginger
¼ teaspoon crushed coriander seeds
¼ teaspoon freshly grated nutmeg
Grated zest of 1 small lemon
Grated zest of 1 medium orange
Salt (optional)
1 generous cup (4 ounces) walnut halves, chopped
½ teaspoon orange flower water

EQUIPMENT
Potato masher

Put all of the ingredients except the walnuts and orange flower water in a medium saucepan. Add water to cover the fruit generously. Bring the mixture to a simmer. Cook, stirring and mashing with a potato masher from time to time, until the water has evaporated and the mixture is a thick jammy paste. If the figs were very dry and hard, you may have to add water and simmer again. Remove from the heat and stir in the walnuts and orange flower water. When cool, taste and add salt (or any seasoning) to your liking. May be kept in the refrigerator for at least 1 month.

PEAR FILLING

Pears brightened with lemon zest and just a nuance of spice.
Makes 1½ cups

INGREDIENTS
2 cups (12 ounces) gently packed diced dried pears
1½ tablespoons honey
Grated zest of 2 small lemons
2 teaspoons sugar
½ teaspoon ground cinnamon
⅛ teaspoon ground cloves
Salt
Couple drops of pure vanilla extract
½ cup chopped almonds

EQUIPMENT
Potato masher

Put the pears, honey, grated zest, sugar, cinnamon, cloves, and a pinch of salt in a medium saucepan. Add water to cover the fruit. Bring the mixture to a simmer. Cook, stirring and mashing with a potato masher from time to time, until the water has evaporated and the mixture is a thick jammy paste. Remove from the heat. Stir in the vanilla. When cool, taste and adjust salt (or any seasoning) to your liking. Stir in the almonds. May be kept in the refrigerator for at least 1 month.

SOUR CHERRY FILLING WITH BLACK PEPPER

Sour cherries love a little vanilla in the background. Don't be afraid of the pepper.

Makes 1½ cups

INGREDIENTS

2 cups (12 ounces) gently packed dried sour cherries, chopped
1 tablespoon unsalted butter
½ teaspoon grated lemon zest
Salt
½ teaspoon pure vanilla extract
⅜ teaspoon fresh, finely ground black pepper

EQUIPMENT

Potato masher

Put the cherries, butter, grated zest, and a pinch of salt in a medium saucepan. Add water to cover the fruit. Bring the mixture to a simmer. Cook, stirring and mashing with a potato masher from time to time, until the water has evaporated and the mixture is a thick jammy paste. Remove from the heat. Stir in the vanilla and pepper. When cool, taste and adjust salt (or any seasoning) to your liking. May be kept in the refrigerator for at least 1 month.

APRICOT VANILLA FILLING WITH CINNAMON AND ALMONDS

Especially good in meneinas with dough flavored with rose water instead of orange flower water.

Makes 2 cups

INGREDIENTS

2 cups (12 ounces) dried apricots, chopped
1 tablespoon unsalted butter
A 4-inch piece of vanilla bean, split
½ teaspoon ground cinnamon
Salt
1 cup (5 ounces) almonds, coarsely chopped

EQUIPMENT

Potato masher

Put the apricots, butter, vanilla bean, cinnamon, and a pinch of salt in a medium saucepan. Add water to cover the fruit. Bring the mixture to a simmer. Cook, stirring and mashing with a potato masher from time to time, until the water has evaporated and the mixture is a thick, coarse jammy paste. Remove from the heat. Fish out the vanilla bean and use the tip of a paring knife to scrape the seeds into the pot. Discard or save the pod for another use. Stir in the almonds. When cool, taste and adjust the salt (or any seasoning) to your liking. May be kept in the refrigerator for at least 1 month.

EASY POWDERED SUGAR COOKIE ICING

This icing, plain white or tinted with ordinary food colors, is an easy option for decorating cookies. Spread it with a small spatula, paint it with a brush, drizzle it, or pipe it from the corner of a resealable plastic bag (fill it, close it, and snip off a corner). Powdered sugar dissolved in just a little liquid dries hard and shiny and takes color well. It is sweet and decorative, though not exactly a gourmet item.

For 1 cup of icing, measure out 4 cups (16 ounces) powdered sugar. Sift the sugar and mix with 3 to 4 tablespoons water or lemon juice (for a lemon-flavored icing) or 5 to 6 tablespoons brandy or rum to the desired consistency. Adjust by adding powdered sugar or liquid. If desired, divide the icing among small cups and tint with ordinary food coloring. Note that food coloring intensifies with time, so tint the icing lighter than you think it should be. To store, press plastic wrap against the surface of the icing. The icing keeps for about 4 days at room temperature.

MINTY WHITE CHOCOLATE GANACHE FILLING OR FROSTING

Begin the ganache a day ahead to allow time for the fresh mint leaves to infuse their flavor into the cream. Need a shortcut? Skip the fresh mint infusion and make plain ganache. Flavor it with a drop or two of mint oil or some peppermint extract to taste.

Makes about 1½ cups

INGREDIENTS
¼ cup lightly packed coarsely chopped fresh mint leaves
¾ cup heavy cream
6 ounces white chocolate (not chocolate chips), very finely chopped

Stir the chopped mint into the cream. Cover and refrigerate for at least 8 hours and up to 12 hours. Strain the cream into a small saucepan, pressing gently on the leaves to drain out as much cream as you can. Discard the mint leaves. Heat the cream to a simmer. Meanwhile, put the chocolate into a clean bowl. Pour the hot cream over the chocolate and stir until the chocolate is completely melted and smooth. Cool; cover with plastic wrap and refrigerate for at least 4 hours and up to 2 days.

To use, remove the ganache from the refrigerator and check its consistency. If it is smooth and creamy, it can be used right away. If the ganache is too fluid or soft to spread without dripping, stir it vigorously with a rubber spatula for a few seconds (it will appear to soften; don't worry) and return it to the fridge for a few minutes, then check again.

CHOCOLATE GANACHE

Decadent chocolate cream to fill sandwich cookies, including French Macarons (page 276), or Nutty Thumbprint Cookies (page 307). Use a good quality chocolate for this world-class filling, rather than chocolate chips. This recipe makes enough for about 48 sandwich cookies or about 200 thumbprint cookies. Leftover ganache can be melted and used to top ice cream.

Makes 1½ cups

INGREDIENTS

6 ounces semisweet or bittersweet chocolate
   (no more than 62% cacao), finely chopped
1 cup heavy cream

Put the chocolate in a heatproof bowl. Bring the cream to a boil in a heavy saucepan. Pour the hot cream over the chopped chocolate. Stir gently until all of the chocolate is melted and the mixture is smooth. Cool the ganache at room temperature (without stirring) until it is thick enough to spread or pipe. May be covered and refrigerated for at least 1 week.

To soften chilled ganache, set the bowl in a larger bowl of hot water or microwave on low for a few seconds at a time until soft and spreadable. Spread about 2½ teaspoons of ganache between two 1½- to 3-inch cookies or pipe into thumbprint cookies.

FAST FUDGE FILLING OR FROSTING

The best and most versatile bittersweet chocolate frosting I know.

Makes about 2 cups

INGREDIENTS

6 tablespoons unsalted butter
1 cup (7 ounces) sugar
1 cup (3.25 ounces) unsweetened cocoa powder
1 cup heavy cream
1 teaspoon pure vanilla extract
Salt

In a medium saucepan, melt the butter. Stir in the sugar and cocoa. Gradually stir in the cream. Heat over medium heat, stirring constantly, until the mixture is smooth and hot but not boiling. Remove from the heat and stir in the vanilla and a pinch or two of salt, to taste. Set aside until cool, thickened, and spreadable. May be covered with plastic wrap and stored in the refrigerator for up to 1 week.

You can let it cool and spread it in swirls like old-fashioned frosting or use it while still slightly fluid for a sleek, luxurious glaze, in which case you turn each cupcake or cookie upside down and dip the tops. Make sure whatever you are frosting is completely cool, or the frosting will slide right off. Store and serve at room temperature for the best taste and texture.

CHOCOLATE BUTTER FILLING

This is an easy alternative to chocolate ganache, and you can use chocolate with any cacao percentage that you like.

Makes ½ cup

INGREDIENTS

4 ounces bittersweet or semisweet chocolate
   (any cacao percentage), coarsely chopped
3 tablespoons unsalted butter

Place the chocolate and butter in a heatproof bowl set directly in a wide skillet of barely simmering water. Or microwave on medium power for 1 to 2 minutes, stirring after the first minute. When the chocolate is almost completely melted, remove the bowl from the heat and stir until completely melted and smooth. Set aside until needed. If the filling hardens before using, soften it gently in a pan of hot water before spooning it into each cookie.

CHOCOLATE FOR DIPPING

All kinds of cookies are festive and fancy—or just plain delicious—dipped or half-dipped in chocolate. Consider Almond Biscotti (page 92) or any of the chocolate biscotti (pages 96–99). Don't forget Alfajores (page 192), butter cookies, sugar cookies, and graham crackers, including any upgrades that sound like they will taste good with chocolate. Of the two recipes that follow, Tempered Chocolate Cookie Dip is the Cadillac choice for dipping cookies, although it takes patience and practice to master; Easy Chocolate Cookie Dip is the easier, but quite tasty alternative.

EASY CHOCOLATE COOKIE DIP

Made with pure chocolate and a little clarified butter (which will prevent the chocolate from blooming for at least a day or two), this dip sets up a little softer than pure tempered chocolate, but it's simpler to use and it tastes great.

Makes about 1⅓ cups

INGREDIENTS

12 ounces bittersweet or semisweet chocolate, coarsely chopped,
   or 12 ounces of milk or white chocolate, finely chopped
2 tablespoons clarified butter (or ghee) if using dark chocolate,
   or 1 tablespoon plus 1 teaspoon clarified butter (or ghee)
   if using milk or white chocolate

EQUIPMENT

Cookie sheets lined with parchment or wax paper
Instant-read thermometer (optional)

Place the chocolate and clarified butter in a small stainless-steel bowl. For bittersweet or semisweet chocolate, set the bowl directly in a wide skillet of barely simmering water. For milk chocolate or white chocolate, turn the heat off under the skillet and wait 60 seconds before putting the bowl of chocolate in the skillet. Stir frequently until the chocolate is melted and smooth. Remove the bowl from the water bath and stir well.

Cookies should be completely cool before dipping. For the best gloss with no streaks on your finished cookie, keep the chocolate warm to the touch (between 95°F and 110°F), rather than hot or tepid, while dipping cookies. Reheat the chocolate in the original water bath as necessary, because dipping cookies cools off the chocolate. Stir the chocolate frequently as you work and especially well after reheating.

Hold a cookie between your thumb and forefinger. Dip the cookie half to two-thirds of the way into the chocolate. Shake the cookie, letting the excess chocolate flow back into the container. Wipe some of the chocolate gently off the bottom of the cookie against the edge of the chocolate bowl. Set the cookie, right side up, on the lined cookie sheet. When you have filled a whole sheet with dipped cookies, refrigerate it for 10 minutes to set the chocolate. Remove the cookies from the refrigerator and let them sit in a cool place until the chocolate is completely set. Store the cookies between sheets of wax paper in an airtight container at cool room temperature.

TEMPERED CHOCOLATE COOKIE DIP

For cookies dipped in chocolate, there is nothing like the intense flavor, crisp snap, and attractive gloss that comes from pure chocolate (your favorite brand) that has been melted and tempered (so it will dry hard and shiny instead of gray and streaky on cookies) before dipping. Here is one of many methods . . .

You will need an instant read thermometer and solid chocolate that is already in temper—a nice shiny new bar right out of the package. You can temper any amount of chocolate but at least 1¼ pounds is convenient. Leftover chocolate is reusable so there is no waste. Have baking sheets lined with parchment or wax paper ready, and if possible a portable. fan. Cookies should be cooled to room temperature before you temper the chocolate.

Start with about 1¼ pounds of chocolate (for example). Set aside 4 ounces (one fifth of the total amount) in one or two large pieces. Chop the remaining pound coarsely and place it in a dry 1- to 2-quart stainless-steel bowl. Set the bowl in a wide skillet of not quite simmering water. With a dry spatula, stir frequently at first, then constantly, until three quarters of the chocolate is melted. Turn off the heat under the bath and remove the bowl. Stir for 1 to 2 minutes to melt the remaining chocolate. Your goal is melted chocolate at about 100°F, so don't be too eager to put it back on the heat yet. If the chocolate is not entirely melted after stirring for a couple of minutes, rewarm it briefly in the turned-off bath. Remove the bowl and stir until the chocolate is completely melted.

If the temperature of the chocolate exceeds 100°F, let it cool to about 100°F. Add the reserved chocolate chunk(s) and stir patiently until the chocolate registers 90°F for dark chocolate or 88°F for white or milk chocolate—the chunks will not be entirely melted. Test the chocolate to confirm that it is tempered by drizzling some on a knife blade and setting the knife in a cool place (or in front of a portable fan). If the drizzle starts to set within 1 to 3 minutes without streaks or mottling, it is tempered and ready to use; if it still looks wet after 3 minutes, stir the chocolate and chunks for a few more minutes and test it again. When the chocolate is tempered, fish out the unmelted chunk(s) and set them aside.* Use the tempered chocolate immediately.

Hold a cookie between your thumb and forefinger. Dip it halfway to two-thirds of the way into the tempered chocolate. Shake the cookie, letting the excess chocolate flow back into the bowl before placing it on a lined pan. Let cookies set at room temperature or in front of a portable fan until the chocolate hardens. Store cookies in an airtight container between layers of wax or parchment paper.

As you work, scrape the bowl frequently to prevent chocolate from hardening around the sides. Before the chocolate gets too thick or cool, rewarm it in a water bath that's 92°F to 94°F, stirring until the chocolate regains fluidity. Do not let the chocolate exceed 91°F for dark chocolate or 88°F for milk or white chocolate, or the chocolate may lose its temper (check this by testing) and you will have to add a new chunk of chocolate and stir until the chocolate is again in temper.

---

*As for the chunk(s) of chocolate that you have fished out, this chocolate is reusable if you refrigerate it for about 10 minutes before storing it unrefrigerated.

SHORTBREAD CRUST

Tender, buttery, crunchy, this is a great base for cheesecake bars, pudding bars, and more.

Makes one 9-by-13-inch or 8-by-12-inch crust

INGREDIENTS

14 tablespoons (1¾ sticks) unsalted butter, melted and still warm
½ cup (3.5 ounces) sugar
2 teaspoons pure vanilla extract
⅜ teaspoon salt
2 cups (9 ounces) unbleached all-purpose flour

Preheat the oven to 350°F. Position a rack in the lower third of the oven. Line the pan as specified in the individual recipe with foil.

In a medium bowl, mix the melted butter with the sugar, vanilla, and salt. Add the flour and mix just until incorporated. Don't worry if the dough seems too soft or oily. Press and smooth the dough evenly over the bottom of the pan. Bake for 20 to 25 minutes, until the crust is a rich golden brown with well-browned darker edges. Let cool on a rack before proceeding as directed in the recipe.

WHEAT-FREE SHORTBREAD CRUST

Here is a tasty, tender, crunchy crust for Wheat-Free Gooey Turtle Bars (page 209), Wheat-Free Rocky Road Bars (page 214), Wheat-Free Chocolate Pudding Bars (page 216), and Wheat-Free Caramel Cheesecake Bars (page 238). To make a single square crust, divide the recipe in half.

Makes one large 9-by-13-inch crust or two 8- or 9-inch-square crusts

INGREDIENTS

⅓ cup plus 1 tablespoon (2 ounces) white rice flour, preferably extra-fine (see Note, page 153)
1¼ cups plus 2 tablespoons (5 ounces) oat flour (see Note, page 153)
¼ teaspoon salt
⅛ teaspoon baking soda
⅔ cup (4.625 ounces) sugar
2 ounces (one quarter of an 8-ounce package) cream cheese, cut into chunks
12 tablespoons (½ sticks) unsalted butter, softened, cut into chunks
1 teaspoon vanilla extract

Preheat the oven to 350°F. Position a rack in the lower third of the oven. Line the pan or pans as specified in the individual recipe with foil.

Combine the flours, salt, and baking soda in a medium bowl, and mix thoroughly with a whisk or fork. In a large bowl, using an electric mixer, beat the sugar with the cream cheese, butter, and vanilla until smooth and creamy. Add the flour mixture and mix just until it is incorporated.

Scrape the dough into the prepared pan and spread to make a thin, even layer. Bake for 20 to 25 minutes, until the crust is fully baked, well-browned at the edges, and deep golden brown in the center.

MOCK PUFF PASTRY

Mock puff pastry is easy and fun to make, once you get over seeing the incoherent mass of butter pieces and flour that you are expected to roll into dough. But it really works and the flaky layered results will thrill you. With mock puff pastry, tiny tartlets/tassies and butterflies are lightning quick and quite fancy. The fillings are so simple that you can easily do several kinds of flaky cookies from a single batch of pastry.

Makes seventy-two 1½-inch tartlets or tassies, or 48 butterflies

INGREDIENTS

1¾ cups (7.875 ounces) unbleached all-purpose flour
¾ teaspoon salt
½ pound (2 sticks) chilled unsalted butter, cut into ½-inch cubes
½ cup ice water, plus additional as needed

In a large bowl, mix the flour and salt together thoroughly. Add the butter. With a large metal spoon, stir until the butter bits are separate from each other and coated with flour. Separate the butter pieces with your fingers if necessary. Drizzle in most of the water and turn the mixture gently with the spoon until the water is absorbed. Lift the mixture to one side and pour the remaining water onto the flour in the bottom of the bowl. Stir and lift the mixture until there is no longer any dry flour in the bottom of the bowl, adding up to 2 tablespoons more water if necessary. The mixture should be very loose and shaggy, literally a bowl full of butter chunks coated with damp flour amid damp raggedy pieces of dough. Do not overmix or let the butter get soft.

Scrape the mixture out onto a smooth surface heavily dusted with flour and shape it into a rectangle. With a floured rolling pin, press and roll the dough out to a rectangle about 8 by 16 inches with one of the narrow sides facing you. You will see distinct pieces of butter and loose pieces of flour in the dough. Run a cake spatula under the dough to detach it from the work surface. Fold up the bottom third of the dough and fold the top third down over it, to make a new rectangle about 5⅓ by 8 inches. If the dough is not cohesive enough to fold without significant breakage, slide a file folder or other stiff paper underneath to help you lift and fold the dough with minimal breakage. As you work, dust the surface, rolling pin, and spatula with flour to avoid sticking. Rotate the dough a quarter turn (there may still be many loose bits) and roll it out again to 8 by 16 inches. By now the butter will have softened somewhat and the dough should be more cohesive, but it may still be breaking up at the edges—this is OK. Run the spatula under the dough, fold the bottom up and the top down to make a rectangle 5⅓ by 8 inches, and wrap it tightly in plastic wrap. Chill for 2 hours.

Lightly flour a smooth surface and a rolling pin. Working rapidly to keep the dough cool, unwrap the dough and roll it out to a rectangle 8 by 20 inches. Fold the bottom edge up to the center and the top edge down to the center. Now fold the new top edge down to the bottom edge (there will be four layers of dough in a rectangle about 5 by 8 inches). Flour the dough and the work surface, rotate, and repeat the last rolling and folding steps. Flour the dough and roll it out to about a 10-inch square. Wrap securely with plastic wrap and chill for at least 2 hours and up to 2 days. Freeze for longer storage; defrost in the refrigerator.

INGREDIENTS

Cookie dough is not a fountain of youth. Don't even consider using up your petrified dried fruit, old currants, slightly stale nuts, old spices, or butter that tastes and smells like the refrigerator in a batch of cookies. Dried fruits should be moist and plump enough for nibbling, spices fresh and lively (toss out the old and bring in the new), butter fresh enough to enjoy on your morning toast. The best ingredients make the best cookies.

BAKING POWDER AND BAKING SODA

Baking powder has an expiration date because it loses its oomph if not fresh and not kept stored in a tightly sealed container. To see if baking powder is still good, add about 1 teaspoon to ¼ cup hot water. If it bubbles vigorously, use it. If in doubt, toss out the old container and buy a new one.

Baking soda appears to last indefinitely (even if the container is not airtight) in the cupboard. If you are unsure, spoon a little of it into a cup and add vinegar. If it bubbles vigorously, it's fine.

BUTTER/MARGARINE/OIL

The recipes in this book call for unsalted butter, which is the usual choice of bakers and pastry chefs. If you use salted butter in a recipe, subtract ¼ teaspoon of salt from the quantity in the recipe for each stick (8 tablespoons) of salted butter. Traditional home bakers may like shortening or margarine for cookies because these fats produce tender cookies. I prefer the superior flavor of butter, regardless. I also know that tenderness can be achieved with good technique. If you must use or prefer to use margarine, choose one that is labeled suitable for baking, as some "lite" margarine spreads and butter substitutes contain too much water for successful baking. Finally, do not expect predictable results from substituting vegetable oils for solid fats.

Extra Virgin Olive Oil

Extra virgin olive oil is a flavor ingredient as well as a fat! I used it purposely in cookies, for its own good taste rather than as a substitute for butter. Choose fully fragrant, flavorful oil and don't hesitate to try different styles from delicate to robust.

European and European-Style Butter

These butters contain 82 to 87 percent fat compared with our American standard 80 percent and thus less water. Some are made from cultured milk (like cheese). The flavor of European-style butters varies considerably from brand to brand. If you bake cookies with European-style butter, its higher fat and lower moisture content may result in cookies that spread too much on the baking sheet and seem too buttery or greasy. Using 8 to 10 percent less butter in the recipe may correct these problems. A butter cookie with 2 cups (9 ounces) of flour and 14 tablespoons (1¾ sticks) of regular butter was perfect with 13 tablespoons of European-style butter. A single tablespoon may seem like a negligible amount, but it can make a difference.

CHOCOLATE

Buy chocolate that you like and choose the best you can afford. Unless otherwise noted in the recipe, the cookies in this book turn out beautifully with common supermarket brands, as long as they are the type of chocolate called for in the recipe. However, better chocolate does make better cookies. Note that some premium brands of chocolate are not divided into 1- or 2-ounce portions, so you may need a scale for measuring.

Different kinds of chocolate chips and chunks may be substituted for one another, but when chocolate is melted and mixed into batters, you will get better results if you stick with the type of chocolate called for in the recipe: do not substitute bittersweet for unsweetened chocolate or milk chocolate for bittersweet; avoid using a bittersweet or semisweet chocolate with a radically higher cacao percentage than the one called for.

Roasted Cacao Nibs

Cacao (or cocoa) nibs are pieces of roasted and hulled cocoa beans—the essential ingredient in all chocolate. In the manufacture of chocolate, nibs are roasted and ground to a molten paste (called *chocolate liquor,* aka *unsweetened chocolate*) and further processed to make all kinds of sweetened chocolate. But nibs are also available to home cooks for use in baking and cooking. Crunchy and relatively bitter, nibs have all of the flavors and nuances that may be found in chocolate—toasted nuts, wine, berries, tropical fruit, citrus, grass, or spice, to name just a few—as well as some of the (frankly) rougher, earthier, more tannic flavors that are normally eliminated in the processing that would transform them into chocolate. Crushed, ground, chopped, or left in their natural form, nibs add unique chocolate flavor and texture to cookies. I vastly prefer the flavor of nibs that are roasted (rather than raw), and I prefer to purchase them from a company that also manufactures good chocolate.

Unsweetened Chocolate

Technically called *chocolate liquor* (though it contains no alcohol), unsweetened chocolate is pure ground cacao nibs, often with a fraction of a percent of lecithin as an emulsifier. Some companies include a little vanilla, but most do not. Some unsweetened chocolate may be labeled "99% cacao" (to account for that tiny amount of lecithin and/or vanilla). The highest quality unsweetened chocolate is smooth enough and palatable enough to use chopped or ground up in recipes as well as melted and blended into batters.

Semisweet and Bittersweet Chocolate

Bittersweet and semisweet chocolates are sweetened dark chocolates: pure ground cocoa beans, optional added cocoa butter, sugar, optional lecithin and/or vanilla. A small amount of milk product is permitted, but the best usually contain none. Although the legal minimum is lower, the old standard brands in the baking aisle contain 50 to 60% cacao and thus 40 to 50% sugar (assuming no milk, the percentage of cacao is inversely proportional to the percentage of sugar). But there are dozens of semisweet and bittersweet chocolates with ever higher cacao percentages. And, while bittersweet is generally less sweet than semisweet, the industry does not make an official distinction between them, so one brand of bittersweet may be sweeter than a semisweet made by a different company. Cacao percentage is a better predictor of sweetness and chocolate intensity than these less specific terms.

Since bittersweet chocolate with 70% cacao behaves very differently in a recipe from bittersweet chocolate with 60% cacao, my recipes always specify a cacao percentage (or range of percentages) that will produce successful cookies. Using chocolate with significantly more cacao than the recipe calls for may result in dry, bitter cookies or curdled fillings. In some recipes I may also include tips for using other types of chocolates, and I always note when you are free to choose your octane, so to speak!

Milk Chocolate

Milk chocolate is sweetened chocolate that contains at least 10 percent cocoa beans and a minimum of 12 percent milk solids, plus milk fat. Milk chocolate is mild, sweet, and creamy tasting in comparison to semisweet and bittersweet chocolates. The most flavorful milk chocolates exceed the minimum cacao requirement considerably, resulting in chocolate with more chocolate flavor and less sweetness.

Gianduja

Gianduja is sweetened chocolate, usually milk chocolate, containing toasted hazelnuts ground to a perfectly smooth, unctuous paste. A few companies make gianduja with a base of semisweet chocolate instead of milk chocolate.

White Chocolate

White chocolate is made from only the fat of the cocoa bean (called *cocoa butter*)—rather than the whole cocoa bean—combined with sugar, dry milk solids, milk fat, lecithin, and vanilla. White chocolate is now recognized and defined by the FDA as a form of real chocolate and should not be confused with "white confectionery coating," which is made from tropical vegetable fats other than cocoa butter and thus contains not a single ingredient derived from cocoa beans.

Chocolate Chips and Chunks

Traditional chocolate chips (and some but not all chocolate chunks), whether semisweet, bittersweet, milk, or white, are specially formulated with less cocoa butter than bar chocolate so that they hold their shape when baked into cookies. They may also help keep cookies from flattening out during baking. Since chocolate chips (and chocolate chunks formulated similarly) stay thick when melted and are usually fairly sweet, they are not recommended for melting and blending into batters.

Because I like to raise the quality bar (so to speak) and I like to have as many choices as possible, and because I don't care if my cookies are a little flat or if the chocolate flows a bit rather than retaining its original shape, I often hand-chop my favorite chocolate bars instead of using commercial chocolate chips.

Chocolate Pastilles, Buttons, Pistoles, Callets, Fèves, and Ribbons Unlike chocolate chips, these small chocolate pieces are formulated like regular chocolate and molded or extruded in small easy-to-melt (no chopping necessary!) pieces for the convenience of chefs, commercial bakers, chocolatiers, and home bakers. You may use them in place of chocolate chips or chunks, keeping in mind that they won't hold their shape when melted and the cookies may bake up a little flatter than normal.

COCOA POWDER: NATURAL AND DUTCH-PROCESS

Cocoa powder is made by removing 75 to 85 percent of the fat (cocoa butter) from chocolate liquor, then pulverizing the partially defatted substance that remains. The result is pure, natural (nonalkalized) cocoa. Dutch-process (alkalized) cocoa has been processed with a chemical alkali to reduce both acidity and any harshness that may be a result of poor quality beans or under- or overfermentation. Alkalizing darkens the color of cocoa and alters its flavor. Chefs and consumers vary in their preferences for these two styles of cocoa, although I have noticed a trend toward natural cocoa as I write this paragraph. Of course, quality makes a difference with either type; it is worth tasting different cocoas to learn your own preference. Fans of Dutch-process cocoa extol its rich color, toasted nutty flavor, and coffee notes, while others find the taste dull, dusty, harsh, chemical, and lacking in fruitiness. Natural cocoa tastes vibrant, fruity, and complex to its admirers (including me) and harsh, bitter, and sour to its detractors. Are they interchangeable in recipes? Generally, in recipes that include leavenings such as baking powder or baking soda, you should stick with the type of cocoa called for to avoid bad results. But absent any leavening in the recipes (such as those for brownies, sauces, fillings, etc.), it is usually safe to use the type of cocoa that tastes best to you.

COCONUT

Unsweetened Coconut

Many of the recipes in this book call for unsweetened dried shredded coconut and/or wide strips of dried shaved unsweetened coconut (aka *coconut chips*). Both have superb true coconut flavor in cookies, and neither has the preservatives and sugar. Both are found in better supermarkets, in specialty markets that sell nuts and dried fruit in bulk, in natural food stores, and online (see Resources). The flavor and quality make it worth finding. To toast coconut, see page 16.

Sweetened Dried Shredded Coconut

This supermarket staple is found in the baking aisle.

COFFEE AND ESPRESSO POWDER

If a recipe calls for freshly ground coffee beans, use freshly roasted beans from a specialty coffee purveyor and grind or crush the beans yourself if possible. For recipes that call for espresso powder, use Medaglia d'Oro instant espresso powder rather than freeze-dried crystals if possible. If you must use freeze-dried crystals or regular powdered coffee, increase the amount by about 25 percent.

CREAM

The freshest, best-tasting cream is simply pasteurized, rather than ultrapasteurized or sterilized (for longer shelf life), and contains no ingredients other than cream.

DRIED FRUITS

These should be moist, plump, and flavorful. Whole pieces are always better, fresher, and moister than prechopped or extruded pellets, even if you have to chop your own. Use an oiled knife or oiled scissors to cut or chop sticky fruit.

Freeze-Dried Raspberries and Bananas

Freeze-dried fruit is just that, whole berries, banana slices, etc., with the water removed and nothing added. The flavors are intense and pure. I buy freeze-dried fruit made by Just Tomatoes, Etc.! It's available in better supermarkets and online at www.justtomatoes.com.

FLOUR

The recipes in this book were tested with unbleached all-purpose flour, although many had been originally developed (by me) using bleached all-purpose. You will get good (though slightly different) results with either.

Bleached flour makes the most tender cookies because it usually has slightly less protein than unbleached flour, because it is more finely milled, and because the bleaching process acidifies the flour, which also has a tenderizing effect. But unbleached flour is a purer, less processed ingredient and has a better taste.

Whole Wheat and Graham Flour

The best whole wheat flour is stone-ground from hard whole wheat kernels. It includes all parts of the kernel, the germ, and the bran as well as the endosperm. Whole wheat flour has an appealingly nutty flavor, and it can produce meltingly tender, elegant cookies as well as those that are hearty and healthy and down to earth. Whole wheat goes well with all kinds of nuts and seeds, especially hemp seeds, cacao nibs, hazelnuts, and walnuts. Keep whole wheat flour in the refrigerator or freezer to preserve its flavor and prevent rancidity. Graham flour is coarsely ground whole wheat flour.

Whole Wheat Pastry Flour

Whole wheat pastry flour is whole wheat flour made from soft rather than hard wheat. Soft wheat has less gluten (thus less protein) than hard wheat and can produce a finer and more tender texture in cookies.

Buckwheat Flour

Buckwheat is actually an herb, not a grain at all. Its seeds are ground into the dark flavorful flour that many Americans may know only, if at all, in hearty pancakes and, possibly (and not always favorably), in buckwheat groats or kasha. Buckwheat has a nutritional profile similar to wheat's but can often be tolerated by those with wheat allergies. The flavor is malty, earthy, and pleasantly bitter—some would say strong. However, used with a light hand, buckwheat flour adds elegant nutty flavor and tender complexity to Nibby Buckwheat Butter Cookies (page 119) and Nibby Buckwheat Linzer Hearts (page 196). Buckwheat flour is available in light and dark varieties, which may be used interchangeably in recipes, though the latter has a stronger flavor. Store buckwheat flour in the refrigerator or freezer to prevent it from becoming rancid.

Buckwheat flour is available in some supermarkets, from health food and specialty food purveyors, and online (see Resources, page 362).

Chestnut Flour

Pulverized dried chestnuts, chestnut flour is used in traditional northern Italian baked goods and deserves a place in American baking. The flour has the sweet, slightly nutty flavor and starchy characteristics appreciated by those of us who love chestnuts in any form. It makes an irresistible meringue with walnuts (see page 282). Imported Italian and domestic chestnut flour are available in better supermarkets and specialty stores and online (see Resources).

Kamut and Spelt Flours

Kamut and spelt are nutritionally superior ancestors of modern wheat and may be substituted for whole wheat flour in recipes. Both flours contain a type of gluten that is more digestible than common wheat gluten. Kamut and spelt impart a rich nutty flavor, and kamut in particular adds a fragrant buttery flavor and lovely yellow color to baked goods made with it. Anyone familiar with the dense, heavy texture of whole-grain breads and "healthy" recipes made with spelt or kamut will be astonished at the delicate, tender texture and sensational flavor of Golden Kamut Shortbread (page 332) and Whole Wheat Sablés made with spelt

(page 320). Keep these flours in the refrigerator or freezer to preserve their flavor and prevent rancidity.

Oat Flour

Oat flour is finely milled oats. It is high in protein, fiber, B_1 vitamins, magnesium, zinc, and antioxidants. Better still, it imparts a lovely oat flavor to baked goods, or just a nuance of nutty flavor when blended with other flours and starches. Oat flour makes terrific Wheat-Free Double-Oatmeal Cookies (page 152), Wheat-Free Chocolate Chip Cookies (page 134), Wheat-Free Butter Cookies (page 44), and more. Store oat flour in the refrigerator or freezer to preserve its flavor and keep it from becoming rancid. For gluten-free baking, buy oat flour specifically labeled gluten-free, which indicates that it's free of cross-contamination from wheat in the fields or during processing. Bob's Red Mill brand is available in good supermarkets and by mail order (see Resources, page 362).

Potato Starch

Not to be confused with potato flour (which is made from the entire potato), potato starch—also called potato starch flour, just to confuse us—is derived only from the starchy part of the potato. Potato starch has less nutritional value than potato flour, but its relatively neutral flavor, lightness, and silky texture is an asset in wheat-free baking. I blend it with brown rice flour and oat flour in sensational Wheat-Free Chocolate Chip Cookies (page 134). Store potato starch in the refrigerator or freezer to preserve its flavor and keep it from becoming rancid. Potato starch is available in the baking aisle and or the kosher food section of good supermarkets; Bob's Red Mill, which is available by mail order (see Resources, page 362), is a good brand.

Rice Flour (Brown or White)

White rice flour is finely milled white rice, not to be confused with sweet rice (glutinous rice) flour. Brown rice flour is milled from brown rice, and thus it includes the rice bran and germ, making it a nutritious whole grain flour. Brown and white rice flours are used in wheat-free baking, often in combination with other flours or starches. Look for Wheat-Free Butter Cookies (page 44), Wheat-Free Cutout Cookies (page 46), Wheat-Free Rugelach (page 252), and Wheat-Free Mexican Wedding Cakes (page 308). Store rice flours in the refrigerator or freezer to preserve their flavor and keep them from becoming rancid. The extra-fine rice flours available from Authentic Foods (see Resources, page 362) are especially nice; cookies made with them have a beautiful texture without the grittiness that rice flours can often impart.

GINGER

Ginger adds a hot, fresh, palate-tingling flavor to any dish. It comes in several forms, which may be used separately or in combination.

Dried Ground Ginger

Buy this familiar pale yellow powder in a jar from the spice section of the supermarket or from a purveyor of bulk spices. It is very pungent and earthy, and it has a slightly peppery flavor, more muted than fresh ginger.

Fresh Ginger

Available in the produce section of many supermarkets, fresh ginger looks like a knobby root or stem (it is actually a rhizome or tuberlike stem) with a brown, papery skin. Buy fresh ginger that feels heavy for its size, rather than light or shriveled (which would suggest that it has lost a lot of its natural moisture). Look for taut, smooth skin with a slight sheen. Young or baby ginger looks fresh and moist with a yellowish green color and even more delicate thin skin. Fresh ginger keeps for at least a week, unwrapped, in a cool dry place. It will keep refrigerated for several weeks as long as you wrap it first in a paper towel (to absorb moisture that might produce mold) and then enclose it in a plastic bag. Peel ginger with a vegetable peeler before slicing, grating, or pureeing. To avoid long, stringy fibers, thinly slice ginger across the grain before chopping, mincing, or pureeing. When fresh ginger is added to recipes that call for ground dried ginger, it imparts pungency and tartness to the flavor.

Crystallized Ginger

Chopped or minced, this sugar-coated candied ginger makes a great inclusion in cookies. The Australian variety is exquisitely tender and somewhat milder than ginger from other sources (such as Thailand).

HEMP SEED

Hemp seed rivals flax and soy, with exceedingly high levels of protein, iron, omega-3 fatty acids, and vitamin E (it has three times the vitamin E contained in flaxseed). Even better, hemp seed is completely delicious; it has a light, slightly fluffy texture and delightful nutty flavor, similar to but more delicate than that of sunflower seeds. I use hemp seed in Hemp Seed Whole Wheat Sablés (page 321), and with pecans and sesame seeds in Honey Hemp Bars (page 157). Hemp seed comes in packages or in bulk, in markets that sell natural and whole foods. Keep it in a sealed container in a cool, dark place or in the refrigerator to prevent rancidity. Hemp seed contains no psychoactive substances, by the way.

NUTS

For freshness and flavor, buy nuts raw, rather than toasted, and in bulk from stores that have a lot of turnover, rather than packaged from the supermarket. Larger halves and pieces stay fresher longer; it's better to chop them yourself. Nuts keep well in the freezer, packaged airtight.

Fresh nuts are delicious raw, but toasting brings out such rich new flavors that almonds and hazelnuts are virtually transformed. Toasted nuts are also extra-crunchy.

SESAME

In North America, we most often encounter sesame seeds sprinkled on breads and bagels. But we taste their nutty flavor in the toasted oil used in Chinese cooking, in the Middle Eastern confection known as *halvah,* and in dips and dressings made with the ground sesame seed paste called *tahini.* I add their nutty rich flavor to Sesame Butterflies (page 270), Sesame Sticks (page 30), and Honey Hemp Bars (page 157). Hulled sesame seeds are off-white or cream; natural, or unhulled, seeds are tan, black, or red (very rare in this country). I use them interchangeably. Sesame seeds turn rancid quickly. Buy them in small quantities from a reliable source and store in the refrigerator for up to 3 months or freeze.

Sesame Tahini

Sesame tahini is 100 percent pure hulled (roasted or unroasted and usually unsalted) ground sesame seeds. It resembles very runny natural peanut butter, although it may be paler in color. Like natural peanut butter, it does not contain emulsifiers, so you must stir to blend in any separated oil each time you use it. Tahini has intense sesame flavor, sometimes including a slight bitterness.

Excessive bitterness or a pronounced metallic flavor is an indication of poor quality. Do not confuse tahini with dips or sauces that contain ingredients in addition to ground sesame seeds, including Tahineh, which contains chickpeas. I prefer the richer flavor of tahini from roasted seeds over that made with raw seeds. Tahini made with roasted seeds may or may not be so labeled. However, raw tahini is always labeled *raw,* so you should not have any problem identifying the type you want. I especially like the family-owned Tarazi brand of sesame tahini (Tarazi Specialty Foods of Chino, California).

SPICES

For the best and brightest flavors, use pure extracts and ground spices that still smell potent in the jar. Grinding one's own spices may seem extreme to many American cooks, but nutmeg and cinnamon are easy to grate on the spot using a Microplane zester. The rewards are significant in terms of flavor and aroma, especially considering the small effort involved.

SUGAR

Professional bakers use sugar with a finer granulation than the regular sugar available at the supermarket. While finer sugar makes cookies lighter and more tender, all of the cookies in this collection were tested with supermarket granulated sugar, and all are tender when made correctly.

Sugar varies in different parts of the country. If your supermarket brand of sugar is coarser than regular salt and/or you think that your cookies could be more tender, switch to C&H bakers' sugar, or use superfine or bar sugar, or process your regular granulated sugar briefly in the food processor before using it.

I use cane sugar rather than beet sugar for baking and dessert making. Chemically, the two substances are the same, yet many bakers and pastry chefs have reported differences and disappointments with beet sugar. After having several cakes fall, I now avoid sugar that contains added fructose. (Granulated sugar is, by definition, a combination of sucrose and fructose, but when fructose is on the ingredient list, it means that extra fructose has been added.) The recipes in this book were tested with C&H granulated cane sugar purchased at the supermarket.

Brown Sugar

The original brown sugars were semirefined, with some of the natural molasses left in them (see Raw Sugars, below). Today commercial brown sugar is retrofitted; that is, it is refined white sugar with added molasses. The resulting light (or golden) brown and dark brown sugars impart pleasing caramel or butterscotch flavors to desserts. Some recipes may specify a preference for light or dark brown sugar, but you can use them interchangeably to your taste. Brown sugar hardens with exposure to the air; store it in an airtight container or tightly sealed in the bag it came in. The sugar should be lump free before it is added to a batter or dough since it is unlikely to smooth out once it is added. Soft lumps can be squeezed with your fingers or mashed with a fork before adding.

To soften hardened brown sugar, sprinkle it with a little water, put it in a tightly covered container (or wrap tightly in foil), and place it in a 250°F oven for a few minutes. Allow it to cool before using it. Brown sugar is measured by packing it fairly firmly into a measuring cup. My recipes are based on 7 ounces of brown sugar per cup.

Raw Sugars

Raw sugars (all of which are actually cooked in processing) are more accurately described as semirefined sugars, with varying amounts of natural molasses left in them. They range in color and consistency from coarse crystals with a light caramel hue (and flavor to match) to amber, russet, or deep mahogany brown with the moist consistency of familiar brown sugar. The best of them burst with complex tastes and aromas.

Turbinado, Demerara, and Evaporated Cane Juice Sugars. These semirefined cane sugars are coarse crystal sugars with delicate caramel toffee flavors. Often served with coffee or tea, they can also be substituted for a little of the granulated sugar in shortbread and butter cookie doughs, adding flavor, crunch, and tenderness. Or sprinkle them, in lieu of white sugar, on top of anything. Demerara tends to be a little darker and more flavorful than turbinado sugar.

Muscovado Sugar (Light and Dark). From Barbados or Mauritius, muscovado sugar is semirefined cane sugar, with lots of the natural molasses left in it. Soft and moist rather than dry and crystalline, it has an earthy, ripe, tropical fruit aroma and flavor with a touch of smoke. Light muscovado has the relative intensity and sweetness of regular dark brown sugar (for which it can be substituted), but with far more flavor and complexity. Almost black, dark muscovado has deep aromatic molasses notes without the bitter pungency of the latter. See Pecan Polvorones with Muscovado Filling (page 200).

Piloncillo. This semirefined sugar, also called *panela* or *panocha,* is a traditional Mexican sugar made from boiled sugarcane juice and molded into cone shapes. In color and relative sweetness and intensity, piloncillo is similar to dark brown sugar, but the flavor is brighter and more interesting, with caramel and molasses notes and a slight flavor of smoke. Grate the hard-as-rocks cones, or put one in a bag and smash it with a hammer; then store it in an airtight jar and use it instead of brown sugar or light muscovado in recipes or on your oatmeal.

Powdered Sugar

Also called *confectioners' sugar* or *icing sugar,* this is granulated sugar that has been pulverized and mixed with a little cornstarch to prevent clumping. I use powdered sugar mostly for dusting—sieved over Linzer Cookies (page 194) or Very Tangy Lemon Bars 2.0 (page 182), for example. I avoid using large quantities in cookie dough because I do not find the added tenderness that it may impart to cookies worth the dull, uncooked starch flavor and powdery sensation on the palate.

VANILLA

Vanilla Extract

I use only pure vanilla extract—Tahitian, Mexican, or Bourbon, depending on the flavor I'm looking for. Tahitian has a floral aroma, like exotic tropical flowers, with flavor notes of cherry, licorice, and raisins. It is a lovely flavor to feature rather than use as a background. Mexican vanilla has aromas of rum and caramel and very ripe fruit. Bourbon vanilla (also called *Madagascar*), the type most familiar to North Americans, is most difficult to describe because it smells and tastes like . . . well, vanilla.

Vanilla Beans, Whole Ground

I like to use whole ground vanilla beans in cookies, instead of (or in addition to) vanilla extract. If you can't find jars of pure ground vanilla beans (not to be confused with vanilla powder that contains dextrose or vanilla paste), you can chop a whole bean and grind it as fine as possible in a

coffee or spice grinder. As a rule of thumb, you can use ¼ teaspoon ground whole vanilla beans to replace 1 teaspoon vanilla extract, but I often use more.

XANTHAN GUM

Xanthan gum is a by-product of cornstarch production, produced through the fermentation of a bacterium called *Xanthonomonas campestris* on corn syrup. Xanthan gum, in powdered form, is increasingly available in the baking aisles of good supermarkets and easily found online (see Resources, page 362). Xanthan gum is used in commercial products to add volume, thicken and stabilize liquids, and hold particles in suspension (in salad dressings, for example). It is also used to create a smooth, ice-free texture in ice creams and frozen desserts. In gluten-free baking, it simulates gluten by binding ingredients and creating chewy textures that would otherwise be lacking. Cookie recipes may use up to ¾ teaspoon per cup of nonwheat flour.

EQUIPMENT

Simple but successful cookie baking requires simple basic equipment rather than a specialized batterie de cuisine. Even a minimally equipped kitchen can turn out good cookies so long as the oven is reliable and the cookie sheets are adequate.

BOWLS

To prevent sugar and flour from flying when beating with a handheld electric mixer, choose mixing bowls that are relatively tall and deep rather than wide and shallow. The weight of glass or crockery bowls makes them nice and stable, but stainless steel is more versatile—and preferable for melting chocolate or heating ingredients in a water bath.

COOKIE SCOOPS

Nonessential but wonderful—cookie scoops with squeeze-and-release handles are the fast and easy way to make lots of evenly sized drop cookies, or balls of dough in specific sizes. Scoops are found at cookware stores or by mail order. Manufacturers use different names for the sizes, but I like a small (2 level teaspoons to form a 1-inch ball), medium (slightly more than a level tablespoon to form a 1¼-inch ball), and large (2 tablespoons to form a 1½-inch ball) scoop.

COOKIE SHEETS AND BROWNIE PANS

Every pan bakes a little differently, depending on the material, thickness, weight, and surface reflection. If your oven temperature is accurate, but cookies, brownies, and bars bake unevenly or brown too quickly on the bottom and edges, your pans may be too thin or too dark. Parchment paper liners might help promote even baking if your pans are less than ideal. When buying new pans, look for medium- to heavy-weight aluminum pans. Light-colored aluminum works better than dark metal or dark nonstick coatings.

Although air-cushioned baking sheets bake quite evenly, they overinsulate and prevent cookies from getting brown crispy edges.

All of the cookies in this collection were tested with medium-weight 16-by-12-inch "half sheet" aluminum pans with 1-inch rims on all four sides. This is what I mean by cookie sheets throughout the recipes.

COOLING RACKS

Simple and inexpensive from the hardware store, or fancy and French, it doesn't really matter so long as you have some kind of rack so cookies can cool quickly with lots of air circulation.

MIXERS AND SPOONS

Most of the recipes in this book call for a moderate amount of mixing, rather than lengthy beating. Unless specified otherwise, a handheld mixer or a big wooden or metal spoon is the best mixing tool for single batches of cookies and may actually prevent overmixing as compared with bigger, more powerful heavy-duty electric stand mixers. If you double or triple recipes, a stand mixer will be needed, in combination with restraint, where necessary, to avoid overmixing. If using a heavy-duty stand mixer, the paddle or flat beater attachment will work best for most cookies other than meringues.

PANCAKE TURNER

Removing individual cookies from baking sheets is easiest to do with an ordinary kitchen pancake turner/spatula. Choose the thin metal kind; plastic or nonstick-coated ones are thicker and harder to slip under cookies.

ROLLING PINS

I like a rolling pin that is straight rather than tapered. Large and heavy or small and light, with or without handles, use what is comfortable for you.

THERMOMETERS

An oven thermometer is useful for checking the accuracy of your oven dial. An instant-read or candy thermometer is essential if you plan to temper chocolate for dipping cookies. Both are available wherever kitchen utensils are sold, or by mail order.

TIMER

Cookies are easily overbaked if left in the oven a minute or two longer than necessary. A timer that rings or buzzes keeps the busy or distracted cook from forgetting the cookies in the oven.

WHISKS

Wire whisks are better than forks for blending dry ingredients together and fluffing up the flour in lieu of sifting and, in general, for whisking things together.

RESOURCES

Anson Mills
1922-C Gervais Street
Columbia, SC 29201
803-467-4122
www.ansonmills.com
Stone-ground organic whole grains, including whole wheat, buckwheat, and corn.

Authentic Foods
1850 W. 169th Street, Suite B
Gardena, CA 90247
800-806-4737
http://authenticfoods.com
Ingredients for gluten-free baking and the best source for superfine white rice and brown rice flours.

Bob's Red Mill Natural Foods
5209 SE International Way
Milwaukie, OR 97222
800-349-2173
www.bobsredmill.com
An extraordinary array of stone-ground flours, including whole wheat, graham, kamut, and spelt flours, cornmeal, and much more.

El Molino Mills
345 North Baldwin Park Boulevard
City of Industry, CA 91746
Stone-ground whole-grain flours.

India Tree
1421 Elliott Avenue
Seattle, WA 98119
800-369-4848
206-270-0293
india@indiatree.com
A great resource for spices and muscovado sugar and decorating sugars made with natural colors. Products are available in specialty stores and better supermarkets, but you can also order online.

Just Tomatoes Etc.!
www.justtomatoes.com
Freeze-dried fruits and vegetables.

King Arthur Flour
The Baker's Catalogue
PO Box 876
Norwich, VT 05055-0876
800-827-6836
www.kingarthurflour.com
Comprehensive source of ingredients, cookie scoops, and other tools for cookie makers.

Parrish's Cake Decorating Supply, Inc.
225 West 146 Street
Gardena, CA 90248
800-736-8443
www.parrishsmagicline.com
Comprehensive source of ingredients and tools for cookie makers.

The Pasta Shop
5655 College Avenue
Oakland, CA 94618
888-952-4005
www.rockridgemarkethall.com
A fabulous gourmet store with a second location in Berkeley. The buyers and owners solicit advice from an impressive list of local cookbook authors and professional bakers, so the store has a subspecialty in baking ingredients and chocolate. Chocolate and cocoa from Scharffen Berger, Valrhona, Callebaut, E. Guittard, and Michel Cluizel, among others; Madagascar and Tahitian vanilla extracts and whole and ground vanilla beans; honeys; chestnut flour; nut pastes; flavored salts; specialty sugars; olive oils; preserves; and more.

Penzey's Spices
PO Box 924
19300 West Janacek Court
Brookfield, WI 53008
800-741-7787
www.penzeys.com
All kinds of spices; Madagascar, Tahitian, and Mexican vanilla beans; several types of cinnamon. Reading the catalog is an education in flavor ingredients and their uses.

Scharffen Berger Chocolate Maker
www.scharffenberger.com
Some of my favorite semisweet, bittersweet, extra-dark, unsweetened, and milk chocolates; limited-edition special chocolate blends; cacao nibs; and the best natural cocoa powder.

Studiopatró
2832 Lyon Street
San Francisco, CA 94123
415-775-3432
http://studiopatro.com
The source for the beautifully designed eco-friendly linen tea towels used as background patterns in many of our photographs.

Sur La Table
1765 Sixth Avenue South
Seattle, WA 98134-1608
800-243-0852
www.surlatable.com
Premium source for quality tools and equipment for home bakers and cooks; ingredients including Scharffen Berger, Valrhona, and E. Guittard chocolates.

Whole Foods
www.wholefoodsmarket.com
This upscale national natural food chain is a great source of natural and organic ingredients, including specialty flours and sugars; fine chocolates; bulk foods, including seeds, nuts, and grains; unsweetened shredded, dried, and flaked coconut; and more.

Don't forget local treasures: Health food and natural foods stores and ethnic and high-end groceries, for bulk foods, grains, flours, seeds, spices, nuts, and inspiration.

Specialty coffee roasters and purveyors of fine teas.

Restaurant supply stores, for commercial half-sheet pans to use as cookie sheets.

ACKNOWLEDGMENTS

I am privileged to work with people whom I like and who are also superb at what they do. At Artisan, much love and thanks to my editor, the legendary Ann Bramson. Trent Duffy managed an avalanche of details with consummate grace, and Jan Derevjanik went every extra mile to make words and pictures flow gracefully into place; also at Artisan, I appreciate the support of Nancy Murray, Barbara Peragine, and Erin Sainz. In San Francisco, producer and art director Sara Slavin infused the entire project with magic, as always. Deborah Jones redefined cookies on film as no one else could have done, and made our studio time intensely productive, creative, and fun. Jennifer Morla designed a stunning modern book and conjured the perfect concept—cookies categorized by texture. Maya Klein was, for the umpteenth time, a cherished source of ideas, wisdom, and testing. Anya Wayne, Hannah Hoffman, and Jenny Richards helped with testing along the way. Finally, I thank my agent and friend, Jane Dystel, for always being there.

SMART SEARCH

These lists will help you find cookies (and variations) for special audiences, interests, or requirements, regardless of texture. Recipes in each section appear in alphabetical order. Use the index to find the recipe.

WHEAT-FREE

Almond Macaroons
Amaretti
Apricot Nut Wheat-Free Rugelach
Banana or Raspberry Meringues
Chestnut Walnut Meringues
Chocolate Hazelnut Wheat-Free
 Rugelach
Chocolate Latkes
Chunky Hazelnut Meringues
Cocoa Nib Wheat-Free Rugelach
Coconut Meringues
Date Nut Wheat-Free Rugelach
French Macarons
Honey Hemp Bars
Melting Chocolate Meringues
Meringue Mushrooms
Milk Chocolate and Salted
 Almond or Cashew Meringues
New Classic Coconut Macaroons
 2.0
Not-So-Plain Chocolate
 Meringues
Pannelets
Peanut Butter Clouds
Sesame Kisses
Spicy Carrot Masala Macaroons
Sweet and Salty Nut Meringues
Wheat-Free Butter Cookies
Wheat-Free Caramel Cheesecake
 Bars
Wheat-Free Chocolate Chip
 Cookies
Wheat-Free Chocolate Pudding
 Bars
Wheat-Free Cutout Cookies
Wheat-Free Double-Oatmeal
 Cookies
Wheat-Free Ginger Cookies
Wheat-Free Gooey Turtle Bars
Wheat-Free Mexican Wedding
 Cakes
Wheat-Free Nibby Nut and Raisin
 Cookies
Wheat-Free Nutty Thumbprint
 Cookies
Wheat-Free Pecan Spice Cookies
Wheat-Free Rocky Road Bars
Wheat-Free Rugelach
Wheat-Free Sablés
Wheat-Free Toffee Bars

DAIRY-FREE

Almond Biscotti
Almond Macaroons
Amaretti
Banana or Raspberry Meringues
Chestnut Walnut Meringues
Chocolate Biscotti with Less Fat
Chocolate Chip Biscotti with
 Less Fat
Chocolate Latkes
Coconut Meringues
Chunky Hazelnut Meringues
Dairy-Free Caramel Rocky Road
 Squares
Dairy-Free and Wheat-Free
 Chocolate Chip Cookies
French Macarons
Fruit and Nut Bars
Honey Hemp Bars
Melting Chocolate Meringues
Meringue Mushrooms
New Classic Coconut Macaroons
 2.0
Not-So-Plain Chocolate
 Meringues
Orange Chocolate Chip Biscotti
Pannelets
Peanut Butter Clouds
Sesame Kisses
Spicy Carrot Masala Macaroons
Supercrunch Cinnamon Almond
 Biscotti

COOKIES WITH WHOLE GRAINS

Aniseed and Almond Shortbread
Breakfast Biscotti
Cornmeal and Fruit Biscotti
Cornmeal and Olive Oil Biscotti
 with Walnuts and Pears
Flaky Whole Wheat Walnut
 Cookies
Golden Kamut Shortbread
Great Grahams
Honey Hemp Bars
Nibby Buckwheat Butter Cookies
Nibby Buckwheat Linzer Hearts
Oatmeal Cookies
Wheat-Free Double-Oatmeal
 Cookies
Whole Wheat Biscotti
Whole Wheat Chocolate Chip
 Cookies
Whole Wheat Hazelnut Cookies
 with Currants and Cacao Nibs
Whole Wheat Rugelach
Whole Wheat Sablés

RIDICULOUSLY QUICK AND EASY

Here are the cookies or bars that you can mix up and bake in short order with such simple ingredients that you might even have them on hand in the pantry or fridge.

Almond Macaroons
Almond Sablés
ANZAC Cookies
Basic Butter Cookies
Blondies
Cakey Brownies
Chocolate Chunk Cookies with
   Cherries and Pecans
Chocolate Wafers 3.0
Cocoa Brownies
Dairy-Free Caramel Rocky Road
   Squares
Fruit and Nut Bars
Hazelnut Gianduja Chunk Cookies
Less-Is-More Overnight Brownies
Lucy's Chocolate Minis
Macadamia and White Chocolate
   Chunk Cookies
Mexican Wedding Cakes
My Chocolate Chip Cookies
My Ginger Cookies
Oatmeal Cookies
Peanut Butter Blondies
Peanut Butter Cookies
Robert's Brownies My Way
Rocky Road Bars
Snicker Doodles
Steve Ritual Brownies

Sugar Crunch Cookies
Wheat-Free Butter Cookies
Wheat-Free Chai Butter Cookies
Wheat-Free Chocolate Chip
   Cookies
Wheat-Free Double-Oatmeal
   Cookies
Wheat-Free Mexican Wedding or
   Russian Tea Cakes
Whole Wheat Chocolate Chip
   Cookies
Whole Wheat Sablés

LESS FAT AND 2-POINT TREATS

Cookies on this list are low to moderate in fat, or else small enough so that eating 2 or 3 can still be considered moderation! In parentheses I've let you know how many cookies you can enjoy for 2 Weight Watchers points (calculated using the Recipe Builder on the Weight Watcher member Web site). I've listed only those cookies that I think deliver a lot of delicious satisfaction for your 2 points or a few fat grams.

Almond Biscotti
   (1 cookie for 2 points)
Amaretti (2 cookies for 2 points)
Banana Meringues
   (6 cookies for 2 points)
Banana Pecan Meringues
   (3 cookies for 2 points)

Breakfast Biscotti
   (1 cookie for 2 points)
Chestnut Walnut Meringues
   (2 cookies for 2 points)
Chocolate Biscotti with Less Fat
   (2 cookies for 2 points)
Chocolate Chip Biscotti with Less
   Fat (2 cookies for 2 points)
Chunky Peanut Butter Clouds
   (1 cookie for 2 points)
Coconut Banana Meringues
   (4 cookies for 2 points)
Fruit and Nut Bars
   (1 small bar for 2 points)
Great Grahams (two 2-inch
   cookies for 2 points)
Less-Is-More Overnight Brownies
   (1 brownie for 2 points)
Lighter Lemon Bars
   (1 bar for 2 points)
Melting Chocolate Meringues
   (2 cookies for 2 points)
Meringue Mushrooms
   (4 cookies for 2 points)
My Ginger Cookies(2 cookies
   for 2 points)
Not-So-Plain Chocolate
   Meringues (2 cookies for
   2 points)
Orange Chocolate Chip Biscotti
   (2 cookies for 2 points)
Peanut Butter Clouds
   (2 cookies for 2 points)
Sesame Kisses
   (3 cookies for 2 points)
Whole Wheat Biscotti
   (1 cookie for 2 points)

COOKIE DOUGHS THAT FREEZE WELL

Almond Sablés
Aniseed and Almond Shortbread
ANZAC Cookies
Basic Butter Cookies
Bittersweet Decadence Cookies
Bourbon Pecan Butter Cookies
Café de Olla Sticks
Cardamom Sugar Stars
Chocolate Chunk Cookies with
   Cherries and Pecans
Chocolate Espresso Cookies
Coconut Sticks
Coffee Walnut Cookies
Crunchy Seed Cookies
Golden Kamut Shortbread
Great Grahams
Hazelnut Gianduja Chunk Cookies
Hazelnut Molasses Cookies
Hazelnut Sticks
Lemon Ginger Thins
Linzer Cookies
Macadamia and White Chocolate
   Chunk Cookies
Maya's Lemon Thins
Mexican Wedding Cakes
Mock Puff Pastry
My Chocolate Chip Cookies
My Ginger Cookies
Nibby Buckwheat Butter Cookies
Nibby Buckwheat Linzer Hearts
Nibby Nut and Raisin Cookies
Nibby Pecan Cookies
Nut Slices
Oatmeal Cookies

Peanut Butter Cookies
Pecan Penuche Shortbread
Pecan Polvorones with
    Muscovado Filling
Rugelach
Salted Peanut Toffee Cookies
Sesame Sticks
Sugar Crunch Cookies
Twice-Baked Shortbread
Ultrathin Chocolate Chunk
    Cookies
Vanilla Sugar Cookies
Wheat-Free Chocolate Chip
    Cookies
Wheat-Free Cutout Cookies
Wheat-Free Double-Oatmeal
    Cookies
Wheat-Free Rugelach
Whole Wheat Chocolate Chip
    Cookies
Whole Wheat Hazelnut Cookies
    with Currants and Cacao Nibs
Whole Wheat Rugelach
Whole Wheat Sablés

Cardamom Sugar Stars
Chestnut Walnut Meringues
Chocolate Biscotti
Chocolate Biscotti with Less Fat
Chocolate Chip Biscotti with
    Less Fat
Chunky Hazelnut Meringues
Chunky Peanut Butter Clouds
Coconut Meringues
Coffee Walnut Cookies
Crunchy Seed Cookies
Fruit and Nut Bars
Great Grahams
Meringue Mushrooms
Nibby Buckwheat Butter Cookies
Nibby Pecan Cookies
Not-So-Plain Chocolate
    Meringues
Pecan Penuche Shortbread
Supercrunch Cinnamon Almond
    Biscotti
Twice-Baked Shortbread
Vanilla Sugar Cookies
Whole Wheat Biscotti

COOKIES THAT KEEP AT LEAST 2 WEEKS

Almond Biscotti
Almond Sablés
Amaretti
Aniseed and Almond Shortbread
ANZAC Cookies
Banana or Raspberry Meringues
Basic Butter Cookies
Bourbon Pecan Butter Cookies
Breakfast Biscotti

INDEX

CONVERSION CHARTS

Here are rounded-off equivalents between the metric system and the traditional systems that are used in the United States to measure weight and volume.

FRACTIONS	DECIMALS
⅛	.125
¼	.25
⅓	.33
⅜	.375
½	.5
⅝	.625
⅔	.67
¾	.75
⅞	.875

WEIGHTS

US/UK	METRIC
¼ oz	7 g
½ oz	15 g
1 oz	30 g
2 oz	55 g
3 oz	85 g
4 oz	110 g
5 oz	140 g
6 oz	170 g
7 oz	200 g
8 oz (½ lb)	225 g
9 oz	250 g
10 oz	280 g
11 oz	310 g
12 oz	340 g
13 oz	370 g
14 oz	400 g
15 oz	425 g
16 oz (1 lb)	450 g

VOLUME

AMERICAN	IMPERIAL	METRIC
¼ tsp		1.25 ml
½ tsp		2.5 ml
1 tsp		5 ml
½ Tbsp (1½ tsp)		7.5 ml
1 Tbsp (3 tsp)		15 ml
¼ cup (4 Tbsp)	2 fl oz	60 ml
⅓ cup (5 Tbsp)	2½ fl oz	75 ml
½ cup (8 Tbsp)	4 fl oz	125 ml
⅔ cup (10 Tbsp)	5 fl oz	150 ml
¾ cup (12 Tbsp)	6 fl oz	175 ml
1 cup (16 Tbsp)	8 fl oz	250 ml
1¼ cups	10 fl oz	300 ml
1½ cups	12 fl oz	350 ml
1 pint (2 cups)	16 fl oz	500 ml
2½ cups	20 fl oz (1 pint)	625 ml
5 cups	40 fl oz (1 qt)	1.25 l

OVEN TEMPERATURES

	°F	°C	GAS MARK
very cool	250–275	130–140	½–1
cool	300	148	2
warm	325	163	3
moderate	350	177	4
moderately hot	375–400	190–204	5–6
hot	425	218	7
very hot	450–475	232–245	8–9